Innovation and Scaling for Impact

Innovation and Scaling for Impact

HOW EFFECTIVE SOCIAL
ENTERPRISES DO IT

Christian Seelos and Johanna Mair

STANFORD BUSINESS BOOKS
An Imprint of Stanford University Press
Stanford, California

Stanford University Press
Stanford, California

Special discounts for bulk quantities of Stanford Business Books are available to corporations, professional associations, and other organizations. For details and discount information, contact the special sales department of Stanford University Press. Tel: (650) 725-0820, Fax: (650) 725-3457

Printed in the United States of America on acid-free, archival-quality paper

Library of Congress Cataloging-in-Publication Data

Names: Seelos, Christian, author. | Mair, Johanna, author.
Title: Innovation and scaling for impact : how effective social enterprises do it / Christian Seelos and Johanna Mair.
Description: Stanford, California : Stanford Business Books, an imprint of Stanford University Press, 2017. | Includes bibliographical references and index.
Identifiers: LCCN 2016036938 (print) | LCCN 2016037328 (ebook) | ISBN 9780804797344 (cloth : alk. paper) | ISBN 9781503600997 (e-book)
Subjects: LCSH: Social entrepreneurship. | Social responsibility of business. | Nonprofit organizations—Management. | Social entrepreneurship—India—Case studies. | Social entrepreneurship—Bangladesh—Case studies.
Classification: LCC HD60 .S436 2016 (print) | LCC HD60 (ebook) | DDC 658.4/063--dc23
LC record available at https://lccn.loc.gov/2016036938

Typeset by Thompson Type in 10/15 Sabon

CONTENTS

ACKNOWLEDGMENTS

Generous and wise colleagues, advisors, friends and professionals at many organizations laid the foundation for our learning journey and the insights we share in this book. Their knowledge and observations paired with well-weathered theories and perspectives from the social sciences helped us to understand the innovation trajectories of social enterprises that address persistent social problems.

Many of the insights in this book draw on research from numerous scholars. This book stands on the shoulders of giants such as Edith Penrose, Jim March, Karl Weick, Peter Drucker, Philipp Selznick, Robert Merton and many others. The context in which their theories were developed differs from ours. We selected, combined, and advanced their insights to develop our own unique perspective on the role and characteristics of innovation and scaling in social enterprises in a developing country context.

We wanted to write a book that brings rigor to current debates about innovation in the social sector and at the same time informs decisions and actions. The Rockefeller Foundation not only generously supported our research but also made us see the relevance of our work for a broader community of practice. Together, we convened scholars and leaders in the social sector in Stanford, New York, and Berlin to inform, test, expand, and correct emerging findings. We benefited greatly from comments by Adrian

Ely, Alnoor Ebrahim, Amira Ibrahim, Andy Hargadon, Banny Banerjee, Brian Trelstad, Chris West, Claudia Juech, Dean Karlan, Evan Michelson, Harry Barkema, Helmy Abouleish, Heloise Emdon, Jacob Harold, John Gaventa, Juree Vichit-Vadakan, Kadria Motaal, Kamal Munir, Kippy Joseph, Kristina Jaskyte, Laila Iskandar, Marc Ventresca, Mary Crossan, Noshua Watson, Oana Branzei, Peter Frumkin, Peter Uvin, Stephen Osborne, Steve Luby, Tom Lawrence and Zia Khan.

Kim Meredith and Woody Powell at the Stanford University Center on Philanthropy and Civil Society (PACS) supported us in a myriad of ways. PACS has been a wonderful incubator for this research. Jim March, Jeff Pfeffer, and many other faculty members at Stanford University have generously shared their thoughts and insights. Margo Fleming and the team from Stanford University Press have become valuable sparring partners in the publishing process. Jenna Nichols and Joanna Wylegala provided important research support.

We feel deeply indebted to the many people that make BRAC, Gram Vikas, Aravind, and Waste Concern the inspiring and impactful organizations that they are. At BRAC, we thank Sir Fazle Abed, Asif Saleh, Maria May and the social innovation team, Andrew Jenkins, Golam Samdani, Safiqul Islam, Mahabub Hossain, Sukhendra Sarkar, Rabeya Yasmin, Shabiha Sultana, Susan Davis, and Imran Matin for providing insights into a social enterprise that operates at a massive scale.

Joe Madiath, Sojan Thomas, Chitra Choudhury, Urmila Senapati, and US Mishra at Gram Vikas helped us to understand local realities in rural India and to appreciate the entrenched nature of inequality.

At Aravind and Aurolab we thank Thulsi Ravilla, Dr. Aravind, Fred Munster, Dr. Kim, Dr. Ravindran, Dr. Nam, Dr. Venkatesh, Dr. Haripriya Aravind, Dr. Balakrishnan, Vishnu Prasad, Mr. Sriram, Ganesh Babu, Shash Karumanchi, Pavita K. Mehta, David Green, and Susanne Gilbert.

Melanie Walker, Adnan Aliani, and the founders of Waste Concern, Iftekhar Enayetullah and Maqsood Sinha, showed us what it means to be serial entrepreneurs and how to diffuse innovations to ensure scale and impact.

We dedicate this book to those who have the courage to set up an organization to address a social problem and to those who support them.

Innovation and Scaling for Impact

INTRODUCTION

Social Enterprises Require a Distinctive Perspective on Innovation and Scaling

Social innovation as a field of practice continues to flourish and expand. Yet few have explored the roles, governance, and consequences of innovation and scaling in social enterprises. An overoptimistic and often naïve discourse about innovation may create unintended negative consequences for organizations. It might even hinder them in helping the people and communities they serve. Building on a decade-long research project studying social enterprises, we hope to offer a fresh and realistic look at how innovation and scaling enable social enterprises to create impact. We hope to strengthen understanding of the roles of innovation and scaling, to expose the potential but also the limits of innovation for creating impact, and to propose a number of practical frameworks that support decision making and long-term strategizing in social enterprises.

First, let's clarify some key terms. What do we mean by *social enterprises*, by *innovation*, and by *scaling*? In this book, we use the term *social enterprises* to refer to established organizations that enact a primary objective of catering to important social and environmental problems of disadvantaged people and communities. They often focus on problems that are not effectively addressed by public sectors or businesses, and they provide products, services, or interventions by working with and also on behalf of their beneficiaries. These organizations come in a variety of different legal structures and sources of capital. Some social enterprises generate profits; others use external funds to cover costs. Our use of the term *social enterprise* thus integrates a wide set of organizations in the social and development sectors.

Our perspective on *innovation* positions it as a process by which organizations create and develop ideas under conditions of uncertainty. Innovations generate uncertain future outcomes. If successful, innovations create new products, services, or interventions that have potential for positive impact. The term *scaling* refers to actions that use established products, services, or interventions to serve more people better. Scaling creates predictable positive impact today.

Numerous field visits, interviews, workshops, and active discussions with various stakeholders in the field of social innovation have led us to realize that productive decisions about innovation and scaling in the social sector necessitate a much more strategic organizational perspective than the one we typically encounter. We hope that our readers will treat this book as a joint learning project. It provides a number of tools, frameworks, and case studies that will enable readers to reflect deeply on similarities to and differences from their own organizations or organizations they are interested in. Working with this book is an investment in understanding and learning that pays off in informed decision making about whether, when, and how to innovate for impact. Making smart long-term decisions about innovation and scaling is crucial for organizations, their funders, and their supporters in the form of consultants, researchers, or observers. The book also supports educators interested in understanding innovation and scaling as part of organizational efforts to create impact.

More than fifteen years ago we embarked on a research journey to understand how social enterprises dealt with stubborn social and environmental problems and catered to basic human needs by developing novel solutions. What triggered our interest as scholars and educators in strategic management was how these organizations created value. Value creation in social enterprises goes beyond generating financial returns, the principal measure of value creation in business. It explicitly integrates the creation of positive impacts on the lives of the individuals and the communities they serve. We found that the most inspiring and novel solutions were enacted by organizations from the Global South. These social enterprises engaged deeply and on an eye-to-eye level with the people and communities they served. They generated unusual combinations of resources and capabilities to attack persistent needs and pressing problems. They deployed different organizational forms and structures that included nongovernmental organizations (NGOs), not-for-profit enterprises, and for-profit firms. They created hybrid arrangements by combining and integrating these forms in novel ways. What impressed us most was their determination and commitment to making a real difference in the lives of the poor or alleviating environmental problems over long periods of time.

To us, these social entreprises and the people that created these organizations appeared tremendously innovative. A nascent but vibrant community that formed around the topic of social entrepreneurship agreed with our view. For example, Ashoka, an organization that supports and promotes social entrepreneurs, states that "social entrepreneurs are individuals with innovative solutions to society's most pressing social problems."[1] *The Economist* expressed a similar view: "A social entrepreneur is, in essence, someone who develops an innovative answer to a social problem."[2] In the spring of 2004, we embarked on our first field trip to Bangladesh to examine more diligently how these organizations managed to be so innovative. We learned that the local realities in which they operated did not match our romantic and somewhat glamorized image about "social entrepreneurship." The organizations had tremendous impact on the constituencies they served. But innovation played a relatively minor (although very specific) role in creating that impact.

Filling the gap between what we think these organizations do and how they really do it is the main motivation for this book. We want to provide space not just for the usual success stories but for reflections on failures, unintended consequences, and false assumptions. We strongly believe that a more realistic depiction is a solid foundation for making better decisions about innovation and scaling to achieve what we all aspire to: supporting organizations to provide disadvantaged people and communities with solutions for their fundamental problems and to create fruitful spaces for development.

SOCIAL INNOVATION

Social innovation as a growing field of practice involves social entrepreneurs and their organizations, impact investors and foundations supporting them, companies that partner with them, and governments that rely on them. We aim to reveal, challenge, and go beyond commonly held assumptions about social innovation on a number of topics, as discussed in the following subsections.

On Glorifying the Individual

It is popular to reduce social innovation to the actions of individuals and consider social entrepreneurs as "the new heroes"[3] and "change makers" who singlehandedly change the world.[4] Instead, we focus on the organizations that these entrepreneurs built. Organizations comprise not only visionary leaders but also their followers. Most people in social enterprises are not social entrepreneurs but regular staff who care about having a job. The inner workings of social enterprises are often treated as a "black box" in social innovation discourse. Yet they are where innovation and impact creation happen. How innovation and scaling are done in established social enterprises is the central lens of this book.

On Taking the Term Innovation for Granted

Innovation is considered the key to business success. In today's hypercompetitive markets, success or even survival without innovation seems unlikely. Because innovation is so strongly associated with business success, the term has been eagerly adopted by the social sector, which addresses problems related to poverty and development. Innovation is good, the more the better!

The word *innovation* is now widely used in the social and development sectors, and yet few ask what it really means. Unfortunately, research on the role of social innovation or how social enterprises actually innovate has been scarce.[5] The lack of a shared understanding prevents learning, accumulation of knowledge, and consistent decisions by social enterprises and their supporters. We critically evaluate the characteristics of innovation—rather than glorify it—and clarify its meaning. We portray innovation as an organizational process and provide a conceptual framework that emphasizes learning as the main requirement for productive innovation. A central tenet of this book is, "If you don't know how to learn, don't innovate."

On the Overoptimistic View of Innovation's Potential

The role of innovation in generating impact is hardly ever questioned. Eric Schmidt, the former CEO of Google, says that the company does not care about incremental ideas that allow them to be 10 percent better.[6] They care about radically innovative ideas that allow them to be ten times better to cater to and to create a myriad of dynamically evolving needs and wants of relatively wealthy customers.

Developing countries suffer much greater and more persistent needs of poor people and communities, and they generally have much lower levels of competition and available resources than developed countries. Is investing in the improvement and scaling of existing products, services, and interventions potentially more urgent than innovating different ones? Investing in being 10 percent better may not count for much for Google or its customers but may make a real difference for the poor.

We assert that innovation per se does not create impact. Innovation generates the *potential* for impact creation. Scaling creates impact from innovation. Another central message of this book is, "If you don't know how to scale, don't innovate!" Innovation and scaling are often treated as separate ways to create impact. This division is unproductive. The two processes need to be integrated. We offer frameworks and conceptual tools for systematically assessing how to productively integrate innovation and scaling for impact.

On Ignoring the Cost of Innovation Failure

Innovation often fails and has uncertain outcomes. In modern markets with fluid capital, knowledge, and labor the innovation failure of one business is a positive opportunity for a competing business. Stakeholders are protected from negative effects of failed innovation, for example through diversification, legal mechanisms, and insurance and welfare systems. The dynamic is very different for organizations operating in developing countries where the cost of innovation failure may be significant. In poor communities the legacy effects of failed innovations may be severe in the long run. For example, the introduction of a novel service provided free by a development organization may create the expectation that other services will also be provided free. This unintended consequence of innovation persists even if the innovation has failed. Subsequent organizations may find it difficult to introduce services in an economically sustainable way. Innovation failures of a single social enterprise may deprive whole communities of essential services for a long time because their needs are not targeted effectively by the public or private sectors.

Poor people without any safety net may be extremely vulnerable to failed innovation, which affects them directly. This vulnerability provides a strong argument for a critical view of the potential of innovation in the social sector. The benefits from innovation may not always justify the associated risks. Any innovation efforts need to be made very productive. Innovation in the social sector is thus neither naturally legitimized by its potential benefits nor a necessity for competitive reasons, as it is for businesses. For that reason, we do not provide innovation recipes but explore how organizations potentially can innovate and grow at lower degrees of uncertainty and risk to improve the quality, predictability, and scale of their solutions. We replace an innovation logic with an impact-creation logic.

On the Dominance of the Technical View of Innovation

Innovation is often associated with technical problems that can be solved with technical solutions. We differentiate between technical and relational problems and distinguish the different challenges that technical problems (dealing with economic resources, technology, and cognitive challenges) and relational problems (dealing with norms, traditions, politics, and power relations) present for innovation and scaling. Furthermore, case studies of four organizations (see Part II) remind us of the critical role that an organization's identity—its core values, beliefs, and sense of mission—plays as it makes productive decisions about innovation and scaling.

A GUIDE TO READING THIS BOOK

Here is a guide to the learning journey that we hope this book sets you on. In Chapter 1 we challenge widely held assumptions and the popular use of the word *innovation*. Even in experienced organizations, the term has ambiguous, unclear, and inconsistent meanings and uses. This is not a productive basis for decisions, learning, and supporting long-term efforts to create impact. We therefore explicitly link innovation to the objectives and potential for impact creation in organizations. Because our focus is on innovation in established organizations, we present a framework that clarifies the relation between innovation and the impact-creation logic of organizations. The term *impact-creation logic* refers to the ability of organizations to purposefully create impact by acting on accumulated knowledge in three important dimensions: the problem space that defines the needs that an organization targets in a particular environment, its mission and strategy, and its resources and capabilities. *Innovation* in that framework refers to creating and developing ideas that deal with uncertainties in some or all of these dimensions. Because innovation deploys organizational resources for uncertain future outcomes we propose that innovators keep an eye on six types of uncertainties.

We explicitly distinguish innovation from scaling. We refer to scaling as activities that act on and improve already existing knowledge, processes, products, services, or interventions to serve more people better. Scaling creates more immediate and more predictable positive impact than innovation. This distinction between innovation and scaling has serious implications for decisions about allocating resources to either innovation or scaling. The frameworks in Chapter 1 provide a consistent terminology and an analytical perspective for comparing and for drawing important distinctions and insights from the four case studies in Part II.

In Chapter 2 we further explore the important distinction between innovation and scaling. Building on Chapter 1, where innovation and scaling are treated as distinct sets of activities, this chapter explicitly links the two. Doing so generates a generic innovation process that consists of the creation and development of new ideas (innovation) and the subsequent operational delivery of the resulting products, services or interventions, their improvements, extensions, and growth (scaling) that generate impact. This perspective sensitizes readers for a critical distinction between *innovation or scaling* as two fundamentally different processes and *innovation and scaling* as two processes that are joined over time and fundamentally depend on each other. This distinction is an important and useful lens for evaluating our featured social enterprises' long-term decisions about scaling and innovation and how this creates positive impact.

A process view of innovation opens up an opportunity to diagnose innovation pathologies, unproductive innovations that waste scarce organizational resources. We develop a diagnostic tool that enables mapping innovation pathologies. An objective assessment of these pathologies supports decisions about how to make innovations more productive and how to integrate innovation and scaling into an organization's long-term impact-creation logic.

In Part II we dive deeply into four social enterprises. The case studies in Chapters 3 through 6 invite reflections on their particular approaches to innovation and scaling. They also illustrate the conceptual frameworks in Chapters 1 and 2 to emphasize distinct challenges to innovation and scaling, depending on the particular impact-creation logics of the organizations. The chapters also introduce the particular environment that defines the operating space of the social enterprises in this book: developing countries with many social and environmental problems. The cases give us a rich set of data to support a comparative analysis and let us draw conclusions and insights. We compromised between providing mere narratives and providing "raw" data. We have integrated many direct quotes by members and observers of the featured organizations into the case narratives. Their words let readers draw their own conclusions before reflecting on the more analytical Chapters 7 and 8.

At the end of each case study we synthesize insights and important distinctions from each organization. We distinguish among four innovation archetypes that represent a distinct sequencing and purpose of innovation and scaling over the lifetime of an organization. Innovation archetypes enable organizations to think systematically and explicitly about how to integrate innovation and scaling over time and how this integration contributes to establishing and strengthening a distinct impact-creation logic.

In Chapter 7 we compare the histories and the innovation archetypes of the four organizations in a systematic manner. We also show how impact-creation logics change over time and potentially become broader and deeper. This evolution has important implications for the relative innovation advantages of organizations that organizational decision makers and potential funders should explicitly consider.

In Chapter 8 we reflect on a prominent feature that seems to define almost all of the most effective social enterprises we have studied: a deep engagement with local communities, a willingness to learn from them and to understand what makes them tick. This chapter therefore focuses on problem spaces, the ways in which needs and problems associated with poverty are embedded in local characteristics of their socioeconomic and political environment. We introduce a crucial distinction between two types of problem spaces, technical and relational problems. The factors that create and sustain important poverty-associated needs and problems of individuals and communities can be identified and mapped as a distinct problem space. This mapping approach is the basis for a diagnostic framework that organizations and their supporters can use to understand the implications of these factors for intervention design, for innovation, and for scaling. It guides the design of adequate measures and it helps establish more realistic expectations about the time required for translating interventions into beneficial outcomes. It is also a simple yet powerful tool for learning within and across organizations and geographic areas. This diagnostic tool facilitates innovation efforts where constant and systematic learning is crucial, as well as project evaluation and benchmarking efforts.

The closing chapter summarizes and synthesizes our main findings and makes practical recommendations for how to use and to integrate the tools and frameworks presented in this book for other organizations. A central message is that productive innovation rarely comes from trying to make organizations more "innovative." Rather, productive innovation is the result of investment in organizational infrastructure, and this often means innovating less. And, although routine work and small improvements to existing products, services, and interventions do not have the "sexiness factor" of innovations, organizations are well advised to resist the innovation hype and concentrate on building committed, productive organizations based around a clear, consistent, and well-developed impact-creation logic. Doing so requires patience, realism, and a willingness to invest in building and nurturing enduring organizations that develop their own unique character and approach to innovation and scaling for impact.

INTRODUCING THE SOCIAL ENTERPRISES FEATURED IN THIS BOOK

Because we occasionally refer to our case studies in Chapters 1 and 2, a brief introduction to the organizations is in order. First we want to clarify the purpose of the case studies. We provide rich histories of two decades of each organization, from its founding until today. We integrate many direct quotes to give the organizations voice and to reduce our own biases and tendencies as researchers for selective editing and overinterpretation. By letting the organizations speak for themselves, we hope to encourage you to do your own analysis and interpretation of the cases before reflecting on the insights and conclusions that we draw from them. Comparing your own findings and impressions of the cases with our analyses and conclusions is a much more fruitful learning method than relying on our findings alone. Compare the differences and similarities between the featured organizations and their environments with your own. How do they think about the problems of innovation and scaling? How does your organization? A keen sense of contextual scope and boundary conditions facilitates generalizations from a few social enterprises to other organizations that are valid and therefore of practical use.

In the past decade we have studied many inspiring and effective social enterprises. For this book, we have chosen to feature four. Our choices were based on four criteria:

1. We wanted to provide sufficient variety in the missions and approaches of organizations to reveal the broad range of roles that innovation and scaling play in social enterprises, how the processes are enacted and with what consequences.

2. The organizations were founded in two developing countries, Bangladesh and India. Their location gives the book a particular lens that reduces effects introduced by country-specific differences. This also means that we need to be sensitive to these particularities when

TABLE I.I
Brief summaries of the four organizations featured in this book (data from 2014).

	Gram Vikas	Aravind (Aravind Eye Care Services)	BRAC (Bangladesh Rehabilitation Assistance Committee/Bangladesh Rural Advancement Committee)	Waste Concern
Formal founding year	1979	1976	1972	1995
Mission	To promote processes that are sustainable, socially inclusive, and gender equitable to enable critical masses of poor and marginalized rural people or communities to achieve a dignified quality of life	To eliminate needless blindness	To empower people and communities in situations of poverty, illiteracy, disease, and social injustice. Our interventions aim to achieve large-scale positive changes through economic and social programs that enable men and women to realize their potential.	To contribute toward waste recycling, environmental improvement, renewable energy, poverty reduction through job creation, and sustainable development
Regional presence	India	India; International through collaborations with partner organizations	BRAC: Bangladesh; BRAC International: Afghanistan, Pakistan, Sri Lanka, Philippines, South Sudan, Tanzania, Uganda, Sierra Leone, Liberia, Haiti	Bangladesh; International through collaborations with partner organizations
Main program areas	Inequality; gender and social discrimination; water, sanitation, and hygiene; social housing; education; livelihood and food security	Hospital services, community outreach, education, training, consulting, manufacturing ophthalmic consumables, research, eye bank	Agriculture and food security; community empowerment; disability inclusion; disaster relief; environment and climate change; education; gender justice and diversity; health, nutrition, and population; human rights and legal aid services; integrated development; microfinance; road safety; migration; social enterprises targeting extreme poverty; water, sanitation, and hygiene	Solid waste management and resource recovery, clinical and hazardous waste management, waste water treatment, community-based environmental improvement, urban environmental management, municipal services planning, environmental impact assessment, climate change and clean development, organic farming
Staff	About 260	About 2,500	About 120,000	About 50
Subunits	Gram Vikas	Aravind Eye Care Centers, Lions Aravind Institute of Community Ophthalmology (LAICO), Dr. G. Venkataswamy Eye Research Institute, Aurolab	BRAC, BRAC International, BRAC University, BRAC social enterprises	Waste Concern, Waste Concern Consultants, Waste Concern Baraka Agro Products Ltd., WWR (World Wide Recycling), Bio Fertilizer Bangladesh Ltd., Matuail Power Ltd.

generalizing findings to other environments, especially to social enterprises operating in developed countries.

3. We had followed these organizations and had interacted with them on a number of occasions within and outside their operating environments for more than a decade. We felt that we had established trusting relationships with a number of people within and outside the four organizations, so that they were motivated to share facts and anecdotes about failures, false assumptions, and unintended consequences of innovations.

4. We had collected a broad set of data from these organizations as well as a number of external funders, supporters, and observers. This variety provided us with sufficiently deep accounts to reflect different perspectives of different observers over time, as well as an appreciation of the ongoing changes that defined their trajectories.

Table I.1 compares salient facts of the organizations. Their case studies will be presented in Chapter 3 (Innovation as Learning: The Story of Gram Vikas), Chapter 4 (Innovation in Support of Scaling: The Story of Aravind), Chapter 5 (Innovating and Scaling for Transformative Impact: The Story of BRAC), and Chapter 6 (Innovation that Enables Diffusion: The Story of Waste Concern).

PART I

Innovation, Scaling, and Impact
A Complex Relationship

In the following chapters we develop the argument that a deeper strategic conversation around innovation and scaling enables better decision making and demonstrate how this works. As a first step, we present a central framework that establishes clear terminology. The framework treats innovation and scaling as distinct processes within organizations. Next, we evaluate innovation and scaling based on their potential for creating positive impact. Lastly, we develop a diagnostic framework that enables organizations to identify their innovation pathologies that make innovations unproductive and waste scarce resources. Clarifying terminology and identifying innovation pathologies are essential first steps for organizations that seek productive decisions about innovation and scaling for impact.

1   OF RED AND GREEN ZONES
How Innovation and Scaling Create Impact

Most people feel they understand the world with far greater detail, coherence, and depth than they really do.[1]

We often call things innovative. We talk about innovative people, innovative organizations, innovative products, or innovative approaches to alleviating poverty. But when we ask ourselves what exactly it is that we are trying to say when we use this label, we are often unable to give a clear answer. It can seem as though innovation is merely a subjective judgment about something. The absence of a shared basis for how we use the term leads to inconsistency. This may not be a problem when we use the word *innovation* in a casual conversation. But we have witnessed—in workshops, at conferences, and in discussions with colleagues—how unproductive it is to argue over subjective interpretations of innovation. The ambiguity around the term is a strong barrier to learning and knowledge accumulation and to making productive decisions. This ambiguity also explains why managerial research has largely failed to generate practical insights for organizations and why so many organizations continue to struggle with whether and how to be more innovative.

As we explained in the Introduction, we have had to reconsider our own use of the word *innovative* in relation to social enterprises. These organizations often have unconventional hybrid structures, financing mechanisms, and engagement processes with various stakeholders. All of those differences seemed innovative to us because they did not fit the standard model of a typical organization in Western competitive markets. Eventually, through our fieldwork, we developed a clearer set of criteria for what *innovative* implies. We felt that it was crucial to link innovation explicitly to the creation of impact.

This chapter attempts to deliver a clear perspective and a consistent set of criteria. As a basis for making this book helpful for you, our readers, we specify and operationalize innovation. By *operationalizing* we mean defining it in a practically useful manner that relates to concrete decisions and actions in organizations. That way we also introduce a consistent terminology for analysis of our four featured social enterprises, which we use throughout the book.

Our perspective on innovation is a synthesis of what we consider to be useful frameworks and distinctions offered by the innovation literature and insights derived from our deep engagement with organizations over many years. We will not sell you a paint-by-numbers guide to operationalizing innovation. Rather, we offer a grounded perspective that is conscious of the complexities of innovation and scaling but integrates a minimal, or core, set of concepts that we feel is necessary and sufficient for making productive decisions on innovation and scaling for impact. From this core set of concepts we build frameworks that you can adapt to any type of organization. We strongly believe that organizations that invest time and effort to create clear, internally shared, consistent, and actionable language and mental models around innovation are in a much better position to accumulate knowledge, to measure and compare innovation efforts, and to make strategic decisions about innovation and scaling.

Productive operationalization starts with being sufficiently precise and transparent about the term—something we rarely see in organizations. It requires finding terminology that is clear to decision makers in organizations and distinguishes innovation from other activities that also create impact. What also matters is consistent application of the term and careful adaptations that come from accumulated experience of when, how, and with what consequences innovations are enacted in an organization over time.

In this chapter we show how innovation contrasts with other impact-creating activities to illuminate what it is and is not. Clarifying what innovation actually does in an organization has several advantages: It creates shared and realistic expectations about what innovation can and cannot achieve, distinguishes which types of innovation an organization favors, and develops a shared sense of requirements that clarifies why, when, and at what pace an organization can and wants to innovate. This perspective on innovation is clearly different from the view of innovation as a competitive necessity in the business sector, where the dynamics in your industry in many ways define the why, what, and when of innovation. As we said in the Introduction, a number of organizational and environmental factors necessitate a much more conscious, careful, and intentional approach by social enterprises deciding about innovations. Otherwise, innovation is too often just a distraction for organizations that undermines the potential to create long-term impact at a meaningful scale. Let's explore those factors now.

ILLUSIONS OF UNDERSTANDING

Cognitive scientists believe that we all suffer more or less from illusions of understanding. Studies have shown that we are overconfident about the extent to which we know and can explain the workings of seemingly simple objects that we use in our daily lives, the terms we use in our work, or organizational phenomena that we observe.[1,2] But, when challenged, our explanations often reveal significant holes, invalid assumptions, and inconsistencies. In the social sector, we confidently and frequently use ambiguous words such as *impact, resilience, scaling,* and *innovation.* These terms resonate with many, perhaps because there is plenty of room for various interpretations of their meaning. Consequently, anyone can choose his or her own favorite meaning. This is how buzzwords are born and readily diffuse through a sector. The development sector, where the painful reality of fundamental needs of millions creates a constant state of desperation for new solutions, is an easy victim of this dynamic. Unfortunately, deciding and acting on illusions of understanding often have negative consequences. Reality has little patience for well-intended ignorance.

Innovation is a good example. It is among the most frequent terms used in almost any field these days. The development sector has readily adopted it from the business sector with little reflection on fundamental differences. When we ask social enterprises or funders what innovation is and how they use the term internally, we get a bewildering range of definitions, assumptions, and expectations. It seems that anything that appears novel or surprising is called an innovation, even if the act of creating it was not innovative and did not involve any significant risk or uncertainty.

Here is an example: when we first visited BRAC in Bangladesh, more than ten years ago, we were taken to one of its field sites. BRAC staff encouraged us to interact directly with the villagers. We visited kindergartens where boys and girls naturally played together, and when asked they voiced aspirations for their future lives that were totally unexpected, given the local circumstances. They wanted to become educators or medical doctors and clearly had expectations for their futures that were very different from their families' current realities. Illiterate women from very poor families worked together in support groups and dealt confidently with money, loans, and interest payments. This was all surprising and novel to us. We saw an incredible innovation in how on-the-ground development work is done. But for BRAC it was a day like any other. All this "innovation" we observed was mostly routine work for them. Its staff had operated kindergartens and organized groups of women for more than a decade. Instead of innovating, BRAC was scaling well-established programs to serve more people better. After many discussions and field visits, it finally dawned on us: If we want to study innovation, we need to suppress our natural tendencies to treat outcomes of organizational work that seem novel and surprising as innovations. Instead, we need to look carefully at the organizational processes that generate these outcomes. This insight raised central questions that we explore in this book: What are the characteristics of processes that we call innovative or innovations? What is the role of innovation in creating positive impact? And what is the relation between innovation and scaling?

Being sensitized by this perspective on innovation, we increasingly noticed that neither leaders of social enterprises nor their funders seem to have a shared and consistent understanding of what innovation means. Therefore, innovation activities are often ad hoc and associated with unrealistic expectations. Organizations may use innovation language and perception management opportunistically to jump on available grants that seem to require the extensive use of the term *innovation* as a prerequisite for funding. It is difficult to coordinate activities within and across organizations if everyone has a different mental model of innovation.

But isn't there a wealth of knowledge available on innovation that could serve as a source for clarification and inspiration? That was our assumption—and hope—when we started reviewing the extensive managerial and organizational literature on innovation. What did we find?

Innovation Research Is Not Practical

To clarify thinking about innovation, one could potentially read the thousands of managerial papers and books that have been published on the topic in recent years. They share insights on many aspects of innovation in organizations and promote solutions and recipes for increasing their innovativeness. A number of authors have reviewed the vast and rapidly expanding organizational innovation literature. Many are skeptical about the practical use of our knowledge. A review from 1994 already noted that "the most consistent theme found in the organizational innovation literature is that its research results have been inconsistent" and that it is "low in explanatory power and thus offers little guidance to practitioners."[3]

Despite this skepticism, today we know a lot about how organizations develop and execute new ideas internally as part of innovation processes. We also have a good understanding of how and under which circumstances organizations adopt ideas and innovations from the external environment. And we know many characteristics of the organizational and environmental factors that influence innovation processes. A comprehensive 2004 review of the innovation literature documents this progress in knowledge.[4] The authors identified a large number of factors that researchers have found to influence innovation in organizations. Despite all this knowledge, however, the authors of the review criticized innovation research as lacking creativity and innovativeness and as portraying innovation as unrealistic, inaccurate, and linear.

Other authors agree. In a more recent review,[5] scholars synthesized thousands of scholarly papers on organizational innovation in an effort to identify actionable determinants within the realm of organizational and individual power. That review documents impressively how our collective understanding of the factors that influence innovation in organizations has grown. We understand quite well how at least some of them work in isolation. But the complexity generated by numerous coexisting factors and their particular constellations in any given organization, whether from the business or the social sector, challenges our ability to translate that knowledge into practical advice. The authors of the review summarized their evaluation of the state of the innovation literature: "However, as our review has demonstrated, innovation research is fragmented, poorly grounded theoretically, and not fully tested in all areas. Even the latest innovation models fail to consistently capture across and within sector factors."[5]

Social Sector Innovation Research Lacks Adequate Depth

Research on innovation in the social sector unfortunately is not particularly useful either. In a recent review of the innovation literature with a specific focus on social sector organizations, we found the knowledge base to be relatively thin and equally problematic for providing guidance.[6] What are the implications of this sobering review of existing innovation research? Research matters, but it does not furnish organizations with recipes they can follow to guarantee "innovation success," despite the hopes raised by hundreds of innovation books. We therefore caution against naïve assumptions that there are easy and quick answers to the questions of what innovation is and how to build innovation capabilities. Unfortunately, organizations are left to translate this fragmented knowledge base into useful decision frameworks themselves. The potential advantage of doing the translation work is that it forces organizations to unearth, question, and—if necessary—correct hidden assumptions. Ideally, they will create an innovation language that is intelligible to decision makers and specifies clear roles and expectations for innovation in support of their longer-term ambitions for the organization. In the next sections we offer some ideas for getting started with this work.

DEVELOPING A FRAMEWORK THAT
LINKS INNOVATION AND IMPACT

We evaluate innovation by its potential for creating impact. The term *impact creation* refers to the benefits created for the people and communities that an organization serves. Linking innovation to impact creation has a number of advantages. It implies that innovation needs to "prove itself." Innovation must be evaluated by its outcomes and the impact it generates compared to the effort expended. Innovations may thus fail or succeed, and innovations may be more or less productive. We replace the positive ideology of "innovation is good" with an evaluative perspective that considers innovation as one potential way to create impact. The focus on impact creation also links innovation to concrete organizational decisions and actions. By treating innovation as a process that has particular characteristics, organizations, funders, and other stakeholders can reflect on innovation more systematically and learn to make better decisions about it.

In the next sections we focus on two important aspects of innovation. One considers the particular roles and challenges for innovation in already established organizations, the main focus of this book. The second aspect focuses on the types of uncertainty associated with innovation. Six distinct types of uncertainty prevent organizations from knowing whether or how they might succeed with innovations. We distinguish innovation explicitly from those organizational processes that create impact by enacting well-established knowledge at low degrees of uncertainty. Existing knowledge in organizations enables impact-creation processes by specifying the why, what, and how of organizational action. In that way, action is legitimized by its ability to generate predictable positive impact in line with an organization's mission, values, and strategic priorities (*why* knowledge). Relevant and effective action is enabled by a deep understanding of the problems and needs of an organization's customers or the people and communities it serves (*what* knowledge). And it is enabled by resources such as trained staff and their capabilities to meet these problems and needs efficiently (*how* knowledge). Under these circumstances, success (in the form of creating positive desired impact) is expected.

Investing time and effort in defining and articulating the nature and role of innovation in an organization is valuable. When organizations clearly lay out the characteristics of innovation and the role they expect it to play, they can transform an illusion of understanding into real understanding. The distinctions about innovation in this section support that work. Step-by-step we will build a framework that clarifies and operationalizes the term *innovation*. We kept the framework as simple as possible to reduce the complexity that reviews of the innovation research have identified as barriers to understanding and making decisions about innovation. The framework builds on three well-established dimensions that determine the impact creation potential of organizations in general. That way we avoid introducing an "artificial" innovation framework that is decoupled from an organization's day-to-day operations. Because the framework is generic, individual organizations can adopt it, modify it, and expand it for their own purposes. Furthermore, the framework explicitly contrasts innovation with other impact-creating activities. This distinction avoids the fallacy of overestimating the potential of innovation, in the sense of "innovation is good—the more the better."

Impact-Creation Logics

We assume that innovation is purposeful. Therefore, innovations are enacted in organizations with the explicit purpose of creating impact. For our innovation framework, we have adopted Peter Drucker's notion "the theory of the business."[7] Drucker asserts that successful organizations that create value operate from a sound theory that aligns three critical dimensions: (1) mission, (2) environment, and (3) capabilities. Successful organizations operate from a high level of relevant knowledge and little uncertainty in these three dimensions. They have a clear sense of mission. They know who they want to be and what they want to achieve. They hire people for whom that mission is meaningful. This clarity of mission guides their actions with appropriate levels of focus, motivation, and commitment (*why* knowledge). Successful organizations also know their environment well, as well as their customers and other stakeholders. They know their competitors and the social, economic, and political factors that define a particular environment. Actions thus cater to well-understood customer problems and needs by providing relevant products and services (*what* knowledge). Successful organizations also understand the essential capabilities they must build to satisfy needs in their markets and to achieve strategic objectives. This understanding makes actions more efficient and effective and increases productivity, quality, and growth potential (*how* knowledge). Relevant knowledge in these three dimensions thus enables organizations to create value.

Drucker emphasizes three criteria that characterize a successful theory of the business: (1) high validity of the knowledge and low degrees of uncertainty in the three dimensions, (2) clarity and a shared knowledge of the theory of the business across the organization, and (3) the ability to create a reinforcing fit between the three dimensions. We use Drucker's model as the principal architecture for our innovation framework. We adapt the three dimensions of Drucker's theory of the business to study social enterprises and group them as (1) mission and strategy, (2) resources and capabilities, and (3) problem spaces, the needs and problems that an organization targets in a particular environment. Instead of *theory of the business* we use the term *impact-creation logic* (see Figure 1.1). High levels of valid knowledge, clarity, and fit of the three dimensions are a hallmark of successful impact-creation logics. This is so because successful impact-creation logics provide adequate why, what, and how knowledge that enables social enterprises to create more positive impact.

Six Types of Uncertainties Define Innovations

How does innovation fit into this impact-creation logic? Novelty and uncertainty are central elements of innovation. This has been an enduring theme in organizational innovation research.[8,9] *Uncertainty*, as we use it here, refers to a lack of knowledge sufficient for creating expected positive impact from organizational action. Innovation thus refers to actions outside an established impact-creation logic. Innovation is characterized by low levels of why, what, and how knowledge, which challenge an organization to realize positive impact.

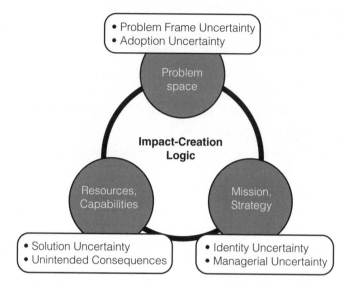

FIGURE 1.1

Organizations should keep an eye on six types of uncertainty associated with innovation, defined as actions outside their established impact-creation logic.

Acting despite uncertainty requires that organizations make a number of assumptions as temporary placeholders for knowledge. Thus a fruitful perspective on innovation views it as an act of finding out whether these assumptions are true or not. Sue Desmond-Hellmann, CEO of the Bill & Melinda Gates Foundation, explains this characteristic really well: "The job of the innovator is to seek truth. My job as a leader is to enable and reward people to seek and to tell the truth."[10] Uncertainty, lack of knowledge, is thus a principal criterion for defining actions as innovative. We therefore define innovation as decisions and actions with the purpose of creating impact whose realization is challenged by various degrees of uncertainty.

This definition has important implications for the impact-creation potential of innovations: Innovation outcomes are uncertain and can be positive or negative for organizations and their stakeholders. This unpredictability explains why innovation often fails and thus potentially wastes scarce organizational resources. For many readers, this may seem to be common knowledge. But organizations that have been successful for a long time sometimes forget about this important characteristic of innovation. For example, a senior manager of a well-established social enterprise told us that his organization could innovate "safely." Imagine how an organization operating under this belief deals with failures when enacting innovations. Blaming people instead of learning about uncertainties might be the default option. A related observation is that some funders seem to demand more innovation from social enterprises and at the same time expect them to demonstrate more impact. We believe this is also a flawed notion akin to "innovating safely." Our innovation framework thus makes the link between innovation and creating desired positive impact explicit. It clarifies both the potential and the limits of this link.

To understand what innovation entails, we recommend that organizations keep an eye on six types of uncertainty that are frequently associated with innovations in the social sector:

DO WE UNDERSTAND THE PROBLEMS OR NEEDS THAT WE WANT TO ADDRESS SUFFICIENTLY WELL?   Often, the observable part of poverty hides many unobservable but important aspects. Our assumptions are crucial. We may assume that women in a particular community are poor because they have no financial means, or because they have cognitive limitations, or because they are discriminated against for reasons of gender or social status. Our assumptions have important implications for how we think about ideas and opportunities for meeting their needs. Gram Vikas, one of our featured organizations, struggled with a number of failed innovations when trying to solve the problems of tribal villages in Orissa, India. The problems of the tribes were complex and multifaceted, and they had historical and unobservable roots. But every failed innovation provided the organization with an additional window into the complexity. It took a long time for their understanding of the villagers' problems to improve and innovations to become more productive. We therefore call this area of uncertainty *problem frame uncertainty*. It is a starting ground for innovation. Investing time and efforts in understanding problems correctly is central to making innovation productive.

DO WE KNOW WHETHER PEOPLE AND COMMUNITIES ARE WILLING AND ABLE TO ADOPT OUR INNOVATIONS?   A storehouse in Ann Arbor, Michigan, has acquired the nickname "Museum of Failed Products." It is a graveyard for thousands of product innovations that failed in the market because consumers did not want them. Two of our featured organizations also illustrate the importance of this innovation uncertainty in the social sector. Gram Vikas built a dairy facility for tribal communities in India. Despite serious investments in time, money, and effort, it could not get the communities to adopt dairy products and had to declare the innovation a failure. Another example is BRAC's search for solutions to the high child mortality rate in Bangladesh in the early 1970s. One idea was to develop and introduce family planning. Unfortunately, BRAC discovered that the acceptance rate of this intervention was low and was thus forced to stop this innovation. We call this area of uncertainty *adoption uncertainty*.

ARE WE ABLE TO DESIGN, BUILD, AND OPERATE EFFECTIVE SOLUTIONS TO PEOPLE'S AND COMMUNITIES' PROBLEMS?   Even if the problem frame is clear and adoption uncertainty is low, we may not know how to configure various resources into an effective solution. Furthermore, the scarcity of resources, dearth of technologies, and lack of markets in developing countries make it uncertain as to whether workable solutions can be designed. For example, the health innovations introduced by the Aravind eye hospital were menaced by uncertainty that the organization could hire, train, or otherwise acquire sufficient numbers of scarce eye doctors and nurses to succeed with its mission "to eliminate needless blindness." And whether their health service innovations could be made financially sustainable was uncertain as well. We call this area of uncertainty *solution uncertainty*.

Even proven solutions often do not work in a different environment from the one where they were established. For example, when BRAC replicated its successful Bangladeshi microfinance operation in Afghanistan, its staff found that there were not enough economic opportunities to make it work. What BRAC thought was a routine replication of a well-established program instead turned out to be an innovation with uncertain outcomes. Thus problem frame uncertainties and solution uncertainties are often closely linked. Many innovation processes go back and forth between striving to improve their problem frame for designing better solutions and using experiments with different solutions to understand problems better.

CAN WE FORESEE ANY NEGATIVE SIDE EFFECTS OF INNOVATIONS? The history of innovations is full of examples that illustrate the importance of this question. Talk to any pharmaceutical company about long-term negative side effects of drugs that had looked promising in clinical trials. Often it is a question of how many side effects of innovations we tolerate, given the benefits they create. This balance is true not only for drugs but for almost all the defining innovations of the industrial revolution. Think about climate change as a long-term unintended consequence of using fossil fuels that undoubtedly also generated a lot of wealth and other benefits for societies. Or, in the social sector, think about instilling bad habits of consumerism in poor communities as a side effect of easy access to microfinance. Gram Vikas also offers an illustrative example about an agricultural innovation aimed at reducing economic inequality among farmers in India. The innovation failed because its adoption counterintuitively reinforced power and dependency structures between poor farmers and landowners. We call this area of uncertainty *unintended consequences*.

DOES THIS INNOVATION FIT OUR IDENTITY AND VALUES? Organizations are made up of people to serve other people. They are not society's toolbox for targeting poverty or funders' instruments for creating impact. An organization's identity—its particular values and sense of mission—shapes its preferences for the why, what, and how of innovation. An innovation may make sense for one organization but not for another. Whether an innovation will require engaging in activities that do not fit an organization's core values and sense of identity may be uncertain.

For example, the founders of Waste Concern were not motivated to run a large organization. Throughout their organizational journey, they faced high degrees of uncertainty about how to create significant impact from innovations while remaining small. Another example is Gram Vikas's successful innovation around developing biogas to improve the livelihood of poor farmers. The innovation created tremendous impact for thousands of farmers. But it was not in line with Gram Vikas's identity and sense of mission. Eventually, the organization could not sustain the required level of motivation and let go of an otherwise very successful innovation. Innovations in BRAC's microfinance unit were explored by setting up two competing approaches that were grounded in different ideologies. The tensions created by evaluating which approach fit BRAC's identity were so high that some staff members even left the organization. Thus innovation is not just learning about hard facts such as designing solutions for particular needs. It is also about soft facts, exploring directions that an organization may be uncomfortable with. This requires testing and clarifying an organization's sense of mission, core values, and identity. We call this area of uncertainty *identity uncertainty*.

HOW DO WE MANAGE INNOVATION PROCESSES PRODUCTIVELY?   Organizations often stifle innovation or make innovation processes unproductive. This possibility increases the uncertainty associated with innovation in their organizations. Research has identified a number of organizational factors that increase uncertainty.[11] The belief mentioned earlier that an organization could "innovate safely," for instance, may generate unrealistic expectations and may stifle learning. If organizations don't have clearly articulated impact-creation logics but rather vague objectives and priorities, staff will find it hard to judge what types of ideas to create, what innovations to pursue, and how their ideas and efforts will be evaluated.

Aravind demonstrated the challenges that organizations face when innovating. It struggled to decide whether to expand into manufacturing to unplug a bottleneck in its supply chain. An observer remembered: "There was a shouting match between the founder and his sister, who until then had never raised her voice against her brother. That was unheard of." Innovation can be quite stressful! Innovating productively requires that organizations find ways to manage the process well. We therefore call this area of uncertainty *managerial uncertainty*.

We propose that uncertainty is a defining characteristic of innovation. Creating knowledge through learning is thus a much more realistic outcome of innovations than expecting the development of valuable new products, services, or interventions. This view is consistent with much organizational research.[12,9] The quality of learning—and a bit of luck—determine the quality of innovation outcomes. But although any fool can get lucky once, in the long run, innovation favors the smart, not the fool.

Keeping an eye on the six types of uncertainty gives you an opportunity to load the innovation dice in your favor. A keen awareness of the principal uncertainties involved in a particular innovation makes explicit the areas in which learning should occur. This awareness helps organizations to stay on a productive innovation path. It gives innovation efforts direction and legitimacy in several ways: First, it provides organizations with explicit areas for intentional learning as a central objective of innovation. For example, if you are participating in innovations you might work with everyone involved to map expected areas of uncertainties. As you proceed with an innovation you can update your assumptions and thus document the ongoing learning effort. Second, it reduces wasted efforts by highlighting opportunities for enacting fast and inexpensive ways to reduce at least some types of uncertainty before you commit significant resources to innovation. Third, it enables evaluation of the relative riskiness of different innovative ideas. Enacting ideas that have lower degrees of uncertainty in some dimensions is associated with lower innovation risk. This may also help funders to monitor their investment portfolio and to visualize the relative riskiness of their investments. At the same time, this map may help funders to identify particular areas of support that are adequate for innovations with different uncertainty profiles.

Keeping an eye on the six areas of uncertainty also lowers the threat of organizational silence (when no one wants to communicate bad news about innovation failures). All news is good news when it results from explicit learning about the pertinent uncertainties. Explicit learning creates organizational knowledge as a key outcome of innovations in line with Sue Desmond-Hellmann's notion of "to seek and to tell the truth."

The organizations we feature in this book will illustrate and bring to life our more conceptual arguments. They offer rich contextual information for understanding how individual areas of uncertainty relate to each other and what this implies for productively embedding innovation in a long-term organizational trajectory.

THE RED AND GREEN ZONES OF
INNOVATION AND SCALING

As we have discussed, the validity, clarity, and fit between three dimensions of knowledge determine the strength of an organization's impact-creation logic and thus its potential for creating impact. Figure 1.1 depicts this argument. It proposes that an impact-creation logic refers to enacting three dimensions of knowledge that are vital to social enterprises: (1) knowledge about the nature of the problems and needs that an organization caters to in a particular *space* or environment and the likelihood that solutions will be adopted by those in need, (2) knowledge that accumulates as resources (for example, trained staff) and capabilities (the things that an organization does really well) as the basis for enacting effective solutions and understanding the likelihood and properties of unintended consequences of solutions, and (3) knowledge and clarity about its core values and identity that is formalized as a clearly understood mission, as well as knowledge formalized into a long-term strategy around concrete objectives and priorities and a managerial infrastructure such as particular organizational structures and processes.

Impact Creation: Enacting the Green Zone (Scaling)

All established organizations are repertoires of implicit and explicit knowledge that they have accumulated over years of operation. They all operate from some impact-creation logic, even though it may not always be a very good one. They provide established products and services that cater to well-understood needs. This is the day-to-day routine work by which organizations create immediate and predictably positive impact. Effective social enterprises with successful impact-creation logics constantly search for ideas that allow them to improve what they are already doing in an effort to create more impact. They identify problems and opportunities that emerge directly from ongoing work. This exercise creates ideas for improvements and expansions of existing processes, products, or services. The ideas are generated by routine work, and therefore they are well understood by an organization.

The impact potential of these types of ideas and their costs of implementation are relatively clear. Implementation is feasible because they fit organizational capabilities and thus leverage accumulated knowledge. Resources are available to implement the ideas. Enacting these ideas can be safely expected to improve performance and thus create more impact. The ideas usually fit prevailing mental models and an organization's value system and sense of mission. They support current priorities and established organizational objectives and measures. Ideas are likely to fit the agendas of decision makers and support the career ambitions of general staff. Evaluating these ideas is thus straightforward; they make immediate sense. In effective organizations, no tensions are involved in communicating, evaluating, and deciding to implement them.

We refer to these ideas and their execution as scaling. Scaling means that organizations do more of what they are good at or do things better or both. Scaling thus allows organizations to create immediate and predictable benefits and positive impact. Scaling generates a stream of improvements and expansions of current activities, products, and services. Individually these improvements may be unremarkable, but they accumulate and thus deepen and expand an organization's knowledge over time. The focus, commitment, and repetitiveness of scaling refine an organization's routines and capabilities. Specialized resources and other types of implicit and explicit knowledge accumulate. The positive impact scaling creates is highly motivating and reinforces a shared sense of mission. This accumulation strengthens an organization's impact-creation logic. Scaling over time dramatically improves an organization's ability to serve more people better.

We refer to this important link between scaling and impact-creation logics as an organization's green zone, as depicted in Figure 1.2. The term *green zone* captures two important organizational characteristics. First, it consolidates the essential criteria of successful impact-creation logics: high levels of valid knowledge (low degrees of the six types of uncertainty), clarity (being consciously aware of it and consistently acting from this knowledge), and a reinforcing fit between the three dimensions: problem spaces, resources/capabilities, and mission/strategy. And, second, it captures the dynamics by which scaling further strengthens an organization's impact-creation logic as a result of improvements and knowledge accumulation. The term *green zone* thus specifies the organizational context in which successful and effective scaling and impact creation occur.

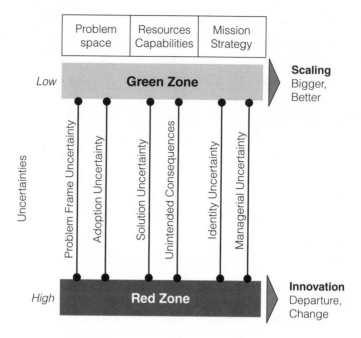

FIGURE 1.2

Mapping the green and red zones of scaling and innovation in established organizations.

Every organization has an impact-creation logic. Unfortunately, few have a distinct green zone. Without a green zone, organizations create little impact and are limited in their abilities to scale. Why? Because they do not have a successful impact-creation logic. Or, if they do, they do not push themselves hard enough to constantly improve their operations. Reflecting on the particular characteristics of green zones and how to build them will be a principal focus of Parts II and III. At this stage you might want to ask yourself, "What is the distinct impact-creation logic of my organization or the organization I support? What are its characteristics? Is it a weak and not clearly defined impact-creation logic that creates stagnant or unknown levels of impact, or does it have characteristics of a green zone reflecting years of knowledge accumulation? Should I even think about innovation if my organization does not yet have a green zone?"

Impact Exploration: Enacting the Red Zone (Innovation)
Innovation has characteristics very different from scaling's. Innovation is inherently uncertain, and ideas that give rise to innovations lie outside an organization's impact-creation logic. The ideas do not fit business as usual and challenge an organization's "immune system."[13] The immune system protects organizations from elements that are "alien" to its impact-creation logic, such as innovative ideas. Usually this happens for good reasons: Too much innovation may really make an organization "sick" if it limits impact creation from focused scaling. Many novel ideas outside an organization's impact-creation logic may actually have little potential for creating impact. Without an immune system to challenge these ideas, their development would waste resources with little benefit. An organization's immune system may react quite aggressively against unfamiliar ideas and may eliminate any hope that they will ever be executed. This makes their development an uphill battle.

Scholars have identified many factors of this immune system.[12,13] And most people who have ever voiced an unusual idea in an organization probably know what we are talking about. "Not now," "Won't work," "We don't have the resources," "This is not something we do," and "You will be responsible if it fails" are some of the usual killer arguments that give innovative ideas the lifespan of a mayfly.

In contrast, idea creation and implementation as part of scaling processes are fully compatible with an organization's immune system—they make immediate sense. But the needs and problems that innovative ideas address are not fully understood. They don't make sense from the perspective of established mental models or knowledge in use in organizations. The potential of these ideas for creating impact compared to alternative options is therefore hard to evaluate and remains uncertain. Because they are not necessarily grounded in existing capabilities, the resource requirements and costs of executing these ideas are unpredictable. Innovative ideas often seem like distractions from current priorities and ongoing efforts, particularly when things are generally working well. Innovations may not conform to prevailing organizational beliefs, values, and culture or to its sense of mission. Decision makers in organizations may have objectives and incentives that do not support enacting innovative ideas. For example, requirements for short-term positive results to advance careers, an organization's or manager's reputation, or performance based on established impact metrics are rarely aligned with the uncertainties of innovation. The time between starting an innovation and any observable effect can be uncomfortably long. Whether an innovation works is usually clear only at a late stage in an innovation effort. Innovation therefore refers to a set of activities that creates unpredictable positive or negative outcomes sometime in the future. That's scary.

We refer to this important link between innovation and impact-creation logics as an organization's red zone, as depicted in Figure 1.2. Innovations lie outside the knowledge base that defines an organization's impact-creation logic. They are thus contested and often fail. Table 1.1 contrasts the characteristics of ideas that are generated by an organization's green zone with those that lie in its red zone.

By using the terms *green zone* and *scaling* for routine ideas that involve low uncertainty and *red zone* and *innovation* for those with high uncertainty, we emphasize the fundamental differences for organizations as they evaluate and enact either type of idea. We also believe that the terms *green zone* and *red zone* capture important organizational aspects and distinctions that justify their introduction (rather than just using *innovation* and *scaling*). They specify important characteristics of an organization's context and potential for creating impact. Our specification of impact-creation logics shows how this potential is constituted.

The terms *innovation* and *scaling* refer to the actual processes by which this potential is enacted. We believe that this subtle distinction focuses organizational attention on how impact creation from either scaling or innovation is enabled and which particular challenges and outcomes can be expected from either action. For example, the question, "Does this organization have a green zone, and what are its characteristics?" potentially provides much more valid and useful information than just capturing data on how an organization "scales." We also feel that using *green zone* and *red zone* helps us avoid limiting ideologies that are often associated with discourses about innovation and scaling, as we said earlier in this chapter.

TABLE I.I

Characteristics of green zone ideas versus red zone ideas.

Green zone—Scaling	Red zone—Innovation
Problem space	
Problems and solutions are well understood.	Problems and solutions are not fully understood.
Ideas arise regularly from ongoing activities.	Ideas do not make immediate sense.
Impact potential of ideas and alternatives can be reasonably evaluated from existing knowledge.	Impact potential of ideas and alternatives is uncertain.
Resources and capabilities	
Resources are available.	Resource requirements and availability are uncertain.
Organization is designed to respond to these ideas (leverages past learning).	Organizational capabilities and knowledge are not sufficient to enact these ideas (requires new learning).
Unintended negative consequences are unlikely.	Unintended consequences are valid concerns.
Mission and strategy	
Ideas align with levels of ambition and strategic objectives.	Ideas may not fit objectives and incentives of decision makers.
Ideas fit current priorities and prevailing norms.	Ideas may depart from current priorities or organizational beliefs and cultures.
Success is expected and likely.	Failure may not be considered appropriate.
Creates predictable positive impact today.	Creates uncertain outcomes tomorrow.

The green and red zone distinction firmly attaches innovation and scaling to the characteristics of an organization's impact-creation logic.

Other authors sometimes use the distinctions of incremental versus radical innovation to refer to what we call the green zone/scaling (incremental) versus the red zone/innovation (radical). Our framework illustrates that there is a fundamental difference between scaling and innovation. When organizations fail to adequately differentiate between these activities, they send the wrong signal to internal and external stakeholders. Using the term *incremental innovation* for idea creation as part of scaling implies that this activity is something "special" or "unusual" that occurs infrequently. However, in effective organizations this constant idea creation that characterizes strong green zones is business as usual. We therefore do not recommend using *innovation* (incremental or radical) to refer to both green- and red-zone activities.

The case studies in Part II and our analysis will provide a more dynamic perspective on these issues and on how impact-creation logics evolve over time into strong green zones. The cases also enable us to expand this fundamental distinction between innovation and scaling to integrate additional questions that arise in organizations: "What defines the boundary between our green and red zones, and how does this shift over time? How do we think about innovations as part of scaling efforts? How does innovation relate to or even depend on green zones?"

Implications for Organizations

The distinction between green zones and red zones is grounded in one of the most enduring perspectives in the innovation management literature. It was most prominently developed by Jim March of Stanford University,[12] and we have adopted it for our purposes. Figure 1.2 shows a framework that clearly contrasts innovation with scaling. The distinction arms organizations with a clear specification of terms that can be integrated in concrete decisions. In a way, this specificity removes uncertainty and ambiguity about what innovation or scaling is, what their execution entails, and what results might be expected. The distinction also permits a more fine-grained mapping of the relative "innovativeness" of ideas by considering that, in reality, most innovations lie within the "playground" defined by the two extremes of the green and red zones. It highlights that there is a gradient of ideas between more or less innovative to the extent by which they depart from existing knowledge in the three dimensions of an organization's impact-creation logic. When an organization evaluates innovative ideas, mapping its assumptions about uncertainties will help it learn more objectively and more explicitly. It can trigger a search for quick ways to lower uncertainty, for example through a focused survey or by reaching out to experts or other sources of potential knowledge. It may set up parallel competing pilot studies to explore uncertainties more systematically. If it formally documents the uncertainties before resources are

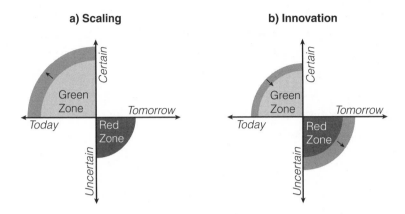

FIGURE 1.3
Consequences of allocating limited resources to scaling (certain benefits today) or innovation (uncertain outcomes tomorrow).

allocated, innovation failures are less likely to be blamed on the people involved. And progress can be documented more objectively by asking the question "Are we still learning something?" when we decide to abandon or continue with an innovation.

The distinction between green zones and red zones implies another crucial question: "Given that every organization has only limited resources, how many should it allocate to scaling to create positive impact immediately or to innovation and creating uncertain future outcomes?" This choice has important implications for an organization's impact-creation potential, as illustrated in Figure 1.3. Investing more resources into scaling effectively expands the green zone because the level of resources is a critical dimension of an organization's green zone. Investing in scaling thus generates higher levels of predictable positive outcomes today (Figure 1.3a). Investing in innovation—given limited resources—reduces the green zone, and fewer resources can be allocated to scaling. When more resources are allocated to innovation, the potential for uncertain future outcomes increases. But short-term performance and impact creation may decline (Figure 1.3b).

Figure 1.3 triggers a number of additional questions: "How do or how should organizations balance innovation and scaling? Does this balance change over time? How do these decisions influence the overall performance of organizations and their abilities to create impact?" As with all tricky organizational topics, there is no straightforward answer, only more or less productive ways of thinking about it. The frameworks we have discussed so far enable us to be more consistent and clearer when we investigate these questions by reflecting on the long-term trajectories of our featured organizations.

2   MAPPING INNOVATION
PATHOLOGIES

Right now, your company gets the results—good or bad—that it was designed to get. If your vision of the future differs from your current situation, if you want to get better results, then you must change the way you do things. If you don't, how can you expect results that are any different from what you've already achieved?[1]

How can we make innovation more productive? Or perhaps a better question is, "How can we make innovation less unproductive?" Organizations are not good at innovation. They suffer from what we call *innovation pathologies*. This is the central claim in this chapter: When organizations understand their particular innovation pathologies, they can innovate much more productively. Why?

Two reasons account for that. First, organizations can avoid ideas whose development is most likely to be derailed by its particular innovation pathologies. For example, some social enterprises are not good at or do not believe in collaborating with the private or public sectors. Being conscious of this limitation avoids adopting innovative ideas that require such collaborations. Fewer resources are wasted on bad ideas. Second, awareness and acknowledgment of innovation pathologies allow targeted interventions that reduce or eliminate pathologies instead of searching for scapegoats to heap the blame for innovation failures.

Some pathologies may be explicitly accepted as expressions of an organization's identity. Our four featured organizations provide a rich context for exploring this argument. Being conscious of its particular identity and the innovation pathologies helps an organization avoid the pitfall of adopting some random recommendations or recipes provided in "innovation books." But first we need to understand how these pathologies reduce the productivity of innovation and how an organization can diagnose them.

In Chapter 1, we already met one villain of unproductive innovation, the illusion of understanding. It tempts organizations to innovate for the wrong reasons and with unrealistic expectations about innovation's potential. The illusion of understanding is best dispelled by defining what innovation really means, its characteristics, and its role in the impact-creation logic of an organization. We have discussed useful approaches to overcoming this illusion in Chapter 1. And the cases of our featured organizations will offer additional ideas and inspiration. But organizations can easily fall victim to another illusion, the illusion of competence. And that one can best be overcome by using the innovation pathology framework that we propose in this chapter. What is the illusion of competence, and how does it make innovation unproductive?

An important cause of this illusion is the attention and admiration that successful social enterprises get from funders, the public sector, and the media. They are praised for their entrepreneurial spirit and their innovative DNA. New labels are constantly invented to refer to these organizations and their founders. They include "social entrepreneurs," "change makers," "the new heroes," or "frugal innovators." Joe Madiath, the founder of Gram Vikas, shared his view of these buzzwords:

I was amused recently because somebody from some university wanted to interview me, because they identified me as a "frugal innovator." [Laughter] I had not heard of this. I also had not heard of social entrepreneurship before Schwab told me that I was a social entrepreneur. [Laughter] Then I was told that I was an innovator. I had not thought about that. Now they attach that word *frugal*. [Laughter]. This is not what we are. Some people are saying that to us. "OK, you are an innovator, you are a social entrepreneur," all this comes.

Even the most realistic and down-to-earth organizations are liable to believe in magic when the whole world tells them how magical they are. Over time, the flattery may create an illusion of competence, or what one of our interviewees, the director of a large foundation, called a "celebrity effect." It tempts organizations to take on and execute innovative ideas confidently although they are ill prepared for the difficulties of innovation. And because failure is not expected, tolerated, or talked about much in the social sector, we never hear the real stories of funds wasted on bad ideas or on organizations that really have few innovation capabilities.

Overcoming the illusion of competence is tricky. Managers in organizations tend to overestimate their competence.[2] When things go well, they attribute success to their smart decisions and sound strategies. When things don't work, someone else or some unexpected external factors are to blame. Managers also overestimate their ability to improve the innovativeness of their organizations. How else do we explain the hundreds of books published each year with titles that sound like "the secret recipes of successful innovators" or "the five steps to innovation success"? They promise quick fixes and claim success factors that generate optimism about the potential of organizations to "engineer innovation." If quick fixes such as installing an idea box don't work, the staff is usually blamed. We have witnessed the same tendency in social enterprises.

Unfounded optimism is not a fruitful basis for productive decisions about innovation.[3,4] Instead, a useful approach to making innovation more productive starts by explicitly focusing on barriers to productive innovation rather than on success factors. Our diagnostic tool for mapping innovation pathologies helps with that. Numerous conversations, observations, workshops, and systematic studies with social enterprises are the basis for this diagnostic tool. It was built around two simple questions: (1) What constitutes unproductive innovation efforts—or, in other words, what are innovation pathologies? and (2) what are the organizational factors that generate them—or, in other words, what are the organizational barriers to productive innovation?

Building this framework takes seriously the claim that innovation is a process in organizations. In Chapter 1 we discussed the general characteristics of innovations. Here we take a dynamic view on the overall innovation process and how it unfolds. Then we can map innovation pathologies to particular parts of the overall innovation process.

INNOVATE AND SCALE—IT'S NOT JUST A MATTER OF CHOICE

In the previous chapter, we contrasted innovation and scaling as two fundamentally different types of activities. One implication was that an organization at any given time has to decide whether it wants to allocate more resources to innovation, creating unpredictable outcomes in the future, or to scaling, creating positive outcomes today. But what if we look at innovation and scaling as processes over time instead of at one moment in time? A new perspective opens up: Innovation and scaling are also connected in an overall innovation process over time. Figure 2.1 illustrates this point of view.

Innovation Is an Investment

The framework in Figure 2.1 portrays innovation, creating and developing ideas that lie in an organization's red zone, as an investment. Because of the uncertainties of red zone ideas, innovation is risky. Innovation rarely produces expected outcomes. Setbacks and failures are frequent. Political resources, such as relational power and influence, need to be invested to make sure that an idea receives the attention of decision makers and to

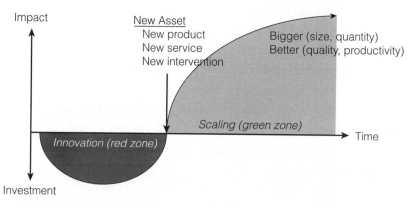

FIGURE 2.1
Innovation is an investment, and scaling creates impact from innovation.

protect the innovation from the organization's immune system, as described in Chapter 1. Financial and other tangible resources need to be invested to explore and to develop ideas. Emotional resources need to be invested to keep up the motivation to continue the effort despite frequent setbacks.

How big is this investment? Two principal factors that we discussed in the previous chapter determine its size: (1) the degrees of uncertainty involved in developing an idea, and (2) the strength of the organizational immune system. Enacting ideas at higher degrees of uncertainty requires more experimentation, more adaptation, changing assumptions, and many other "costly" activities associated with innovation processes. Higher degrees of uncertainty thus consume more time and effort. Likewise, the stronger the organizational immune reaction, the more innovation becomes an uphill battle. Ideas are likely to be dismissed, and this requires expending efforts toward influencing decision makers and getting resources. Many meetings may take place before any constructive action occurs. Momentum and motivation easily get lost. Decision makers may withdraw key resources from innovation efforts prematurely. All this effort makes innovation more resource intense and less likely to succeed. We offer the following "formula" to represent this relationship:

Innovation Investment =
(Degree of Uncertainty) × (Strength of the Organizational Immune System)

Scaling Creates Impact from Innovation

In our framework, innovation is an investment. It does not create impact. Innovation, if it succeeds, creates an asset: a new product, service, or intervention. There are many more potential types of outcomes of innovation processes, such as a new organizational unit, a new hiring process, or a new business model. For the sake of simplicity, we list just three types of outcomes. Our framework can be expanded to include any other type of outcome.

What creates impact from these innovation assets is the ability and willingness of an organization to work hard to standardize, routinize, fine-tune, and constantly improve the new processes, products, services, or interventions. *Bigger* in Figure 2.1 refers to increasing the impact that is created from innovation assets by producing and delivering more products or services to more people. *Better* refers to increasing impact by improving the assets and thus providing higher quality at lower cost more reliably. Consistent with our frameworks in the previous chapter, we call these types of impact-creating activities *scaling* or acting in an organization's *green zone*.

Innovation is an investment and scaling creates impact from innovations. The better an organization's scaling capabilities, the more impact it can create from its investment in innovation. Because we look at innovation explicitly from the perspective of impact creation, we need to integrate both innovation and scaling into an overall innovation process. Just looking at innovation misses the point. This is a central feature of our innovation pathologies framework.

INNOVATION PATHOLOGIES

What do we mean by "pathologies"? In medicine, pathologies are observable manifestations of an underlying disease. Pathologies prevent us from being or feeling healthy, productive, and motivated, thus reducing our ability to perform. Pathologies have causes. The pathology of an itching skin may be caused by an allergic reaction. Good diagnosis starts with establishing that a pathology is present and then proceeds to identify its likely cause. But what does this usage have to do with organizations and innovation?

When we defined the characteristics of innovative ideas in Chapter 1, we pointed out that they easily triggered an organization's immune system and needed to overcome a number of potential organizational barriers (Table 1.1 lists some of them). These barriers are also the causes of innovation pathologies. Taking productive innovation seriously means that organizations need to confront the barriers openly and systematically. As in medical diagnosis, we recommend that organizations first establish their particular innovation pathologies and then find out what causes them.

This method is the basis for targeted interventions to improve innovation performance. Our innovation pathologies framework thus can be used as a diagnostic tool. It helps organizations to map their particular innovation pathologies and the factors that cause them.

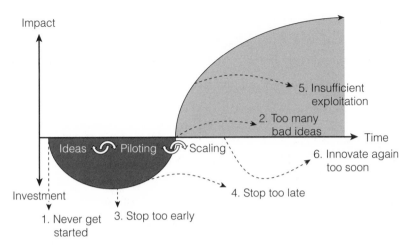

FIGURE 2.2
Main pathologies along the innovation process.

The first step of building the pathologies framework was to recognize explicitly that innovation and scaling are joined in a continuous process. For a diagnostic, we need to look at the overall innovation process more closely. We break it down into three distinct phases, as shown in Figure 2.2:

- Phase I: *Ideas*. This phase involves the creation, communication, and evaluation of innovative ideas.

- Phase II: *Piloting*. This phase focuses on experimenting, designing, or other forms of developing innovative ideas; we use the term *piloting* for general idea development efforts that may or may not include formal pilots.

- Phase III: *Scaling*. This phase considers the adoption of successful innovation outputs and organizing their efficient delivery to serve more people better.

The arrows connecting the three phases remind us that innovation is rarely linear. Innovation involves iterative dynamics that the framework does not fully capture. But this does not limit its usefulness as a diagnostic. Innovation pathologies can occur in all three phases. In the following sections we will discuss the major pathologies that are associated with each phase of the innovation process and factors that typically cause them. The factors that we provide in Tables 2.1 through 2.3 originate from various discussions and workshops. The tables list those factors that were mentioned most frequently in interviews or by workshop participants. Some factors also reflect our interpretations of existing innovation research.

Phase I: Ideas–Idea Creation, Idea Communication, and Idea Evaluation

Innovation starts with the creation of an idea. Organizational research perceives creativity, the generation of ideas that are both novel and useful, as a precursor to innovation.[5] Where do ideas come from? Sometimes we stumble across them by accident or random inspiration. In organizations, ideas frequently result from a more or less conscious search for solutions to a challenge or problem. Ideas may also diffuse from the external environment to an organization.

Individuals usually create or find ideas. This can happen in a group situation or as a lone act of reflection. Most innovative ideas probably never see the light of the day. They reside within individuals as mental assets with an unknown impact potential. Innovation in organizations requires that ideas be actively and convincingly communicated. They get evaluated before organizations provide resources and legitimacy for their development. This phase of the innovation process is marked by an important tension within an organization between individuals with ideas and groups who may have different ideas, preferences, or agendas.

Idea creation in organizations needs to be understood as a process over time. For example, past failed innovations may inhibit creativity. Negative interpretations of ideas after failed innovations may lay the blame falsely on the idea creator. This tendency is exacerbated by a lack of formal documentation and learning systems that objectively follow innovation from idea creation to implementation. The consequence is that the staff are less motivated to engage in innovation processes and to supply ideas in the future.

Two pathologies make this early phase of the innovation process unproductive. One is the "never get started" pathology, and the other is the "too many bad ideas" pathology. Both have a number of potential causes.

NEVER GET STARTED   To accept the claim that "never get started" is an innovation pathology necessitates the assumption that innovation is beneficial in social enterprises. The alternative would be that an organization innovates once and then scales the outcomes of this innovation forever, or at least as long as scaling creates impact. That way, it would never need to start innovating again. But why and how often do or should social enterprises start innovating? We don't really know. Research has not systematically explored this question.[6] All we know is that the situation is more difficult than in the business sector, where the dynamics of competition determine both the legitimacy and pace of innovation. At this point, all we want to say is that, even in the social sector, "never get started" may limit the ability of organizations to generate impact. But understanding the particular triggers of innovation, its role and purpose, and the pace of subsequent innovation episodes requires a deeper reflection on the trajectories of our featured organizations in Part II.

Apart from the link between particular innovations and creating impact, we believe that a basic level of innovation is a general requirement for keeping organizations healthy. Medical doctors know that triggering the immune system from time to time is necessary for good health. Innovations—regardless of their outcomes—potentially have a health-promoting and even rejuvenating effect on organizations as well. Who wants to work in an organization where every day looks the same? Innovation is also a mechanism by which organizations can develop their staff. It provides a space for exploring their ideas and talents, solving nonroutine challenges. Innovation is a great practice ground for developing leadership, communication, and management qualities. And although too much innovation may kill an organization if it takes on too much risk, never getting started is equally an innovation pathology.

TOO MANY BAD IDEAS   People find it easier to accept that too many bad ideas really is a pathology. Investing scarce resources in bad ideas that never create much impact cannot be good for an organization. Jim March of Stanford University famously said, "Most new ideas are bad ideas."[7] Many innovative ideas are readily eliminated by an organization's immune system, often for good reasons.

TABLE 2.1

Causes of two pathologies in the innovation phase *ideas*.

Never get started

- Everyone is too busy all the time limiting the available attention span required to seriously consider and evaluate innovative ideas.
- The most innovative people tend to leave the organization, limiting the variety of ideas produced in an organization.
- The organizational impact-creation logic is unclear or shifting, so people do not know when ideas are desired or for which problems and thus undersupply ideas.
- Competitive organizational cultures foster little trust in the support of others; ideas tend to be "shut down" rather than constructively evaluated, limiting the motivation to communicate ideas.
- Idea creators are unable or unwilling to communicate and defend their ideas; staff may have been socialized in hierarchical cultures where expressing ideas at their level is not considered appropriate.
- Innovation and change may not fit an organization's identity; organizations may openly resist the "business logic" of innovation.
- Low levels of ambition or illusions of achievement fail to trigger an action threshold (ambition minus status quo) for searching for new ideas and new possibilities even if an organization creates little impact.
- Past innovation failures are incorrectly attributed to individuals rather than innovation uncertainties or organizational pathologies; therefore people will not be motivated to engage in innovation.
- "Professionalization" of social enterprises adopting strict financial evaluation and allocation processes may not be compatible with the uncertainties and timescales inherent in exploring innovative ideas.
- Learning deficiencies from both failures and successes prevent knowledge accumulation; deep knowledge in specific domains strongly enables the creation of relevant ideas and their constructive evaluation.
- The organization's decision makers are exposed to homogeneous networks, lowering exposure to novel ideas.

Too many bad ideas

- Senior managers push their favorite innovation ideas to impress funders or other stakeholders or because they need a new story to tell in Davos; innovations are not driven by an organization's long-term impact-creation logic and may not fit the organization or its environment.
- Senior managers are removed from the realities of the needs that they cater to, impairing their judgment of the potential of innovative ideas.
- Lack of objective idea evaluation criteria prevents learning about how to evaluate ideas productively and more consistently and may let more bad ideas slip through.
- Staff misunderstand an organization's mission, vision, and priorities; they may therefore produce too many ideas that-if coupled with inconsistent evaluation criteria-waste resources on developing the wrong ideas.
- Inability or unwillingness to learn systematically and objectively from past innovation prevents organizations from defining the uncertainties that it can productively deal with to understand which types are a better fit for its impact-creation logic.
- Lack of objective evaluation of an organization's strengths and weaknesses due to failure to critically self-assess and self-reflect prevents it from defining an objective and shared understanding of its impact-creation logic, thus creating ambiguity about the organization's potential and capacity for innovation.
- Immature and inexperienced innovation team members that frequently change and other quick-fix efforts to build "innovativeness" actually prevent learning and accumulation of knowledge.
- Preconceived ideas come with resources, for example from large foundations or development organizations, thus tempting organizations to say "yes" regardless of the quality of the idea.
- The emotional power of the direct experience of the misery of life in poor communities urges organizations to act and target problems and needs, triggering ideas that do not fit an organization's belief system, level of competencies, or understanding of community needs.
- Solutions such as microfinance or particular technologies are promoted as panaceas by influential stakeholders triggering ideas for adopting solutions that may not fit an organization or its environment.

What triggers the creation and adoption of bad ideas? We have often observed that, as organizations get bigger or more "professionalized," hierarchies and priorities may increasingly isolate decision makers from operational realities. They may spend too little time with staff and in the field with the communities their organizations serve. Furthermore, senior management and board members may be replaced too frequently, with a concomitant loss of crucial knowledge and trusted relationships with internal and external constituencies. Succession planning seems to be important in this regard—for example, when the founder must be replaced by an external director because there are no sufficiently senior and experienced internal candidates. New senior appointees in organizations often are motivated to do things "their way" and to leave a distinct footprint rather than following the path created by their predecessors. This may have negative consequences for the quality of new ideas, particularly if idea generation and evaluation are dominated by senior personnel.

Table 2.1 lists factors that organizations frequently report as the causes of their innovation pathologies in this stage of the innovation process. The list is not exhaustive but is intended to inspire your search for the plausible or actual causes of pathologies in your organization.

Phase II: Piloting—Experimenting and Developing Solutions

Organizational approaches to experimentation, piloting, and other forms of idea development differ widely. Much depends on the particular problem or need that an organization caters to, the types of solutions that are considered, and the particular environment. For example, piloting a health intervention based on a well-developed drug that creates immediate, observable, and unambiguously desirable effects has dynamics and challenges different from those of piloting an intervention that deals with human rights or gender issues. For these problems, well-developed solutions may not exist. The act of innovating a solution jointly with people and communities may be more important than "providing a solution." Effects may not be desirable to all stakeholders and may take a long time to materialize. All this complexity creates unique challenges for idea development efforts.

Experimenting and designing solutions to develop innovative ideas is primarily an act of discovering the nature of uncertainties involved in innovation, as discussed in Chapter 1. Innovators often discover that their assumptions were wrong. Critical challenges for organizations and individuals in this phase of the innovation process are to maintain the momentum and motivation to deal with failures and to learn productively.

In general, we see two pathologies in this phase of the innovation process: "stop too early" and "stop too late."

STOP TOO EARLY   One pathology is the premature withdrawal of resources for experimentation and piloting. Because organizations underestimate the uncertainties of innovation, too many efforts are insufficiently resourced. When scarce financial resources, essential staff, and management attention are shifted elsewhere, even promising pilots easily come to a grinding halt. We call this the "stop too early" pathology. Potential opportunities to create impact remain undeveloped. Premature abandonment of innovation projects is inherently costly—it deprives the organization of the potential for eventual success. Organizations that do not have committed resources for innovations and the willingness or formal decision to sustain their allocation are particularly liable to this pathology.

Piloting new ideas requires the creation of new knowledge in many dimensions of uncertainty. The learning process itself is potentially extremely valuable for an organization. Innovation often exposes flawed assumptions about a proposed solution to a perceived problem or need. Stopping too early deprives organizations of the opportunity to test and correct assumptions. It also prevents the nurturing of capabilities for designing and running productive pilots and understanding the intended and unintended consequences of innovations for various stakeholders. If organizations are unable or unwilling to learn from pilots and to update their problem and solution frames, they are likely to abandon potentially fruitful innovation endeavors prematurely.

Standard project management and budgeting processes for innovations usually assume linear progress. But many innovations have drawn-out learning curves and experience multiple ups and downs. One particular challenge for this phase of the innovation process is the tendency to put measures of progress on a linear project timeline. Real progress is nonlinear, and observable results may emerge only at late stages. Comparisons between expected (linear) project outcomes and real (nonlinear) achievements may display huge gaps for a long time. The discrepancy may trigger premature abandonment due to a seeming lack of progress. This decision wastes scarce organizational resources, demotivates staff, and lowers their willingness to articulate and champion new ideas and participate in future pilots.

STOP TOO LATE   A second pathology in this innovation phase is the extension of pilots beyond their usefulness. The costs to the organization are obvious: Resources are not used productively, there is no hope of creating impact, people resign and treat the pilot just like any routine project. Many factors potentially contribute to this pathology. Perhaps a pilot is championed by a senior manager and no one wants to communicate the bad news that it is not working. Or past experiences where the honest reporting of failure was punished instead of rewarded lower the willingness of staff involved in pilots to raise the flag. Hiding errors and tinkering with data may hide a lack of progress from decision-makers. This can happen, for example, in organizations that have a strong performance culture where delivery on targets is expected and strongly incentivized.

Abundant resources may sometimes also cause this pathology. Big funders need to spend significant amounts of money every year. Spending more per organization is a convenient way to lower administration costs. Abundant resources can mean that efficiency is not a high priority. Pilots may become "too big to stop" when signs of failure emerge. Organizations may continue innovation processes unduly and with little learning and progress until budgets are spent.

Somewhere we picked up a pertinent quote: "Innovations only ever fail if one gives up." How do organizations know when it's time to let go? Deciding on the appropriate time to stop is tricky. Perhaps reflecting on two criteria might help. One is continuity of learning. As discussed earlier, an important objective of innovation processes is not to "succeed" but to learn about important uncertainties. An absence of insights or learning from pilots might indicate that the effort may no longer be warranted. If this is coupled with the phenomenon of "no good news" (see the following discussion), then perhaps it's an important signal to discontinue an innovation. The characteristic ups and downs, the many small wins and setbacks typical of innovation processes can be taken literally: If there are only *downs* and no signs of any *ups* or *small wins*, people get exhausted and may not be willing to invest in a continuation of the pilot. Perhaps the phenomenon of "no good news" coupled with the perception of "no new learning" is a valid signal that you're going in the wrong direction and warrants stopping an innovation.

Table 2.2 lists factors that organizations frequently report as the causes of their innovation pathologies in this stage of the innovation process.

Phase III: Scaling—Creating Impact from Innovations

Scaling past innovations is by far the dominant activity of most organizations at any given time. Scaling is how they create impact from their investments in innovations. But it's tough to build and manage an efficient organization that can execute and deliver valuable products and services. Few social sector leaders have the stamina, dedication, and experience to scale up effectively. We sometimes sense that social enterprises are legitimized by doing the right thing and not necessarily by being efficient and using resources productively. Investments into organizational infrastructure that are required for building and nurturing a green zone and for efficient scaling are generally perceived as mere "overhead" by funders and ought to be minimized.

Developing countries suffer from a lack of experienced management talent. A manager at BRAC told us that young graduates in Bangladesh are much more likely to go to better-paid jobs in the private industry or the public sector than into the social sector. Building scaling capacity may require internal investments into developing management talent.

We also notice that innovation gets privileged over scaling by many young, motivated entrepreneurs who show tremendous passion for developing technological solutions to tackle poverty-related needs and problems. Few of them, however, seem to be motivated to build a large, efficient organization. Most of them may also lack the required skills and patience. We wonder whether the bottleneck to development is indeed innovation, as the prevailing social innovation discourse implies. The bottleneck may actually be the ability and willingness of people to

TABLE 2.2

Causes of two pathologies in the innovation phase *piloting*.

Stop too early
- Unclear and shifting responsibilities for execution make it unlikely that anyone champions and adequately supports the pilot.
- People are expected to do piloting "on the side," so low willingness to contribute effort and invest in learning may stifle the progress of pilots.
- Without dedicated resources, resources may be withdrawn by powerful decision makers for other urgent matters.
- Failures or unmet expectations trigger blaming people rather than acknowledging the inherent uncertainty of innovation and learning from it; this tendency reduces their willingness to accept responsibility and leadership for pilots.
- Assumptions of linear progress with prespecified milestones do not match the real nonlinear progress of innovations; even successful pilots may be abandoned in the face of apparent lack of progress.
- Essential innovation champions are stretched across too many initiatives; pilot leaders are more likely to abandon some pilots prematurely to reduce stress and complexity.
- Failures waste resources and cannot be sustained if they are not coupled to learning; a "learning fast" focus designs experiments that maximize learning, not failing.
- Managers set specific goals and objectives for developing ideas with high degrees of uncertainty; this ambition tends to restrict efforts and searches for alternative problem frames, ideas, and solutions and limits learning as well as the likelihood of innovation success.
- Pressure to show results prematurely migrates innovations from piloting to scaling at a very immature stage; little impact is created from insufficiently developed innovations.
- Hyping technical innovations and generic solutions creates a quick-fix attitude; the resulting expectations of fast and predictably positive results easily get frustrated by lengthy and uncertain innovation processes.

Stop too late
- Lack of timely and continuous oversight of projects delays decisions required to stop innovations when appropriate.
- Lack of evidence-based monitoring of innovation progress prevents decision makers from knowing when to stop innovation efforts.
- When innovation team members are afraid to acknowledge "failure," they may hide data that indicate a lack of progress.
- If trust and transparency are absent, no one wants to communicate bad news or feel accountable for doing so.
- If learning from successes and failures is superstitious, ideology driven, and anecdotal rather than objective and systematic, it contributes to ignorance about the lack of objective signs of progress.
- When an organization is married to new technologies and solutions, a strong expectation of positive outcomes leads to dismissing signs of failure.
- The "sunk cost fallacy" means that when many resources have already been invested, organizations are hesitant to pull the plug and thus realize significant costs.
- If dedicated innovation funds from donors come with explicit expectations of positive results, organizations are unlikely to admit failure until all resources have been spent.

build efficient and productive organizations. To operate at the scale of social needs and problems requires organizations that deliver reliable products and services and accumulate deep knowledge into a green zone that enables them to really make a difference. People who can do that are in short supply.

The potential of scaling and its challenges are dependent on the actual scaling mode. In our work with social enterprises, we have identified four distinct scaling modes.[8] Distinguishing among these modes may focus discussions when we are actually mapping an organization's innovation pathologies. Different scaling modes may suffer from different pathologies. Our case studies will provide us with rich "data" to reflect on these scaling modes more deeply and to understand ways to lower pathologies. We therefore will briefly sketch the main characteristics of various scaling modes here to enable readers to keep them in mind as they go through the cases.

SCALING THROUGH PRODUCTIVITY INCREASES   This is the crucial work that organizations can do within their green zones. Many small improvements over time to use resources more efficiently and productively enable organizations to create more impact from a given stock of resources. For example, high-quality cataract surgeries per doctor would be an illustrative measure of this scaling approach for the Aravind eye hospital. The fact that Aravind doctors perform five to ten times as many surgeries as the global average indicates that it has a well-developed green zone. Many factors listed in Table 2.3 might lower the potential of this scaling mode. For example, when organizations allocate resources to innovations instead of increasing productivity, impact-creation through this scaling channel will be limited (see also Figure 1.3b).

SCALING THROUGH ADDING RESOURCES   Hiring more staff, getting additional funds, increasing income, and expanding existing infrastructure are ways for organizations to increase their scaling capacity. Productivity increases and capacity increases from added resources ideally combine to generate tremendous benefits from innovations over time. But adding resources may not always be the best option. Its effects are strongest if the innovation has achieved a certain level of robustness, maturity, and efficiency. Adding resources to an unproductive organization with a weak impact-creation logic may not increase its impact very much. Unfortunately, because development funds are abundant, it is usually easier to get resources, particularly financial resources, than to invest in productivity. We have observed that some organizations in the social sector have developed tremendous fundraising capabilities. Resource abundance results in a disincentive to investment into building efficient organizations or innovations that use resources productively by design. The result is often what we call "lazy business models."

The following story illustrates this argument. One social enterprise recently piloted a new initiative that trained local entrepreneurs. Having received sizeable external funds for this innovation they gave away all initial trainings for free. The pilots worked, and the incomes of local entrepreneurs went up. But entrepreneurs who are joining the program now do not want to pay for trainings because the rumors about "free trainings" have widely spread. The social enterprise thus struggles to scale this innovation.

SCALING THROUGH REPLICATION   Replicating a program of a social enterprise is another strategy for increasing the impact from innovations. Organizations may scale through replication for different reasons. They might want to expand operations to a different environment. Or they might want to keep operational units below a particular size. Adding resources to an organization to increase its capacity adds value as long as things don't get too complicated. As an organization gets larger, its complexity increases. For example, it's more difficult to keep all its resources and staff efficiently aligned and productive. Balancing operative with administrative functions gets more challenging. Anyone who ever worked in a large organization knows what we mean. Replication is a way to avoid dealing with this complexity and to keep units to a manageable size.

But replication may be impeded by environmental variance and the scarcity of specialized resources. Experienced organizations with well-developed green zones may have "blinders" for environmental variance and may overestimate their abilities to adjust their programs. BRAC, one of the most experienced social enterprises in Bangladesh, had to abandon its microfinance replication in Afghanistan. It could not make it work in that environment. Often replication necessitates going back to pilot mode to adapt innovation assets to a different environment. Thus pathologies in earlier innovation phases are also relevant for this scaling mode.

SCALING THROUGH KNOWLEDGE TRANSFER   Transfer of knowledge to other organizations may be a productive scaling mode, particularly when resource scarcity prevents scaling through replication. This is a more *indirect* scaling mode. It transfers the impact-creation potential of an innovation to other organizations to enable them to create impact. But knowledge transfer generates benefits only if the adopting organization can integrate the knowledge efficiently. If it does not already have a green zone, the effect of transferring isolated knowledge assets may be marginal. Adopting and acting on knowledge may thus be an innovation for the receiving organization. In this case, applying our pathologies diagnostic may be particularly helpful. It allows organizations and funders systematically to evaluate the potential of adopting organizations for creating impact. This scaling mode also has implications for innovation. For example, an organization might ask, "Can we design and pilot our innovations in such a way that they are easier to transfer to other organizations?" You may want to keep this question in mind when reflecting on the case study of Waste Concern.

Scaling creates impact from innovation, and organizations can enact different scaling modes to achieve this result. Two pathologies in this phase of the innovation process limit the impact-creation potential of innovations: "insufficient exploitation" and "innovate again too soon."

Insufficient Exploitation

A preference for innovation over building efficient organizations contributes to an important pathology that we call "insufficient exploitation." If no one creates impact from the investment into innovation, the return on innovation, measured by the impact created for an organization's constituents, will be negative. When organizations don't build a green zone, they will not exploit the impact potential of an innovation. A drastic thought experiment illustrates this argument. During his tenure as an employee in the Indian health sector in the 1960s, an Indian eye surgeon invested much effort and personal sacrifice to develop a community eye surgery model. The innovation asset it created was a highly efficient surgical practice for treating cataract patients from very poor communities. When it was time to retire, he could reasonably have decided just to lead a comfortable life. After all, his innovation had helped thousands of poor patients. Instead, he built the Aravind eye hospital with the objective of scaling his innovation. We can easily imagine how much of the potential of his innovation would have remained unexploited had he retired or decided to innovate and start something new. Instead, he built one of the most efficient eye care centers in the world and scaled his innovation for more than twenty years. Millions of people regained their eyesight because of his choice.

Scaling accumulates deep knowledge in particular organizational and environmental domains. This strengthens an impact-creation logic and aids the production and identification of relevant ideas and their efficient evaluation and development. Much organizational innovation literature has reported and described this phenomenon.[9,10] Insufficient investment in building scaling capabilities thus lowers an organization's impact through a potential double pathology: (1) The potential of past innovations does not get fully exploited and realized, and (2) the lack of accumulated knowledge due to insufficient scaling efforts leaves many potentially relevant and good ideas unnoticed. Instead, less relevant ideas may get developed. Thus, a weak impact-creation logic prevents both efficient scaling and productive innovation.

In addition, a lack of transparency and accountability and a tendency to hype achievements mask poor performance. It seems that overstating the scale of one's impact has become a competitive game. Observers unfortunately promote an inflation of accounting for scaling impact. They see a "new paradigm" of scaling in which the concept of scaling not only encompasses perspectives of organizational size and efficiency, but also the "number of spin-offs it created," the "number of projects that have been taken over by other actors," the "degree to which it contributed to the social and intellectual diversity of civil society," the "number of beneficiaries or even the specific policy changes won," "local capacity built," or "intersectoral contacts developed," as well as "norms of trust and cooperation strengthened" and "democratic space and social diversity reinforced."[11] This tendency is concerning if it leads to telling richer stories rather than building more efficient organizations.

TABLE 2.3

Causes of two pathologies in the innovation phase *scaling*.

Insufficient exploitation
- Under funder pressure for short-term results, organizations may adopt pilots at an immature state; the problems then become visible during scaling and limit its potential (we also call this the "scaling too early" pathology)
- "Illusions of understanding" and "illusions of competence" limit the potential of innovations; when innovators are ignorant of the necessity of scaling to create impact from innovation or their ability to build an efficient organization, the impact potential of innovations remains largely unrealized.
- When innovations remain invisible to headquarters, as happens in very decentralized organizations, even successful innovations may remain local and fail to diffuse through the organization.
- Innovation driven by a project focus without a clear consideration of a long-term impact-creation logic tends to undersupply vital resources and capabilities for scaling and may reduce the motivation to sustain scaling innovations that do not really fit an organization's identity.
- A power and leadership vacuum may prevent a successful innovation from being formalized and adopted by an organization; it will thus likely remain understaffed and underresourced.
- Rapid and opportunistic cycles of innovations can easily overwhelm an organization's scaling capacities even if it has a green zone.

Innovate again too soon
- If an organization has a project focus that follows donor money rather than a clear organizational strategy grounded in building a green zone, the perception that it is innovative may attract funds even if little impact is created from the innovations.
- Organizations often fail to intentionally integrate the need for scaling and the acquisition and building of scaling resources and capabilities into their innovation processes; when they struggle with scaling they may start another round of innovations rather than investing in building and nurturing adequate resources.
- If the organization operates in a complex environment that is insufficiently understood while desperately seeking to demonstrate impact, urgency and pressure to show success will drive a constant search for new ideas instead of the patient learning required to develop an explicit impact-creation logic.

Innovate Again Too Soon

This leads us to the second pathology in the scaling phase: "innovate again too soon." As Jim March said, too much innovation may be detrimental to organizations because it may create little impact. He warned that organizations that focus on innovation and exploring new possibilities to the exclusion of productively enacting what was learned and developed in the past risk failure caused by "too many undeveloped new ideas and too little distinctive competence."[7]

Many factors may contribute to the pathology of innovating again too soon. Managers may attribute the success of past innovations to their superior ability rather than luck or chance factors that were not under their control. This "overconfidence bias" is well documented in the literature. It creates a naïve illusion of competence that "innovation is easy," and leads to subsequent rounds of blame games when failure occurs.

Scaling often takes much more time and effort than organizations expect. It's easy to underestimate the efforts and difficulties involved in creating impact from innovations. People may prefer the adrenalin rush of innovation to the perspiration of scaling. They may be tempted to innovate again too soon by abandoning scaling work prematurely for new rounds of more exciting innovations. They leave important opportunities for creating impact underexploited. Organizations openly shared with us their view that too many NGOs never develop any distinct competencies and rather opportunistically jump from one "innovative" grant proposal to the next. But the returns on innovation remain low when scaling capabilities are underdeveloped.

Table 2.3 lists factors that organizations frequently report as the causes of their innovation pathologies in this stage of the innovation process.

What should an organization do when it has mapped its innovation pathologies? The next chapters, featuring four social enterprises, suggest that these pathologies play out in different ways. You will see that there may be no generic recipes and solutions to deal with the pathologies. Much depends on the particular impact-creation logic of an organization.

PART II

Case Studies

In the following four chapters we sketch the histories of four social enterprises. These case studies elucidate the roles innovation and scaling play and how these activities relate to impact. The four organizations have distinctive histories and trajectories. Innovation and scaling play particular roles that reflect the impact-creation logics that define the organizations and make them unique. The distinct ways innovation and scaling shape and are integrated into their trajectories thus constitute particular innovation archetypes. We conclude each case study with an analysis of its innovation archetype and how the archetype relates to the central frameworks and concepts developed in Chapters 1 and 2.

3   INNOVATION AS LEARNING
The Story of Gram Vikas (India)

I think in most of the innovations, because I took the initiative, I had an advantage. I happen to be the boss. The boss can innovate and fail. So there was the feeling, "OK, let Joe do it. Then if it fails, it would be he who fails." But it's very, very difficult initially to cut through the resistance in the organization. For example, the first idea for a gravity flow. I asked my colleagues and the engineers to implement it. But they were not convinced and they would not do it. They said: "You are wasting the organization's money," which is a big challenge. So I said: "OK, if it does not work, I will pay for the entire thing, I will slowly pay it back to the organization. At least on that moral ground, you cannot now refuse to work with me."   —Joe Madiath, founder of Gram Vikas[1]

START OF THE INNOVATION JOURNEY:
BELIEVING IN A MORE EQUAL WORLD

The roots of Gram Vikas lie in a student society at Madras University called the Young Students' Movement for Development (YSMD). It came into being at the end of the 1960s, a time when students all over the world began to express their concerns about the inequality and injustice they saw around them. They rejected accepted ways of doing things, were concerned with equality, and wanted to participate actively in changing the system. This upwelling of dissatisfaction inspired the creation of the YSMD, with

Joe Madiath (who later became the executive director of Gram Vikas) as its leader. According to some of the founding members, the students did not engage in spending their time naïvely "romanticizing about the poor and calling for the overthrow of the existing social order." Instead, they wanted to channel their dissatisfaction in a positive manner and to "commit ourselves, in ways that were as yet not fully known, to the challenge of social transformation."

A strong influence on the YSMD was Mahatma Gandhi's emphasis on village life as the core of Indian society and his philosophy of *Swadeshi*, or self-rule, for India's development, rather than reliance on Western trade and Western ideas of modernization:[2]

India had twenty-five years of independence at this time. But we realized that, even during these twenty-five years, the villages were losing out; the poor were becoming poorer. So some of us thought that we should listen to the call that Gandhi gave at the time of independence. He said: "Go back to the villages." And that is how we started the young students' movement for development.

Two events galvanized the YSMD into action. The first was the fallout from the Bangladeshi war for independence in early 1971, when millions of refugees flooded across the border into West Bengal. The Indian government responded to this humanitarian disaster, as did volunteers from all over India. Joe Madiath led a team of 400 YSMD volunteers to help with relief and rehabilitation efforts in West Bengal. The second event was a devastating cyclone that hit the east coast of Orissa (an Indian state adjacent to West Bengal) later that same year. The cyclone killed approximately 25,000 people and left many more homeless. Most of the original 400 volunteers returned home, but Joe and forty of the most dedicated members of YSMD went to Orissa to offer assistance.

TECHNICAL INNOVATIONS BASED ON
INADEQUATE PROBLEM FRAMES

After about a year and a half of relief work and rehabilitation assistance, nearly all the YSMD members had returned to Madras. Joe Madiath, however, decided to stay in Orissa. His reasoning was: "Orissa seemed to be much worse than any other place in India—why don't I work here?" The small remaining group of YSMD members remained to search for ways to improve the livelihoods of poor people in Orissa "in an equitable way."

Lift Irrigation and Community Farms

Several factors focused YSMD's search for ideas on agriculture. The members observed that the cyclone-affected areas in Orissa had rich soil and plenty of water from several rivers. Another source of inspiration was the program priorities of large charitable organizations, such as the Ford and Rockefeller Foundations, which were both present in India. These organizations were championing research and development in agricultural technologies to respond to widespread concerns that developing countries might succumb to famine.

YSMD decided to start agricultural cooperatives. The group thought it could improve agricultural productivity by pumping water from the river to irrigate the land in a more controlled manner. That way, instead of one rain-dependent cultivation of rice, several crops could be produced. A particularly visible problem in Orissa was the predictable fate of the landless poor, who had neither the economic means to acquire land nor the training and skills to increase crop production: "We bargained with the people who had more land that they would set aside some land for the landless. That way they could cultivate it on a community basis and divide the produce later among the people."

The initiative achieved the intended outcome: quickly increasing the farmers' crop yields. But another, more important outcome had not been achieved: to include the poor in the direct benefits of the new irrigation system. Once the irrigation was completed, the landowners did not keep their initial promise. They kept all the land and the extra profits from the advanced irrigation technology. The unintended consequence of the innovation effort was to reinforce the inequality that had already existed in the village. The YSMD members viewed this outcome as an anomaly and repeated the experiment with irrigation in seven more villages. But the results were always the same. Although the richer landowners would agree to donate land in order to start the project, they always took it back when the benefits began to be realized:

Each time the same thing, more or less, happened. Through our work those who had land got the most benefit. And those who had no land got very little benefit. And this very little benefit was increased labor, which was also good, but we were not happy. Though we found increased agricultural production not a crime by itself, that was not the purpose for which we had come there. We wanted to lift agricultural production, but we wanted to do it in an equitable way.

The unintended outcome of the innovation was to reinforce rather than reduce inequality. The group decided to finish the irrigation projects they had started and hand them over to the farming cooperatives after some initial training. Although the YSMD deemed these experiments failures, the experience from that innovation clarified the principal motivation for their work and made it more explicit: targeting inequality.

After some reflection, the YSMD members decided to work more directly with the poorest population of Orissa, the Adivasis. These were tribal people who lived in remote regions and formed nearly one-quarter of the population. The YSMD focused its search for ideas on technical projects, such as irrigation, where the members already had some expertise from their first initiative: "We needed to concentrate our energy and the little knowledge that we had gained into seeing if we could do anything to work with this tribal population—the indigenous people." Nevertheless, a lack of trust and a lack of understanding of the particular situation of Adivasis created serious challenges for implementing and developing this idea. YSMD desperately searched for legitimate ways to engage with the tribal communities.

The Dairy Project

Earlier, in 1970, Indira Gandhi had launched Operation Flood, the code name for the creation and promotion of a nationwide milk grid by India's National Dairy Development Board with support and funding from the World Food Program and the European Economic Commission. Conceived as a vast network of small-scale dairies that would form cooperatives and help the producers retain more of the profits from their efforts, the dairy grid was seen as a pivotal instrument of development in rural areas over the next decades.[3] In 1976, the Ganjam District Administration and the Milk Union invited the YSMD team to come to Ganjam in Orissa and start a dairy cooperative for the Adivasis of that region. The group deemed the dairy cooperatives idea worth pursuing. But they first needed to understand how dairying worked. They were offered land near Mohuda village to set up their headquarters and a demonstration farm. They also started to engage with the tribal villages in the area. YSMD got training as "barefoot veterinarians" and in artificial inseminators and then expanded the idea to the local communities. But the outcome was an unwelcome surprise: "The community did not like the idea; they would not want to hear about it. We did not know that the tribals considered it a crime to milk animals because they say just like mother's milk is for the baby, so also the cow's milk or the goat's milk is only for its calf."

The tribal people did not adopt the innovation, and YSMD had to abandon dairying as an income-generating project for them. YSMD realized that its innovation approach was flawed: "We have not made the field study, and we have not understood. So we thought we were energetic people; we wanted to do something for these people, so we did it. But that was a mistake. Anything you do—you should have field preparation."

It dawned on the group that their focus on solutions and technicalities was not a productive starting ground for innovations, given the particular context of their work and the types of problems they wanted to solve. Perhaps a different approach was needed, one that deepened their understanding of the most prevalent and agonizing problems of the people but also deepened the levels of engagement and relations with the local communities:

We were soon forced to realize that we should no longer waste our time and resources on implementing a scheme that could hold no real hope for the category of people we wanted to reach. We felt that we ourselves were more concerned about the animals, the repayment of the loan, the sale of milk, and so on, than about the people, their acceptance of a new way of keeping cows. We perhaps overmanaged the scheme for the people, with the result that they never really got sufficiently involved, and soon most of them opted to sell the cows.[4]

INNOVATIONS TO GAIN TRUST AND TO ADDRESS
ROOT CAUSES OF COMMUNITY PROBLEMS

YSMD now prioritized advancing the members' understanding of the local communities and their problems. This required gaining the tribal people's trust to build productive channels for communication and collaboration. They launched a simple survey to gather some data and to establish a friendly rapport with the locals. The survey was also meant to signal that YSMD was ready to listen, rather than just imposing preconceived answers and solutions.

By accident, YSMD discovered an entry point into the communities. During their visits, doctors brought along malaria treatment that was put to good use and created immediate benefits. This was expanded to a larger program by a qualified nurse and a doctor who were working with the group. YSMD started to train village health workers, who provided simple curative services, services for mother and child health, and treatment for chronic diseases.

The acceptance and confidence in the YSMD members, gained through the provision of health services, turned into a great resource for the organization to unearth the real problems:

The people did not believe us initially. There are so many fly-by-night people—either politicians, bureaucrats, or people who styled themselves as such, people who said they were concerned with the welfare of this tribal population—coming and really fleecing them. So they did not believe us. They thought we were also one of these types of people. As we stuck through thick and thin with them, they began to confide in us. As we started the medical program—that is the one that started their confidence in us. So slowly they gained faith in us. Then they started telling about all these problems.

The tribes suffered from a number of economic problems. For example, a lack of credit prevented agricultural development and more efficient use of land and water. Other problems had a stronger cognitive or reasoning dimension. Tribals had generally lost hope and a willingness to act. They lived from day to day and rarely considered the consequences of their decisions and actions over a longer time frame. They never saved anything and thus became dependent on expensive loans from moneylenders, who charged annual interest rates of up to 150 percent. The resulting levels of debt prevented any escape from the misery of day-to-day survival. Some problems had a strong normative component. (*Normative* refers to the values the tribes held about themselves and their relations with others.)

They suffered from low self-respect and thought of themselves as "only tribals" who thus never demanded that their rights be respected. Power relations and abuses by powerful actors also contributed to their misery. These actors included moneylenders, but also illicit liquor sellers who forced the tribals into slave labor and controlled them by nurturing chronic alcoholism, withholding salaries, and increasing indebtedness that often was inherited. Abuses originated also from nontribal elites who deprived the tribals of government subsidies, which were appropriated by people with power and influence. In a systematic process of exploitation, the tribals slowly but steadily mortgaged away ownership of their best land and property.

Establishing an Organizational Home for Their Innovations

YSMD also experimented with various engagement models. The principle of working with an entire village or community had been attempted in the early days of irrigation projects. This time the group was much more experimental and tried to introduce various new ideas through particular meeting structures and village committees. The innovations fueled a steep but also painful learning curve. Many idealistic early projects were abandoned after an initial trial period. Examples are attempts to form farming cooperatives, to create a young farmers' club, or to cut out exploitative tribal middlemen who had long-standing patron–client relationships in most market transactions. Despite some failures, a deep sense of injustice fueled the work of the small group of YSMD members. It motivated them to keep going and to keep learning about the problem spaces and needs they wanted to target. Eventually their innovations began to succeed more often.

In 1975, Indira Gandhi and the Congress Party introduced a moratorium on rural indebtedness. YSMD recognized the moratorium as an opportunity to solve some of the fundamental problems that the tribals faced. They drew on their experience with organizing village meetings from their earlier experiments and trusted relations with the tribals to initiate a campaign of collective action. The tribes could not have pulled that off by themselves:

Around the summer of 1978, faced with this glaring injustice of usurious exploitation, the team decided to take this up as an issue of education and liberation through collective action by the tribals. Not one of the tribals knew of the existence of the moratorium on rural indebtedness. This ignorance speaks for itself of the effectiveness of so many government policies and the state of their implementation.[4]

This knowledge awakened the tribe's self-respect and their willingness to stand up for their rights. Slowly, liquor sellers were removed from the villages, and indebtedness to moneylenders and landowners was reduced.

Overcoming some fundamental causes of tribal poverty traps led to the discovery of other needs: "We could chase away the distiller, but now the tribals asked: Who is going to provide us money at the time of need?" Most of the innovations were triggered by the emotional pain of observing all the problems that kept the tribals suffering.

YSMD increasingly was drawn into an expectation that they would solve a never-ending number of complex problems. Innovations were enacted in many areas, such as goat and pig rearing, housing, and an early savings and credit scheme in collaboration with a local bank. YSMD decided to implement a more explicit organizational structure that was aligned with their current priorities and activities: "We began to realize that we had very little in common with the YSMD back in Madras. It was time to set up a new organization." On January 22, 1979, the remaining group registered as an organization with the name Gram Vikas, meaning *village development*, with its headquarters in the village of Mohuda. And they decided to integrate their various activities under an operational umbrella that they named the Integrated Tribal Development Program (ITDP).

The signs of progress were encouraging. Requests from additional villages for support were frequent, and the organization had managed to reach out to 100 villages within a few years. But its broad focus on multiple problem areas, its limited material resources, and a lack of legitimacy in the region made it difficult for Gram Vikas to have a significant impact beyond some small and relatively homogeneous tribal communities. The members found it hard to achieve meaningful scale. Even the successful and comparably large training program for village health workers began to suffer when the emphasis of the organization shifted toward other activities in the 1980s. This episode illustrates the potential negative impact of innovations on the performance of existing initiatives, as schematized in Figure 1.3b.

The focus on solving a myriad of problems clearly helped many tribal people to see new opportunities and to regain self-respect. But it did not transform whole communities. Successful interventions in one problem often created other problems and unintended consequences. For example, progress in freeing tribals from their dependencies on powerful nontribal actors created a power vacuum that was filled by tribal individuals. The power thus shifted from external to internal actors. The exploitations, abuses, and their negative effects on people and communities remained. Despite all these difficulties, Gram Vikas's beliefs and motivation to help the tribals grew stronger during that time. One effect of the stress from enduring multiple innovations and failures during these years was that only a small group of YSMD members remained. But those who stayed formed a tough and deeply committed band who jointly shaped the trajectory of Gram Vikas going forward. Their understanding of local needs and problems and the various economic, cognitive, and normative forces, as well as the power and political structures that created and sustained these needs, had also improved. An important insight would influence later program designs: Gram Vikas had realized that people were reluctant to act and change their minds and hearts unless their fundamental material needs were satisfied first. This discovery was invaluable to the design of Gram Vikas's later signature program, which eventually allowed it to make a difference for thousands of villages in the region.

CREATING SCALABLE INNOVATIONS: BUILDING AN ORGANIZATION WITH A FOCUSED AGENDA

In the early 1980s, Gram Vikas was aware that it remained relatively powerless, given the problems it wanted to solve. It reflected deeply about its next steps and developed two strategic objectives that provided focus and clarity:

To change the situation, they should not be depending on an organization like us or any other organization that may have a short life span. How can we see a sustainable development? For that, we have to take the responsibility of at least educating one generation of children so that they get some kind of education, some kind of exposure, some kind of idea what the world is like.

Therefore, one strategic objective was to find ways of achieving a scale appropriate to the size of the problems Gram Vikas targeted. This and the issue of sustainability, understood as development work that could be sustained beyond the organizational life span, became the strategic objectives that remain with the organization today. The objectives focused the search for new ideas. A first effort targeted education as a crucial missing ingredient that limited the impact and sustainability of any innovations. Gram Vikas's educational innovations first revolved around general adult education in literacy and numeracy.

After some years, the organization recognized that this type of education made little difference for the adults. It abandoned the program for a more practical approach, which delivered information about citizens' rights and other concrete issues relevant for their lives. The focus also shifted to experimenting with offering nonformal education to the tribal children. But these activities too were not fulfilling the organization's mission: "Then we realized that is such an inferior thing. None of us send our children to nonformal education. So by giving nonformal education to these tribal children, we are always keeping them a level or several levels below the others."

After attempts to compensate for the lack of government-delivered education in the tribal areas through ad hoc informal schooling, Gram Vikas decided that nonformal education would not give the local children the opportunity to join the mainstream education system and fully reach their potential. This realization led to the opening of the first formal Gram Vikas residential school in 1982. With time, Gram Vikas also realized that its own educational services would not be sufficient to change the educational situation in the country: "We have taken the responsibility that each of the children will study up to the tenth standard. . . . Then we said OK, even after hundreds of years our work might not change the whole situation. And no government worker would turn up here. So that was not the best way to do it."

The organization then used its skills to organize collective action. It devoted its efforts to strengthening communities so that they could put pressure on the government and demand that teachers be posted to their villages: "So, simultaneously, we have started bringing people together, raising these issues, making them go and ask for such services and complain." As a result of its educational and other tribal work, Gram Vikas started getting the attention of the government. And its greater visibility proved to be an important asset that would trigger a major innovation and shape the next decade of work for Gram Vikas.

Innovate and Scale: A Decade of Biogas

Gram Vikas had been experimenting with biogas since the early days of the dairy experiments at its headquarters in Mohuda. With no electricity, all cooking and heating had to be done using firewood. With the cow dung produced at the demonstration farm, the group began producing biogas for its own needs:

We built one biogas plant for our means, for cooking and for light. Then what happened? The tribals with whom we were working came. They saw this light, so they got attracted, and they said: "Even after thousands of years, our villages won't get electric light, so why can't you help us in building biogas in our villages?"

Gram Vikas experimented with various types of biogas plants. A particular model was promoted by the government, but it did not work well. So the group members decided to change the design.

Their first biogas community plant was opened in 1981 in Toda village. By the end of 1982, the organization had constructed twenty-five biogas plants. At the same time, the Indian government was promoting the use of biogas technology through its National Biogas Extension Program. It asked Gram Vikas to provide training for engineers. Later the government asked the organization to replicate its training activities across Orissa: "We conducted trainings in different parts of Orissa. Thousands of workers—lower level up to executive engineers—were trained. Then the government asked us: 'Why don't you construct biogas plants? If you have all the technical know-how with you, why don't you be the main implementing agency?'" In 1983 Gram Vikas accepted the offer and became an implementing organization for the National Biogas Extension Program.

The organization wanted to popularize biogas technology for the benefit of communities. It also wanted to strengthen its reputation: "We thought that if we can also become an agency, we could show people that without any corruption, without parting with any subsidy which the government was providing, they can get biogas plants." Its biogas activities received the financial backing of the Canadian Hunger Foundation.

Gram Vikas kept scaling up its biogas program for the next decade. It radically increased the number of employees and constructed almost 55,000 plants in more than 6,000 villages in various districts of Orissa. This number accounted for 80 percent of all biogas plants in Orissa and about 4 percent of India's total installed capacity. It built more plants than expected and below budget. Gram Vikas trained masons and supervisors, who in turn encouraged local communities to construct biogas plants. And it helped communities obtain bank loans. With the scale of its activities steeply increasing and exceeding targets, Gram Vikas solidified its reputation as a reliable and cost-effective organization. And it gained access to rural, nontribal communities in Orissa, learning about their needs and gaining their trust:

We had a presence all over the state; in some of the villages we had more plants. More plants meant we knew more people. So initially that helped us. Biogas was instrumental in learning about the state and its problems. Otherwise we knew only the problems of the tribals, or at maximum maybe the problems of this part of the district.

Early on, Gram Vikas experienced internal conflicts and tensions between the part of the organization that continued implementing the ITDP program and the large biogas program. For a decade, the two programs operated in different structural units. But the tensions grew:

We got into such a large-scale biogas implementation by accident. But then we said: "Here is an accident, and we go ahead with the accident to disprove this particular thought about what an NGO or a voluntary agency is." And we felt that by twelve years we had disproved that. So the raison d'être was no longer there except to build more and more plants. And that, we said, can be done by our employee—without our organization going behind it.

In 1994, Gram Vikas decided to withdraw from biogas. Its leaders wanted to reconnect with the deep-rooted sense of mission that motivated them most: to enable social transformation of whole communities to fight injustice and inequality. Gram Vikas employees were actively encouraged to take over biogas activities on their own, and Gram Vikas provided some incentives and helped them deal with the potential risk of failure: "Why don't you go out, and if this is not something you want to do, within two years you can come back and you will have your job."

THE FINAL INNOVATION: CONFIGURING NEEDS, ORGANIZATIONAL CAPABILITIES, AND A CLEAR SENSE OF MISSION INTO A LONG-TERM STRATEGY

The decade of scaling the biogas program had important implications for the organization's future ability to innovate and to scale more productively. During that time, Gram Vikas for the first time developed crucial organizational capabilities. The leaders now knew how to manage a large staff for efficiency and productivity. They had also built external relations with multiple stakeholders that provided legitimacy and resources. They had a new awareness and sense of the power that comes from focus and discipline, enacting a long-term strategy without getting distracted by constantly reacting to problems and opportunities as they emerged. And they had experienced the tremendous impact they could create for villagers by scaling their biogas innovation for a long time, constantly improving and tweaking their approach.

The impact accrued not only to the people and communities Gram Vikas served but also to the organization itself. External actors had changed the perception of it as just an inefficient NGO and a group of well-intended but naïve do-gooders: "We were known as a particularly competent agency who delivered what they promised." Gram Vikas decided to use this trust as a resource to expand its activities. It realized that the biogas program was consistent with what it had learned from the tribals: (1) One needs an entry point into communities that creates immediate and clear benefits, such as health or energy, and (2) satisfying fundamental needs of villagers is not just an outcome of development work. It is also a necessary basis for tackling more challenging and more contested problems that cannot be solved with technical fixes or predefined solutions. The latter point was an insight derived from the biogas program, on whose successes Gram Vikas was able to build more sensitive and complex ITDP initiatives.

The shortcoming of the biogas program was that it targeted only people with sufficient economic means to invest. And it was aimed at individuals; it did not transform communities. But the strongest beliefs and passions of the Gram Vikas members lay in changing the ways people related to each other to counteract the inequalities sustained by the traditional caste system. Gram Vikas went back to the drawing board to search for answers that integrated and built on its experience over the past fifteen years. The search for ideas was now guided by much more explicit design criteria:

- Initiatives had to work in challenging, diverse, multicaste villages, not only in homogeneous communities.
- Initiatives had to include every member of a village to truly transform the whole community, not just individuals.
- Initiatives had to be financially and socially sustainable, in the sense that Gram Vikas could withdraw from a program after some time without the initiative collapsing or the community reverting to past behavior.
- Initiatives had to generate a fundamental, quick improvement of material and emotional well-being if Gram Vikas hoped to sustain the motivation of the community to invest in long-term progress and development by confronting sensitive relational problems.

The Rural Health and Environment Program (RHEP)

During the biogas decade, Gram Vikas created and strengthened an impressive green zone. It found a fruitful constellation and fit among (1) a deep understanding of communities and their needs, (2) building resources and potent organizational capabilities to cater to one particular set of needs, and (3) nurturing a passion for affecting many more villages beyond just the tribal communities. The staff felt a sense of pride and accomplishment.

Scaling the biogas intervention also created a new awareness of community inequality. In the beginning, YSMD had focused only on tribal communities and the problems of their exclusion. But now Gram Vikas had experienced a much more prominent level of exclusion in many more villages: "So we were very troubled by the fact that there was almost an apartheid system working in Indian religion—of exclusion of Dalits, exclusion of Adivasis, exclusion of certain categories like widows and single mothers, and exclusion of women in general, exclusion of differentially abled people." Taking on this problem became the new focal point for the search for ideas.

Gram Vikas needed an entry point into the communities to start working on this troubling problem. The staff ran a survey to identify the most prevalent community needs. Health turned out to be the biggest issue. Gram Vikas analyzed its survey data and concluded that most of the health problems were caused by a lack of clean water for drinking and cleaning. A particular problem was the practice of open defecation that polluted communal water resources. Water and sanitation became the hallmark of the next initiative, the Rural Health and Environment Program (RHEP), which was started in five pilot villages in 1992.

A big asset that the biogas scaling created was Gram Vikas's presence in more than 6,000 villages. It could thus choose the villages that had the best chance of success for the first RHEP pilots. And owing to the organizational resources it now had available, it could run several pilots in parallel with different innovation designs. This ability allowed Gram Vikas to test various intervention designs and quickly find what worked best. And Gram Vikas's reputation, earned during the biogas project, helped to spread the message about the new program throughout the village networks. The organization got the attention of potential supporters, funders, and the government. Despite all those advantages, it found only five villages that were willing to engage in the pilot:

Even with our presence at that time in around 6,000 to 8,000 villages, only five of the villages accepted it. In those villages where we had constructed more biogas plants, our rapport was much better, because the whole community knew us. The other agencies, even government agencies, when a subsidy is given to a particular scheme for a particular farmer, they wanted a share. But in our case, we have never asked a single percent from any of the biogas beneficiaries. So in such villages they have taken an interest in implementing it [the RHEP pilot]. So 1992 to 1995 we called the pilot phase of the program.

Gram Vikas knew that to achieve social transformation and for the people to change their minds and hearts, it needed to go into villages with a big carrot: "We use water and sanitation as an entry-point program, and water and sanitation is maybe the only program where we are able to reach to the whole community, the rich, the poor, the literate, the illiterate, the high caste, the lower caste. Because everybody is in need of water." The idea was to provide running water and operational toilets to satisfy immediate material and emotional needs of the villagers. But the central objective was to use the carrot to transform how people related to each other.

At the core of the program was an emphasis on full inclusion of all villagers from the beginning:

Early on we realized that any intervention of this kind would not work by involving just a few families. For total sanitation to happen, the entire habitation needs to be treated, involving all families without exception. Even one family continuing to defecate in the open or using the pond would be a potential factor in perpetuating diseases. We also realized that the intervention would have to be designed in a manner so that it would be self-perpetuating for all times to come. From the outset, it was clear that the intervention would not succeed as an externally managed affair—it had to be owned and managed collectively by the community to succeed.[5]

Persuading every single family in a village to achieve 100 percent participation in the program was no easy feat. It was met with strong resistance from people of higher castes, who were appalled by the prospect of using the same water source as people of lower castes. Gram Vikas sold the idea of 100 percent inclusion by arguing: "We say that unless those people also have a toilet and actually use it you will be ultimately eating the shit of those people because the fly that sits on the shit of those people won't distinguish between you and them."

In the beginning, only the good faith that Gram Vikas had built up in villages where it could achieve scale with the biogas project allowed it to formalize agreement to participate in the RHEP pilot. Much of the resistance centered on caste and political affiliations that dictate the status of particular families and groups within the village. In some villages, 140 meetings were required before women were allowed to participate for the first time.

Piloting and Improving

Between 1992 and 1995, Gram Vikas ran the first RHEP pilots in five villages. Initially, the design was based on providing a toilet for every family and one standpost for clean drinking water for every five families. One of the main problems with implementing RHEP was the length of time it took Gram Vikas to gain agreement in a village that all families would participate and benefit equally. Reflection on the outcomes of these pilots triggered changes and adaptations in the next wave of pilots, begun in 1995:

Then we found that if there's only one pond, where animals are bathing, children are bathing, men are there. Women also come, but they wear their sari and blouse. Whatever clothes they wear, they go and take a dip, and then go back. So out of sheer shame, she's not able to unclothe and clean herself properly. Why can't we build a small bathroom? It is not a great cost. There is a wall already, because you have a toilet, and then make another three walls and have privacy so she can take a bath without any problem.

Thus toilets were extended to provide a private bathroom for every household. Eventually Gram Vikas also installed a third tap for clean drinking water in every house. The pilots produced a steep learning curve. For example, the organization learned that it had to create a sense of ownership by the communities, or they would just lean back and rely on Gram Vikas to finish the project:

The moment we made the first input into a village, people realized that now there's no way out for Gram Vikas. The people said OK, now let Gram Vikas do.

So people sat back, and instead of taking the next four or six months to complete, we have gone on for two years or so. So it became in their eyes more our need than their need.

Gram Vikas was meeting some resistance to its 100 percent inclusion target. And some Gram Vikas employees argued for a decrease in the initial target. Gram Vikas bent the target on some occasions, but this deviation did not work for the organization in the long term and ultimately was not accepted internally: "In all the places, we follow the same method all the time because we know that wherever we have not got a consensus and we have tried to cut short those methodologies, we have suffered for it." These experiences helped Gram Vikas to solidify the various facets of implementation into a strict engagement process and timetable of events marked by certain commitments and agreements by both the village and Gram Vikas. It started to implement the same procedure in all villages and formalized a three-phase process with clear milestones.

By 2015, Gram Vikas had transformed more than 1,200 villages, following a defined procedure in every one of them. Even attitudes toward the lowest caste, the Dalit, also considered "untouchables," had changed: "So this is a Dalit village to which many non-Dalit people want to come. Before that, nobody would want to live with them. So it is a complete transformation, a real feeling of dignity." By entering with a technical approach revolving around the provision of water infrastructure, Gram Vikas was able, slowly and in a subtle way, to achieve its main objective of lowering inequality:

There are remarks one still hears from men in villages where work has just begun: "Gram Vikas says we must involve women to make decisions, but this is just for RHEP, not for other activities." Little do they realize that once the dent is made, the "cracks" open wider and wider, as evidenced in the older RHEP villages.

Today, more than ten years after the early pilots, these villages are very different. And that creates additional demand for RHEP. For example, women will not allow their daughters to marry someone from a village that was not "treated" by Gram Vikas. And people from higher castes *vol-*

untarily move to villages that have worked with Gram Vikas even if they
have primarily lower-caste populations:

Since we have set such a tall order for ourselves—by saying it has to be 100 percent—we know that our going will be slow. But at the same time, now we have
more examples of villages that are succeeding, and that is exerting a pressure on
the surrounding villages. If this village here has water and sanitation, in the next
village the woman will say: "My aunt in that village, she has all these facilities,
yet I have to go through this dehumanizing process to defecate in the open. Why
don't we do something about it?" So slowly we think that sort of pressure is
working. Another pressure that is working is the pressure of marriage. Girls are
unwilling to go nowadays from these villages to villages without toilets, bathing
rooms, and water supply. They are telling their parents: "Why do you want to
send us there?"

The earlier experience with tribal villages and the lengthy pilots of the
first RHEP experiments have taught Gram Vikas's leaders that introducing
changes or innovations to their current approach to speed up the process
would likely undermine the quality of their initiatives. And, most important, it would undermine their goal to fundamentally change the prevalent
inequality that was holding people and communities back. Unexpected
consequences have usually followed where Gram Vikas has taken short-
cuts or deviated from its standardized approach.

MANTRA PHASE (2003)

To continue its scaling activities, Gram Vikas made a number of strategic
changes. At the turn of the twenty-first century, Gram Vikas developed
what it referred to as its *Millennium Mission.* Its goal was to empower a
critical mass of the population of Orissa, which would have enough political clout to instigate real change for the marginalized and disadvantaged
segments of society, particularly women. Clearly, the plan was a legacy
of the experience of power that came from scaling the biogas program. It
formalized the target: to reach 100,000 families within the next decade.
This explicit goal setting also formalized the organization's strategic objective to continue its slow—but in many ways successful—scaling efforts.

Given that engaging with Gram Vikas is a difficult and demanding process for villages—nothing is given to them free—perhaps the best measure of success is the demand that comes from villages themselves: "Earlier, convincing villagers to join this program took at least two to three years, but now, with proven results, quite a few villages have expressed interest in working with Gram Vikas."

Gram Vikas also introduced structural changes. Until 2003, it worked on two separate programs, the Integrated Tribal Development Program and the Rural Health and Environment Program: "RHEP and ITDP have their own personnel. If things want to move from here to there, people won't easily communicate with each other." The organization realized that it needed to establish the "future direction" that would "make the organization as a whole." Gram Vikas merged ITDP and RHEP into one joint program, now called MANTRA, the Movement and Action Network for Transformation of Rural Areas. It continues to use water and sanitation as an entry point to other development activities in any village.

Scaling, Not Innovating

With time, Gram Vikas gained the acceptance and trust of local communities. It also earned a good reputation with the government, which enabled it to lobby for policy-level changes. Grant-giving organizations also respect Gram Vikas. Good reputation, however, means that grant providers expect a lot from Gram Vikas, especially more innovation. At the same time, they demand more reporting on the positive impact of the work:

Very often what we face is funders that have extremely bright, extremely well-qualified, grown-up boys and grown-up girls. But they have not gone through the grind of getting something done with people in the developing world. They have certain ideas from some universities. They have read about corporate-like innovation, technical innovation. They often push you into where you feel the data are more important than the work that you do. But in an implementing agency like Gram Vikas you need to have your best people interfacing with people out there. They're all in the field, not in front of a computer. We had one donor asking for monthly reports, twenty pages with numbers. We try to make them understand that several of our projects do not even have a telephone. They have to physically go to the village and physically gather data and then travel a hundred kilometers to another place to upload it where they can connect to the Internet. Donors have not experienced that. They have never gone without Internet for a day.

The focus on scaling the core program perhaps fortunately prevented Gram Vikas from being distracted by too many other activities: "Because of our great concentration on this inclusive MANTRA, there is so much of our energy going into that. Not that there are many people whose energies can be spared for these sorts of things [referring to innovations]." As a consequence, Gram Vikas continues to create reliable benefits for villages and their communities.

Gram Vikas is also afraid that innovation might put a large burden of risk on the organization, risk that neither they nor their donors know how to deal with efficiently:

Ninety percent of the risk is with us, and that I think is quite a lot. Even the donors say we accept that there will be a failure. But ultimately, when you fail, you have to explain a lot. They say: "You promised to mitigate risk, and you would do this, this, and this. So most probably you have not done these five things that you were supposed to do to ensure that this failure does not happen." We did a program with the poverty lab at MIT. Ultimately the study came out that there was hardly any impact. My God, the backlash we got. Even in Gram Vikas, a particular coordinator, if one of the villages fails, he is not given an easy time. It's bounced up to his manager. His manager looks at it, then it is bounced up to me or to the management committee, so that person for failing is not having an easy time. While we accept failure in theory, in reality we are not really able to accept.

In addition, Gram Vikas faces the problem of limited human resources. For a long time, the organization did not have any human resource system in place. Currently, a system is in place, but attracting good employees remains the biggest challenge:

Human resource is mostly deficient at the foot soldier level now, at the middle management and also at the management level. Attracting human resources to this organization has become very, very difficult. Even mediocre normal graduates or even undergraduates, we used to get piles and piles of job applications ten years back. Today, no. Because they know that Gram Vikas is working in the most difficult areas, geographically inaccessible, malaria prone, away from markets, away from the TV network or the mobile network, no connectivity; culturally you are away from your community source.

Maybe we should give organizations such as Gram Vikas an "innovation break." Let them continue doing what they do best. Perhaps having a more realistic picture of what it takes to do this type of work and of the pace at which it can be enacted helps us to value the "slow scaling" of Gram Vikas and the achievements they generate from scaling proven recipes rather than inventing new ones. Professor Jeff Pfeffer of Stanford University shared with us an important insight about the dangers of pushing innovation: "The problem of too many organizations is that they get distracted. They lose focus and discipline. I recently asked the CEO of an extremely productive hospital: 'Why does not everyone do what you do?' and the CEO answered: 'Because it's too boring.'"

GRAM VIKAS'S INNOVATION ARCHETYPE
We call Gram Vikas's unique innovation archetype "innovation for learning." The primary role of innovation was to learn and to build crucial knowledge in all three dimensions of its impact-creation logic: problem spaces, resources/capabilities, and mission/strategy. The drawn-out learning curve in the first decade of the organization's trajectory was difficult to sustain for the organization. But this investment was necessary eventually to develop and refine an impact-creation logic that enabled impactful scaling. The focus on scaling instead of innovation in the more recent trajectory of Gram Vikas enabled the development of a green zone that allowed Gram Vikas to generate positive impact for thousands of villages.

Gram Vikas had a long and extremely hazardous learning curve. For many years it did not find an access point to the communities it wanted to work with. It also failed to develop an intervention that really made a difference in the lives of the people it wanted to serve. Why did Gram Vikas struggle so much? Our analysis suggests some factors. The founding team came from a different part of India from the one they started working in. This mattered greatly, because regional heterogeneity is much larger in India than for example in Bangladesh, and experience in one region does not easily travel to another. Gram Vikas had little knowledge of the local needs and circumstances of poor communities. The founders also lacked capabilities in designing and enacting interventions. Furthermore, they were motivated by a relatively abstract mission of fighting inequality and were not able to translate it into an operational reality with priority areas and concrete objectives.

The absence of a successful impact-creation logic as a basis for efficient and effective action meant that anything they did in their first decade of work was an innovation. Not having relevant knowledge also meant that they were liable to reacting to ideas suggested by external actors. After years of trial and error, they switched to a more responsive mode. Active listening and responding to the real needs of communities enabled more patient and careful learning. Slowly, a more formal organization and a clearer impact-creation logic for their integrated tribal development program (ITDP) emerged. But the organization still lacked important organizational capabilities necessary for a distinct green zone. Many innovations within ITDP were abandoned. Those that worked could not be scaled. The young Gram Vikas members did not have adequate knowledge to manage a growing organization and a complex set of needs. They also lacked essential human, financial, and reputational resources. It was uncertain where these resources should come from and whether they could afford them. Stakeholders looked at Gram Vikas as a typical small and inefficient NGO and were not ready to provide much support. This experience illustrates what operating in a red zone looks like.

The innovation into biogas in the 1980s dramatically changed the organization's trajectory. It targeted one specific problem, the lack of electricity, with a technical innovation: building locally adequate and cheap biogas plants. This solution provided the organization with a clear focus and identity. The biogas innovation involved much lower social complexity than the earlier innovations targeting tribal problems. And biogas was supported by adequate external resources, in particular those provided by the government and those of farmers who could afford to pay for it.

Gram Vikas succeeded in building a green zone around its biogas implementation. The characteristics of the green zone were a deep understanding of farmers' needs and priorities, developing a robust technical solution and perhaps enjoying the excitement that came from enacting a program that worked. This excitement created a strong shared identity and clear strategic priorities. Because the biogas innovation generated concrete benefits for poor farmers and was financially sustainable for Gram Vikas, the organization grew rapidly. Gram Vikas developed important organizational capabilities, including hiring, training, and organizing a large staff into a productive delivery machine. Over almost ten years, its people built crucial financial and human resources, changed their reputation from a small inefficient NGO to a large-scale efficient service provider, and nurtured an appetite for scale beyond their wildest imagining in their early tribal years.

Interestingly, in order to build its green zone, Gram Vikas had to de-emphasize one defining organizational characteristic at least temporarily: The original mission of targeting inequality was reduced to a focus on productively delivering a more technical project. This lack of meaning and inspiration eventually limited Gram Vikas's motivation to continue scaling biogas. The leaders decided to spin off the biogas operation and to refocus on its original mission. But this temporary reconfiguration of the elements of Gram Vikas's impact-creation logic succeeded in building a strong green zone as a basis for more productive subsequent innovations.

By now, Gram Vikas was in a much better position to successfully enact their eventual signature intervention, MANTRA. Earlier innovations had provided Gram Vikas with deep environmental knowledge as their explicit design criteria for RHEP illustrate. This accumulated knowledge enabled Gram Vikas to generate ideas with lower levels of uncertainty and thus to innovate more productively and to avoid "too many bad ideas," one of the innovation pathologies we described in Chapter 2. It also had built resources that enabled it to carry innovations through; it was not forced to "stop too early," another potential pathology. Gram Vikas had learned how to scale an innovation and thus how to create impact from investing in new ideas.

The knowledge gained from the biogas decade allowed them to identify appropriate villages for the innovation. They picked those for their initial pilots in which they had already operated and where people trusted them. This enabled quick testing and refining early MANTRA ideas. They now had efficient staff and financial and reputational resources as well as a keen understanding of how the communities ticked. Gram Vikas also set organizational objectives and articulated a clearer overall strategy. They had learned that identifying a technical challenge—in this case convenient access to safe water—could serve as a tangible focal element that provided their innovations with direction. This also enabled entry into communities with something that could generate quick objective benefits. They had also learned that the complex challenge of inequality could best be targeted in an indirect manner on the back of a much less controversial intervention. This enabled much more productive experimentation and learning than their earlier experiments around a vague notion of tribal inequality. And they had organizational and implementation capabilities to scale MANTRA to more than 1,000 villages.

Gram Vikas's early failures acted as a warning against departing from the well-established MANTRA process of engaging communities. So Gram Vikas kept scaling MANTRA over more and more villages with little modification. The directors were aware of the downside of innovations outside their green zone. They refused to give in to funder suggestions to modify some of their program specifics, such as the 100 percent rule. Deviation from their formula might let them make faster progress on tick-box-style reports of delivering water and sanitation facilities. This approach might please some funders, but they knew from deep experience that it would not generate sustainable solutions and would not reduce inequalities. Gram Vikas's impact-creation logic reflected the directors' decision to generate benefits for more than 100,000 people in the poorest communities of Orissa by allocating resources to scaling a proven intervention instead of novel ideas.

Without the failures that came from their earlier innovations, Gram Vikas's leaders would not have been able to build the necessary knowledge to design their MANTRA intervention. And it would have been almost impossible to commit the organization for a long time to a strategic focus on scaling instead of innovation. They are aware of the risks of innovation, and they have no illusion of competence.

Although Gram Vikas has transformed more than 1000 villages, big funders have not been impressed with its record: "Why have you done only a thousand villages; why not ten thousand villages?" is a question that Gram Vikas frequently encounters. Under pressure to innovate more, the new management of Gram Vikas intends to collaborate with other actors from the private and public sectors and to be more innovative in general. In a way, this living case study is unfolding as we write. Reflecting on the insights and frameworks we lay out in this book suggests that this will be a very challenging transition period for the organization. It also shows how important it is to take succession planning seriously in social enterprises.

4 INNOVATION IN SUPPORT OF SCALING

The Story of Aravind (India)

Our goal is to get more patients, not to get patients to pay more. The volume helps us to get better. None of our staff knows how much we are making or financial targets. We never talk about money, only about volume of patients—it's much more fun! —*Senior Manager, Aravind*[1]

START OF THE INNOVATION JOURNEY: AN ELEVEN-BED HOSPITAL

In 1976, Dr. Govindappa Venkataswamy, whom everyone knew as Dr. V, retired from his position as the head of the Department of Ophthalmology at the Madurai Medical College in Tamil Nadu, Southern India. Dr. V had performed more than 100,000 eye surgeries in government hospitals in Tamil Nadu during his career as an ophthalmologist. In the 1960s, working for a government hospital, he developed an innovative approach to high-volume surgeries performed in rural eye camps. What triggered this innovation were particular circumstances that deeply troubled Dr. V's conscience as a doctor. He had only a limited budget to tend to overwhelming numbers of cataract patients. At that time, the established process for cataract treatment was lengthy and costly, limiting the number of patients who could be treated.

Dr. V searched for ideas to bring medical services closer to patients in need. Perhaps his sense of responsibility for the many patients who could not be treated under standard medical procedures was greater than his commitment to established rules and norms. Despite having only a minimal budget and suffering ridicule from the establishment, his team set up temporary surgical rooms in villages. They operated from dawn to dusk and built tremendous goodwill in the communities. Community leaders and even simple villagers provided resources, food, and help with logistics. They started to develop a sense of ownership of the camps.

The concept of community eye camps was born, and it created large demand through word of mouth. Very high surgical volume and ongoing community support enabled the team to learn fast. Over the years, they were able to improve their pioneering approach to community surgery and make a real difference to thousands of patients. There was a clear sense that scaling the initial innovation of eye camps created tremendous impact. But there was also a sense that they had only scratched the surface of what scaling could do, given the huge demand for eye services that mostly called for highly standardized procedures.

When Dr. V reached the mandatory retirement age of fifty-eight, he decided to continue his pioneering work: "I saw hundreds of people blind due to cataract. I realized that with a simple operation, their sight could be restored. It was a simple observation, and I simply decided that I should continue to help people with their sight."[2] A search for answers to a simple question resulted in the establishment of the Aravind eye hospital: Could the community surgery pilot program that he had developed be scaled to the size of the problem and eliminate needless blindness? This became the mission that guided Aravind's journey until today.

Dr. V drew his emotional and ethical inspiration from Indian spiritual leaders such as Mahatma Gandhi and Sri Aurobindo, who emphasized the notion of serving God by serving community.[3] His operational inspiration came from another, more surprising, source:

I was fifty-five when I first saw the golden arches of McDonald's. In America, there are powerful marketing devices to sell products like hamburgers. All I wanted to sell was good eyesight, and there are millions of people who need it. If

McDonald's can sell billions of low-cost burgers, it seemed possible to me that we could sell millions of low-cost sight-restoring operations.[2]

With help from his family and money from a mortgaged house and the sale of personal valuables, Dr. V started an eleven-bed eye hospital in the house of his brother in Madurai in 1976. After the early death of his father, Dr. V, as the eldest son, had taken on responsibility for steering the careers of his brothers and sisters. He also arranged their marriages. So he enlisted the four other siblings and their spouses—several of whom were ophthalmologists—to join him in his mission. They worked grueling schedules in the small hospital during the week and in community eye camps on the weekends. Coming from a family with a traditional agricultural background, they were used to working 365 days with no vacation. The quality and efficiency of their operations built tremendous goodwill and reputation. The project started a steep growth trajectory.

EARLY INNOVATIONS: FINDING AND
STABILIZING A ROBUST BUSINESS MODEL

In 1977, Aravind moved to a larger building in Madurai. Thirty beds were provided for paying patients, and seventy beds were allocated for patients who were too poor to pay. Dr. V, inspired by the efficiency and reach of McDonald's restaurants, reconceived hospitals as high-quality and highly standardized "factories" that could be precisely replicated into a chain of similar hospitals. This image drove pragmatic inquiries into the basic design of the Aravind model of delivering eye care. The group constantly questioned all operational aspects, including costs, types of facilities, hiring, and ways of socializing staff to fit Aravind's explicit values emphasizing dedication and compassionate service. The group nurtured a culture of constant dissatisfaction with the status quo that routinely triggered ideas for making services better and more efficient. This culture still shapes Aravind's journey today. A robust operational model that created tremendous benefits for Aravind's patients emerged. It had developed a robust green zone.

Resources were scarce, but Aravind operated by an unwritten rule, never to turn any patient away. The tension pushed Aravind to find new ways of increasing relative capacity by using bottleneck resources such as nurses, doctors, and facilities more productively. And it needed to increase its absolute capacity at the same time. Banks rejected loan applications, and asking for donations in a neighboring industrial town (which Dr. V found inefficient and embarrassing) was unsuccessful. Aravind developed an aversion to reliance on external funds from the beginning. In 1978, at a time when resources were desperately needed, Dr. V turned down the offer of the CEO of a large company to donate a significant amount of money in return for naming one of Aravind's hospitals after his wife. These decisions both reflected and reinforced the dimension of strategy and mission in Aravind's well-developed impact-creation logic. Since then, collaborations with either the private or the public sector have not been part of Aravind's identity nor strategy—with rare exceptions that tended not to go well (for example, see the later section on managed care). Strategic and identity clarity lent focus and consistency to Aravind's decisions.

As a result, the basic model of Aravind emerged with quality, growth, and financial self-sufficiency as priorities. Instead of relying on external funds, its model was based on paying patients subsidizing the costs of treatment for those who could not afford it. In 1981, Aravind exceeded its capacity of 10,000 surgeries per year. The hospital moved to another facility and expanded to 200 beds for paying patients in 1982 and 400 beds in 1984.

The principle of financial self-sufficiency also influenced Aravind's decisions about human resources. From the beginning, Aravind relied on Dr. V's family members as core managers and doctors. Its doctors had to forgo many of the material luxuries that their peers were accumulating as successful medical professionals. And their peers were also exposed to significantly less arduous work schedules. Dealing with staff turnover became a challenge. Nevertheless, as the organization was growing, it needed people who had not only the right skills but also the right values that defined Aravind. One of the doctors who joined Aravind remembers: "Other organizations, I don't know how they give emphasis on the vision and mission. Maybe they are on paper, but in Aravind it's not like that. It is not a piece of paper. It is actually taught, trained, and they ask us to perform it."

Instead of relying on external hires, it introduced training courses for nurses in 1978. Nurses were a principal bottleneck resource in Aravind's model. The organization competed for girls who traditionally married young rather than working. It took Aravind several years to gain legitimacy as a trustworthy institution, but its consistency paid off: "The families of those girls, they feel that the girls are safe, they are serving for a good cause, they have values of the culture of Aravind, and they're serving the people. So they are very happy. And first year, there is a girl from the family, next year their relatives come here, because it's good here." With time more training courses were developed and added to Aravind's training portfolio. All training involved close mentoring by Dr. V and his core team, whose omnipresence ensured that problems were spotted and resolved fast and that the quality of Aravind's services and its core values were upheld and constantly improved: "When we select a person, both consciously and unconsciously, the most important criterion is organizational fit. At every level. And the more senior they are, the more rigorous is the assessment process." This emphasis created a homogeneous performance-driven organization and the resources needed for further expansion.

Replications: Hospitals in New Locations

To achieve the vision of eradicating needless blindness, Dr. V and his family members worked to increase capacity at the Madurai hospital. As this expansion was deemed insufficient to achieve the vision, new hospitals were started. The second Aravind hospital was opened in Theni in 1985, with the capacity of twenty paying and 130 free beds. In 1988 another hospital, for 135 paying and 400 free patients, was built in Tirunelveli. In 1991 Madurai hospital yet again extended its capacity, to 280 paying and 1,100 free patients. As a result, by the end of 1991 Aravind achieved the mark of 50,000 surgeries per year. Shortly after the Theni hospital opened, Aravind ventured into Nepal, in partnership with the Seva Foundation. They reengineered a small local hospital after Aravind's model. The Nepalese doctors went to Aravind in India for training. The Nepal experiment created hope that Aravind's model could be at least partly replicated in regions outside of Tamil Nadu.

From the start, Dr V's family members worked at Aravind hospitals as doctors and decided on the direction the organization should take. In time the next generation of family members joined Aravind. For example, Dr. V's niece Chitra married Thulsi Ravilla in 1981. Coming from a private-sector background, he became Aravind's first administrator. Slowly, a cadre of senior managers emerged. They were deeply involved in all aspects of Aravind's organization, constantly monitoring and controlling quality, performance, and compliance with Aravind's rules and values. They regularly met and exchanged ideas. Many ideas came from external sources, for instance through travel:

Whenever we see something, we would like to see how it could be implemented for the eye care. That is one thing that, I think, is making us more innovative, because things are there, and we are just going to see how they could be customized for our need, for eye care. So basically almost all senior leader-level people have this kind of attitude; whenever they see something new, they want to see how it could be implemented in Aravind.

During the expansion, improvements of Aravind's model were largely driven by senior managers reflecting on external inputs from international colleagues, funders, and other supporters. But Aravind also had direct and short communication lines and easy access to senior managers, which enabled employees to communicate their ideas directly:

If I want to do something, I can straightaway go and talk to my immediate boss or even up to the chairman; also I can go and share what I have learned. So immediately he would recommend we have to do something similar to this.

For its expansion, the organization tested its model first on a small scale in the Madurai hospital, before scaling it up to other locations. Similarly, improvements in the overall models are usually tested first on a small scale:

Somebody from one of our branch hospitals in Pondicherry suggested we can have a monitor in each doctor's room to show how many patients are waiting for you in the hospital, or in that particular unit. So that was my first request for some resources. So we took that to the management, and then first they wanted to try it in one of their units just to understand whether it is useful.

The consensus building for improvements was often driven by the founders, senior managers, or senior doctors. Decisions about ideas that directly supported Aravind's core mission and priorities and that were enabled by existing resources and capabilities were usually made and implemented quickly. Getting organizational support for innovations that fell outside its explicit remit was more difficult:

Let me give you one example. Lucia in Pediatrics did not have a way of handling cancer in children. But she could find friends in other hospitals who could help. Then she was the champion of that particular innovation. She attracted V's help and my help and VG's help and enough help so that she fought it through the hurdles she had inside the organization. It's now an ongoing program here.

With each expansion, Aravind stayed true to its mission and provided treatment for both paying and nonpaying patients, keeping the ratio at approximately thirty-five to sixty-five. This standard required a sustained focus on cost reduction and financial discipline: "We are not so concerned about the revenue part, but we are very careful about costs!" A critical situation arose in the late 1990s, however, when the number of paying patients sharply decreased to about 18 percent of total surgeries. Higher wealth levels in India had attracted competition for paying patients. Aravind was slow in upgrading its facilities to reflect emerging standards of convenience and to offer a range of eye services beyond cataract surgery.[4] The dramatic loss of revenue triggered a search for ways of upgrading its facilities and services for paying patients. Changes were implemented quickly, and within a few years demand from paying patients had recovered.

Another important element of the Aravind model, which it sustained during its expansion, was the close attention paid to maintaining organizational values that would ensure the expected behavior of all staff. Eliminating behavioral variance is an essential element in a focused, high-efficiency, volume-driven model like McDonald's or Aravind:

If you look at our expansion, any hospital we start the entire team was from our own hospitals, either from Madurai or Coimbatore. We have been comfortable that way. Even if it is a small hospital, we have sourced people who have worked in Aravind predominantly. Even if you are taking people from outside, it has been somebody who has already worked at Aravind, for whatever reason the person has gone out. So far, whatever ten hospitals we have, it has been always like that.

Training also enabled values-transfer and helped to secure manpower: "So far in Aravind we never give any advertisement for ophthalmologists. We have a postgraduation program that produces some twelve to fifteen qualified ophthalmologists every year. All of them join Aravind, 100 percent. A major source of inflow of manpower is always guaranteed." Thus many aspects of Aravind's early impact-creation logic have been maintained and strengthened during its expansion.

Monitoring and data systems were constantly improved to enable measurement of all aspects of Aravind's operation. And although Aravind explicitly does not use individual recognition or rewards, the real-time availability of data using displays visible to staff created a competitive spirit. That coupled with the use of stretch goals further fueled performance:

Sometimes we even set some kind of targets, especially on quality, like pressure-reduced complication rates, or "We should achieve outcomes of this standard." Then we have a fairly robust system for collecting information, analyzing, then reflecting on it. This is, I would say, a formal process, but one that continually evolves as well.

Aravind also earned a good reputation among prospective patients, which helped to shield them from emerging competition by private hospitals:

The reason is that people go for the screening there [alternative hospitals], but come here for surgery, because they trust Aravind. They believe in Aravind for the various cultural values, transparency and various things. So it is really helping us in one way to improve our volume also.

ADOPTING RADICAL INNOVATIONS:
BREAKTHROUGHS IN QUALITY AND PERFORMANCE
In the 1980s and early 1990s, Aravind—like almost all hospitals in developing countries—treated cataracts with aphakic surgery, a well-established procedure. Although the clinical outcomes of the procedure made a significant difference for patients, it did not fully restore normal eyesight.

Patients had to depend on eyeglasses with thick lenses. In 1981, a U.S. ophthalmologist introduced Dr. V to a new technique based on intraocular lenses (IOLs). It had superior clinical outcomes. Dr. V performed successful trials of the new technology. He was immediately convinced that IOL was the future for Aravind. Given his dedication to quality and care for patients, he could not ignore the differences between the two procedures. But he faced at least three severe hurdles to adopting and scaling this innovation. First, the costs of IOLs imported from Western markets were prohibitively high, and there was no local manufacturer in India. Second, India did not have ophthalmologists who were trained in IOL procedures. Both of these hurdles meant that IOLs were not scalable beyond small numbers of surgeries and did not fit the Aravind model. Third, Dr. V faced severe ideological resistance. A number of influential international organizations in the fields of development and health criticized the introduction of IOLs in developing countries as "irresponsible" because it would make these countries dependent on something they could not afford: "In the early 1990s, there was a great deal of debate about the relevance of IOLs to developing countries. Though widely accepted as a better procedure, it was argued that developing countries should not go in for it, as the IOLs were expensive."[5] Consequently, the Indian government did not support Aravind's push to adopt IOLs. Even though Aravind's ambitions were deemed "irresponsible" by some observers, there was no ideological uncertainty within Aravind. The dramatic benefits the new surgery could create for patients fully legitimized the idea from Aravind's perspective. And because it had some of the best surgeons, they could certainly adopt the new technique.

Aravind started training a number of its own doctors in the new technology. International experts and supporters regularly came to Aravind to facilitate training and to bring supplies of IOLs that were available only in Western markets. Unfortunately, none of the international IOL manufacturers was interested in India as a market. They were also unwilling to provide Aravind with lenses at a price point that enabled financially sustainable delivery of IOL surgeries beyond a few donations. Searching for options to overcome this hurdle, Aravind decided to evaluate entering the ophthalmic market itself.

Dr. V again reached out to his family network. One of his nieces had married a research scientist with a PhD in electrical engineering. The couple had been working and living in the United States for a decade. But in 1990, they answered Dr. V's call to help build a manufacturing plant for IOLs and returned to Madurai. Along with an entrepreneurial and extremely dedicated staff member from the Seva Foundation, the duo invested much time and energy for the next two years in implementing the idea. They found a small U.S.-based technology company that was willing to help with the technology transfer to increase its own production capacity.

This period of implementing an innovative idea was difficult for Aravind given the negative attitudes of much-needed international supporters. And it divided the Aravind senior team. Dr. V became increasingly biased against it. He was concerned that running a manufacturing business could expose Aravind to corruption and other ethical hazards that were rampant in the Indian manufacturing industries. It was not unusual for Dr. V to stop projects even at advanced stages if he felt they were not a fit. Before the technology-transfer project was launched, he suddenly pronounced that no Aravind money was to be used for financing the project. A close family member and doctor at Aravind took a personal stance in favor of the project and in an unprecedented act of disobedience passionately opposed Dr. V's decision. Dr. V eventually agreed but limited Aravind funding for the project to a minimum. With the help of Seva Foundation and other funders, Aurolab set up manufacturing facilities in Madurai and started production of intraocular lenses. Aravind's influence in pushing quality and affordability generated a significant analysis and redesign of IOL manufacturing procedures. Eventually, Aurolab produced lenses at a fraction of the price of Western IOL manufacturers. Aurolab was established as a nonprofit organization with the mission of making high-quality ophthalmic products affordable: "When we get into a field we want to make an impact, and that is linked to the ability for price reduction. At some point Aurolab wants to contribute to lowering the cost for treatments. That is the objective."

The demonstration effect of introducing IOLs successfully to a developing country generated a lot of demand for Aurolab's products in India and internationally. But a bottleneck for scaling Aurolab was the absence of sufficient numbers of surgeons trained in IOL procedures. Luckily, Aravind recognized the danger, and in 1993 it started a dedicated training program that welcomed doctors from all over the world. Over the next decade it built up its capacity and eventually graduated about 100 surgeons a year in a two-month training program.

In response to the growing demand, several new manufacturers entered the market. IOL manufacturing was largely unregulated in India. One of Aurolab's concerns was that others might be tempted to produce low-quality lenses to meet Aurolab's low price points while still making a profit. Aurolab thus pushed for achieving ISO and CE Mark certifications of compliance with international quality standards and legislation for its lenses. Certification enabled global exports of Aurolab's lenses and forced the nascent manufacturing industry in India to match not only Aurolab's price level but also its level of quality.

The new manufacturing capability that Aravind had acquired allowed it to target a number of the bottlenecks in Aravind's service delivery model. In 1997 Aurolab expanded its product portfolio to pharmaceuticals and started producing drugs not provided by commercial companies because of their low margins. In 1998, Aurolab began producing suture needles, and several other products followed in the following years. Aurolab's product diversification was always triggered by Aravind's needs and objectives:

If you look at commercial organizations today, the majority of innovation is based on profit margins. All our innovations have always been solutions to a certain problem, never to increase the profit margin. Aravind needed lenses— Aurolab was the answer to that; the market shifted so that Aravind could absorb foldable lenses—Aurolab shifted to foldable lenses. Similar with sutures: Aravind wanted to save costs—Aurolab started to make sutures. We always addressed a certain problem—never addressed a margin.

Aurolab became a major player in the market, driving down the prices of ophthalmic consumables in India and abroad. It also contributed to reducing costs of treatments at Aravind hospitals, bringing Aravind one step closer to achieving its vision. But Aurolab faced limited human resources, constraining its research and development capabilities:

Unfortunately, within Aurolab there are multifaceted divisions, and there are very limited resources that could absorb ideas from external sources. We have not invested that much in these resources and do not have a robust research and development team within Aurolab. If you look at other pharmaceutical companies, they have thirty to forty full-time people only for R&D [research and development]; in Aurolab we try to optimize our resources so that they would also be able to do other things in addition to R&D."

EXPANDING SCALE AND IMPACT: A MULTICHANNEL APPROACH

At the core of Aravind's mission was an ambition to reach every patient in need. The vision of universal coverage required several channels to reach different types of patients, depending on location and economic and social strata. Aravind's first channel was eye camps. This innovation dramatically increased the impact created over the years by Dr. V's original innovation in the 1960s. Aravind made a number of modifications and added services to the original design. In 2014, it was able to screen more than half a million patients through that channel. A second channel was the so-called walk-in hospitals in cities. They were open to patients who were too poor to pay fully or even partially for treatment. By 2014, Aravind had replicated the model in ten hospitals that were purpose-built and fully managed by Aravind staff. The hospitals had separate sections for paying and free patients. Collectively, they screened about 470,000 free patients annually. This screening effort and the identification of so many patients in need of surgery generated tremendous demand and pressure on Aravind's resources. The need to serve all these patients efficiently with high-quality medical services required an extreme focus on monitoring and evaluating performance, eliminating variance in the actions and outcomes of individuals, relentless pursuit of constant improvements, and identifying and eliminating bottlenecks to capacity and productivity. A young hospital manager at Aravind's Madurai hospital said: "Every week we are asked, 'What have you improved? What have you learned?'"

Additional channels were added in the 1990s and 2000s. In 1992, the Lions Aravind Institute of Community Ophthalmology (LAICO) started a dedicated program of outreach through consulting and training in other hospitals. In the mid-2000s, Aravind experimented with a novel program of managed care. And it also started building vision centers and community clinics to build capacity in the form of a hub-and-spokes model.

Consulting and Training through LAICO

In the early 1990s, driven by its success with introducing IOLs and establishing Aurolab, Aravind searched for new ways to expand its impact. Another organization that had a strong focus on "giving sight" was the Lions Clubs International Foundation, established in 1968. Ever since Helen Keller, a renowned advocate for the blind, in 1925 challenged the assembled members at the Lions Clubs International Convention to become "knights of the blind in the crusade against darkness," this precept has become a rallying force behind Lions' global activities. Lions started its ambitious SightFirst initiative in 1990 with a plan to invest more than $200 million in "projects that deliver eye care services, build or strengthen eye care facilities, train professionals and build awareness about eye health in underserved communities."[6] The foundation reached out to Aravind to offer a partnership aimed at improving the capabilities and efficiencies of hospitals that received SightFirst funding. That way, each dollar spent could create more benefits for the people in need of eye services. In other words, it wanted to create more sight for the buck. This proposal came at the right time for Aravind: "Internally, officials began discussing the possibility of opening a training institute to provide instruction for others. This discussion continued while the Lions Club International SightFirst program began looking to support a new hospital in India."[7] Enabled by a generous SightFirst fund, in 1992 the Lions Aravind Institute of Community Ophthalmology (LAICO) was started. The aim of this new organization was to provide training and consulting for health care professionals from within and outside of Aravind. This would also help to alleviate the human resource hurdle that was a crucial bottleneck to introducing IOLs on a larger scale within Aravind and in India.

When LAICO started, it soon ran into a number of challenges. It received many more requests for its services than it could manage with its resources. Some of the requests were rejected because of the risks they posed to Aravind's brand and image. Franchising, for example, was deemed too risky. One of the shortcomings was also that Aravind could not proactively seek and select only those partner hospitals that had the potential for absorbing Aravind's knowledge and methods. Over the years, LAICO consulted with hundreds of hospitals globally.

In July 2006 Dr. V—Aravind's founder and leader—died. Nevertheless, the bonds among three generations of family members remained strong under the chairmanship of Dr. Namperumalsamy, the husband of Dr. V's sister. Some organizational changes followed. Aravind focused on extending its impact through capacity-building activities of LAICO. In addition, LAICO paid special attention to developing monitoring systems for consulting clients:

Now we are really making efforts to ensure that this will be one of our core works and that we will try to have all the hospitals on board. We have just developed a database that will be available even for them. They can directly upload information and see for themselves how they are progressing over time.

The results were mixed. Overall, the effort probably contributed to enabling hundreds of thousands of additional eye surgeries, but the impact of Aravind's engagement varied substantially among hospitals. LAICO's database implied that most hospitals did not show a substantial sustained performance improvement as a result of replicating some of Aravind's processes. Rather, the average performance increase across all hospitals came from a few dramatic positive outliers. In 2006, LAICO and Seva Foundation, its long-term partner and funder, initiated a redesigned effort to build capacity, the Global Sight Initiative. For the first time, Seva put money directly in the hands of LAICO to enable it to identify and handpick hospitals that LAICO thought had the most promising characteristics for developing their own capacity. Once the chosen hospitals had done so, they could become mentors and nurture other hospitals as well.

Seva considered this modification a game changer. The new plan was dramatically different from the previous engagement model of Aravind:

So it wasn't because a donor told the little hospital: "Little hospital, if you want a grant from us, you've got to do this one-week vision-building exercise with Aravind, and basically, Aravind has to sign off on you. And then we'll give you this grant that will enable certain equipment, activity, training to happen."

It is a novel combination of actors, engagement processes, and monitoring and training activities. Building on initial success, the initiative is currently being expanded by a significant scaling effort that will demonstrate how much potential for impact the joint effort has.

It also dawned on Aravind that replications of its model by others may not be the most efficient scaling strategy. It seemed that the principal vehicle for making an impact was Aravind itself. Organizing for efficient implementation and scaling a proven model sounded easy in theory. But it was an elusive goal for organizations that had never developed much of a green zone (see Chapter 1). A much more hands-on model seemed a necessity going forward. This included building more hospitals that were designed, built, and operated by Aravind staff. In 1997 Aravind opened its fourth hospital, in Coimbatore, with a capacity of 775 beds, of which 600 were reserved for nonpaying patients.

In 1998, Aravind partnered with yet another organization, Rotary International. Together, the two organizations opened an eye bank in Madurai in 1998 and additional banks in 1998, 2004, and 2005. The idea for eye banks was triggered by the insufficient numbers of eye transplants conducted at that time in India. Aravind needed eyeballs to conduct eye transplants and yet again extend its impact:

Responsibility means also seeing that our other practices scale, like cataract. It means pushing our clinics and reframing problems. For example, corneal blindness is highly prevalent; a small infection of the cornea leads to ulceration and leaves a scar. We thus need eye donations. That is why we do a lot of promotions through eye banks.

Scaling its eye banks initiative contributed to promoting eye donations in India and thus further extending Aravind's impact. As the organization teamed with external partners, it also developed its partnership capabilities and perhaps its appetite for more partnership arrangements.

Innovating Outside Its Green Zone: The Rise and Fall of the Managed Care Program

In the late 1990s, an empirical study on health services in rural areas came as a wake-up call to Aravind. The study indicated that of all the people in need of eye care who lived in Aravind's service area, fewer than 10 percent could actually get it. The appalling deficiency triggered a renewed search for additional channels to increase Aravind's reach and impact.

One opportunity came in 2000 in the form of the CEO of the Birla Group, a large family-run Indian business conglomerate. She was an elderly woman who was described as very respected but fragile looking, and she was extremely persistent. She really needed persistence, because her proposal did not fit with Aravind's strong reservations about corporate partnerships. But the elderly lady in a wheelchair would not give up. She managed to get a memorandum of understanding for a joint hospital in Kolkata, West Bengal. The project was championed by Thulsi, the managing director of LAICO, and by Dr. Aravind, Dr. V's nephew, one of the best young cataract surgeons at Aravind. Dr. Aravind had just returned from the United States, where he got his MBA—despite strong reservations from the larger "Aravind family," who feared that pursuing an MBA was a distraction from his work as a surgeon.

The young man was energized, though, and championed doing things differently from the Aravind model, providing opportunities for the younger generation to innovate and learn outside the constraints of the established organization:

If you look at Aravind in the past three decades, every decade we have grown four times, and during the last years of the previous decade and the first years of the next decade we have stagnated. That's the time we have taken a newer approach to grow—a new hospital, Aurolab—whatever. Whenever we had a major transition in leadership, we also had major growth opportunities. So today in Aravind, we are going through a transition in leadership from the senior generation to the next generation. The senior generation wants to be very careful in letting the junior, next generation take over. The next generation wants to be very careful, doesn't want to make mistakes. So within the organization everybody tends to be very careful. Nobody moves forward. The only way to move forward is through someone else who trusts you from the outside. They look at me whether I can get the job done or not. Your credibility is much more outside than inside. Managed care really compresses time in an individual's learning. You take leadership positions, people take you seriously, people implement what you suggest, you see for yourself what has been done. You are a failure if you talk about problems in this organization. Because everybody has been so successful. There is no place for you to fail. Managed care lets you fail, lets you fall down, learn. So that is one area where I feel managed care is an amazing opportunity to build leaders within our organization.

Dr. Aravind's design incorporated the operational core of Aravind. But the good doctor felt that the more unobservable parts of Aravind, such as the tight family relationships and the family's values and spiritual influences, were not replicable. Nevertheless, he thought these parts might be replaceable by other elements. Perhaps a more "secular" operational approach to replication could work to increase Aravind's ability to create impact. He thought that an intense, hands-on buildup phase, orchestrated by Aravind but with external resources and ownership, could work. It could potentially overcome the shortcomings of two existing alternatives: (1) on one extreme lay Aravind's plan to build its own hospitals, a form of organic replication; and (2) on the other extreme was LAICO's relatively noncommittal knowledge-transfer model, where the responsibility for replication lay with the partner hospital and its ability and motivation to adopt Aravind practices. Dr. Aravind's idea was somewhere in the middle, thus overcoming the weakness of organic replication, which was extremely resource intense for Aravind, and the LAICO model, which was limited by the weak impact-creation logics of most partner hospitals.

The Birla Group offered an opportunity to test and develop Dr. Aravind's middle way. As a large business conglomerate, they provided financial resources and arranged for land and permits. Aravind's job was to build the hospital infrastructure, train the personnel, and manage the hospital. When Dr. Aravind arrived in Kolkata, however, he found only a small apartment in a residential building. On opening day, only one patient showed up. The doctor responded by pulling many more Aravind resources from its own hospitals into the project. It replicated but had to slightly adapt many important elements of the Aravind model. Training and knowledge transfer eliminated important bottlenecks. By 2006, the team was performing over 3,500 surgeries per year and had moved into a five-story dedicated hospital in the center of Kolkata.

The first pilot thus was encouraging despite taking much longer than anticipated. More requests for affiliated hospitals followed. The Rajiv Gandhi Foundation requested a replication in Amethi. Aravind decided to team up, and the first hospital in partnership with the Gandhi Foundation opened in 2005. This time Aravind had to work with existing hospital resources. The paramedical staff in particular turned out to be a challenge. They seemed unwilling to comply with Aravind's strict rules and expectations that they would overcome strong reservations against working with poor patients from lower castes. Aravind had to hire a set of nurses who were selected much more for their values than their competencies:

Northern girls are very loud and expressive compared to the southern Indian women. But in the hospital setting, you cannot afford being very loud. Everybody knows that operating skill is a skill that if you repeatedly do it, you will get it. But what is important is not the skill—values and attitude makes the difference. My first job is to make them de-learn what they have learned during their under-graduation. After de-learning, then we inculcate the Aravind poison.

The initiative looked promising. In early 2005 Aravind leaders decided to adopt it and to scale it up significantly. They set an ambitious target: conducting one million surgeries annually through a network of about 100 managed hospitals, including Aravind's own hospitals, within a decade. The managed care approach was defined the following way:

The process involves working with a socially conscious local partner—an individual or organization—wanting to invest in eye care as a way of doing social good. While the partner invests the required capital and creates the enabling environment, Aravind implements the project on a "turnkey" basis and continues to run the hospital, in the exact same manner as Aravind Eye Hospitals, by placing a core team from Aravind managing the key functions.[8]

Aravind searched for additional organizations with a social mission and a willingness to open more than one hospital. In 2007, a new partner was found and another hospital built in Amreni. A similar venture was under development in partnership with the Grameen Bank in Bangladesh. A second hospital in partnership with the Rajiv Gandhi Foundation was opened. In 2008 Aravind created a dedicated organizational unit responsible for the managed care strategy. It was named Aravind Managed Eye Care Services (AMECS), with Dr. Aravind as its director. The goal was to build capacity for four new hospitals per year. Projections then aimed to reach twenty-five managed care hospitals with an aggregate surgical capacity of 500,000 per year by 2015. LAICO, with its experience in capacity building, was at the forefront; it organized a leadership retreat to reflect on the lessons learned from managing the first three affiliated hospitals. But already some tensions had arisen within Aravind as to which direction the organization should take: "There was a tension between those who were more conservative and those who emphasized our responsibility. The consensus was to let the needs guide our decisions and stay true to the mission." A crucial problem for each pilot hospital came after a period of stabilization following Aravind's hands-on intervention in the first two or three years. The local management, which was supposed to take over and own the future direction of the hospital, felt constrained by Aravind's rigid processes. After all, they had not participated in the learning that came from going through the innovations that gave rise to the original Aravind model. They misunderstood and questioned the legitimacy of many processes and rules that were the results of experimentation, selection, and retention within Aravind's own hospitals. In addition, the Aravind system did not enable the partner hospital management to innovate and design their own processes and replicate some of that learning. A number of problems with management at partner hospitals emerged: "We could add value in the first years, but then there were too many tensions with the local management and Aravind withdrew." In 2009, Aravind quietly closed AMECS and withdrew from the managed care strategy: "So our original plan to keep managing affiliated hospitals and build many more was stopped."

As several observers familiar with the situation told us, this decision was less critical for Aravind, the organization, but a real tragedy for Dr. Aravind himself. He had promoted and shaped the innovative effort

to replicate managed care. Failure is not something that Aravind was used
to or that was in any way acceptable. One external close observer said:
"It took Dr. Aravind a long time to heal from this. The organization gave
him a really hard time and made him personally responsible for the failure." Meanwhile, Aravind, the organization, kept storming ahead on its
established path, undistracted by all the turmoil. It refocused on its own
values and strengths. In 2010, Aravind had sufficient resources to be able
to build many more of its own hospitals in Southern India. For this more
organic form of replication, it had relevant knowledge, reputation, and its
own financial and human resources. Consequently, Aravind opened five
new branch hospitals between 2010 and 2012.

Community Outreach through Vision
Centers and Community Clinics

Aravind's obsession with identifying weaknesses and bottlenecks in its
impact strategy triggered a deep reflection on expanding the capacity of
its community outreach channel. Aravind was aware that the success of
eye camps depended on the skills and efforts of local organizers, whom
Aravind could not fully control. In addition, eye camps provided only ir-
regular services to people in need of eye treatments. Furthermore, Aravind
was seeking new ways to drive higher patient volumes through its main
bottleneck resources, in particular its pool of scarce eye doctors. And it
wanted to save both its staff and its patients the time and monetary costs
of traveling. The idea for permanent community services emerged:

The idea for telemedicine and vision centers came after the hospital did a utiliza-
tion study in 1996 to look at the efficacy of its rural eye camps—these had been
organized periodically over thirty years in several rural locations. They discovered that these camps addressed only 7 percent of those who needed eye care, as
a camp was usually held only once or twice a year. Before the vision centers were
set up, only 7 percent of those who needed eye care actually got it. This statistic
prompted Aravind to seek out a permanent access model.

In 2003 Aravind was hit by the news of botched eye surgeries conducted during eye camps run by other organizations. Subsequently, the
Indian government temporarily banned eye camps. The closures prompted

Aravind to make some changes in its community outreach strategy, which historically had generated a high inflow of patients for Aravind's hospitals. Dr. V seems to have been inspired to champion the potential of telemedicine by reading an article about a project in Alaska. Others recall that he got excited when hearing about a local Indian NGO that built Internet-enabled telekiosks in rural villages to support farmers with information and education. But not everyone at Aravind agreed. "There was a good deal of internal debate on the approach—it was not clear whether the technology was feasible, and even if it was, whether patients would be comfortable with remote diagnosis."[4] But Dr. V was passionately convinced of the potential of this innovation. And he found an ally in one of Aravind's senior doctors. The two would closely follow progress during the initial pilots and ensure that the pilots did not get stopped by emerging hurdles.

Initial trials in collaboration with the NGO that was running the telekiosks were not successful. But then a team from the University of California, Berkeley, who focused on technologies in emerging regions, was brought in to pilot the idea from scratch. Initial challenges included low bandwidth, which interfered with exchanges of visual and oral communication, and the high cost of available retinal cameras. The latter limitation was successfully resolved by Aurolab's unique ability to develop low-cost diagnostics. New tall buildings often blocked line-of-sight communication channels. But, in little more than a year, a sufficiently stable technical infrastructure was set up, linking the first vision center with Aravind's hospital in Theni. Aravind adopted the innovation and decided to scale it up to forty permanent vision centers with funding from external partners. By September 2004, three vision centers were operational. Each covered between 35,000 and 50,000 people. They were the foundation of a new hub-and-spokes model providing higher capacity outreach to remote rural areas. The centers also improved the productivity of one of Aravind's bottleneck resources, the pool of its trained in-house doctors.

Teaming up with the Right to Sight, a global initiative of the International Agency for the Prevention of Blindness, Aravind started setting up community vision centers. Vision centers provided access to patients and a basic diagnostic capacity at low cost. Aravind developed IT systems that enabled its doctors and staff to interact with remote patients at its vision centers through video conferencing: "We thought about setting up rural centers with connectivity so that paramedical staff can examine the patients and then patients just come to the base for the consultation. Maybe each patient may require two minutes or three minutes for deciding on a [treatment] opinion. So that is how vision centers started." Aravind also expanded the idea of vision centers to building community eye centers or community clinics. These were larger facilities than vision centers and constituted a community establishment for primary eye care more permanent than camps. They are usually staffed by a full-time ophthalmologist, five paramedics, and one paramedically trained receptionist.

From the organizational point of view, Aravind yet again expanded its impact, organizational structure, and channels into patient demand. One consequence was that the organization became increasingly stretched and challenged to manage ongoing workloads and to develop and implement new ideas as well: "We are always busy. For example, Google says 15 percent of the time is free for idea development. We do not have that luxury."

STRENGTHENING ARAVIND'S INNOVATION CAPACITY

Forty years later, despite Aravind's tremendous scaling efforts, demand for its services is undiminished: "We get constant requests from the communities: 'Why can't we have a branch in Chennai or in Kerala? How about a branch in Andra Pradesh?'" But finding the infrastructure and the right place for a new hospital, as well as developing sufficient human resources, remain real obstacles to progress. "We are as stretched today as we were twenty years ago. So we ask new questions: 'Can we train nurses in one year instead of two years, as we have always done?' For example, we would like to have more vision centers. But the bottleneck is staff. Can we replace human labor with technology?" Aravind's expansion—except for the managed care approach in the early to mid-2000s—has always relied on sourcing the teams from within Aravind: "For rapid growth this is a bottleneck. Can we take the risk to do, say, 50/50? Use teams made up of half Aravind and half outside? The main difficulty is: What about our value system and our culture? Because that is the one main glue that keeps everybody together. What happens if somebody from outside dilutes that?" One Aravind staff member shared her belief that Aravind should experiment more with finding solutions to these "soft-factor bottlenecks" to enable faster growth: "Personally, I think we should just go ahead and experiment and do it. When I discussed this with Dr Ravindran, he questioned me: 'Is the eye care problem going to be solved tomorrow?' I said 'No'; 'So then—why do you have to rush so much and talk about growth?'"

Another set of questions relates to Aravind's willingness to partner with actors that have huge influence on and resources for health care services in India:

We have been discussing for the past four or five years whether we should be working with government. We hesitate because getting government buy-in is no easy thing. A concern is that you spend much time working with the government and you are never really welcome and don't know if it will be implemented, so you may waste your energy. We like to be in control of outcomes; with the government we are not.

These questions even prompted Aravind to start an innovation club a few years ago. But apart from a few meetings, nothing came of it. Aravind also experimented with an "idea box." But that did not work either—very few ideas landed in the box. One conclusion was that "we don't have the right staff for innovation." One Aravind doctor remarked: "The third generation is much more risk averse than the founding generation." Others think that the legacy of past and current greatness and success is a heavy burden for the current doctors. Living up to it is already a tremendous challenge. Innovating on top of it may seem like a bad idea.

Some at Aravind question its focus on its scaling strategy:

What does growth mean? Should we look at numbers, for example cataract surgeries, or also horizontally, specialty care, path-breaking research, and so on? At one level we know that if you want to stay relevant we have to do a lot more other things than cataract volume. In cataract we can still grow, but less than previously."

Perhaps to create platforms where questions like these could be considered and further developed, Aravind established Dr. G. Venkataswamy

Eye Research Institute in 2008. It is a dedicated research and development organization for the whole organization:

The people who work there are no different from the ones who worked at Aravind, but now it is a separate organization. All they do today is research, publications, papers, unconstrained by the day-to-day operations of the departments.

Meanwhile, Aravind is growing and creating tremendous benefits simply by doing what it knows how to do best.

ARAVIND'S INNOVATION ARCHETYPE

We refer to Aravind's unique innovation archetype as "innovation in support of scaling." The primary role of innovation was to target operational bottlenecks that emerged as a result of its continuous scaling work. Overcoming bottlenecks to scaling strengthened Aravind's green zone and enabled its health care services to create more impact more efficiently.

When Aravind was established, it already had a significant green zone. Its founder had earlier pioneered an important model of community surgeries that became the operating model of Aravind. Dr. V could hire relatives who brought expertise and relevant skills, he could access small but sufficient economic resources, and he knew how to manage a health service operation efficiently with a limited budget. A clear sense of mission, strong capabilities, and a deep understanding of patient needs in both urban and rural settings all aligned into an efficient and focused health service impact-creation logic.

Scaling and using Aravind's scarce resources productively became its primary strategic objective. Aravind was built for high productivity and for achieving very low error rates in service delivery. Removing any uncertainties in this model was crucial. Even the smallest ideas to improve efficiency immediately benefited patients, and this in turn created the patient demand required for scaling their services:

As a policy we don't do any marketing, but what we do is, we do quality: Our quality speaks. It's the word of mouth that helps us. When you have your surgery done, when you have your satisfied patients, that is your marketing tool. They go to the community and spread their satisfaction. It's not only the surgery, it's the quality of services we provide.

Incremental improvements over many years thus dramatically lowered uncertainty and built essential resources:

- A reputation for high quality and as a deeply caring organization
- Extremely efficient eye doctors, who performed at roughly ten times the productivity of those in comparable hospitals (for example, measured in terms of annual surgeries per doctor)
- A culture of deep commitment to Aravind's mission and to continuous improvements where all parts functioned in a prescribed and controlled manner
- A constantly growing capacity for delivering concrete benefits to more patients
- A financially solid basis that permitted investment in organizational infrastructure and growth
- A network of supporters that brought cheap or free resources and provided funds for larger innovations that eliminated bottlenecks

A razor-sharp focus on these factors made Aravind's impact-creation logic robust and able to accumulate knowledge and also enabled it to be extremely efficient. Interestingly, both Gram Vikas in its last decade and Aravind have been focusing on scaling and continuously creating impact. Why could Aravind accumulate such an enormous resource base while Gram Vikas could not? Perhaps the answer lies in the very different types of problem spaces that the organizations target. We urge you to keep this question in mind when we get to Chapter 8, which systematically addresses the importance of problem spaces for innovation, scaling, and impact.

Aravind developed all the characteristics of a high-reliability, high-performance organization. It did not strive to be a high-creativity, innovative organization. When a number of Aravind's staff recently mapped its innovation pathologies, they revealed a long list of ways in which the organization makes innovation difficult for anyone who is not part of the senior management team:

We often seem too busy to innovate. Only in the last few years did we implement the idea of giving academic staff half a day off for research. At LAICO we often discuss that we want a day off from phone calls and the like. But somehow we are not doing it. We started with one hour off, but that was too short, then one day, let's do Saturday, but then something comes up, and the day is gone.

And growth has created a mature bureaucracy: "Aravind now is a bigger organization. We developed a silo mentality. Best practices are not shared so easily anymore."

But, amazingly, it was able to implement some dramatic innovations very productively. Aravind tended to innovate to remove operational bottlenecks. These emerged as part of its scaling efforts, its push to constantly improve its ability to serve more patients with better procedures. The introduction of intraocular-lens–based surgeries and the subsequent necessity to move into IOL manufacturing is a case in point. Aravind's strategy to aim at extremely high performance levels thus met a real bottleneck in the provision of intraocular lenses. Standard procedures or "business as usual" could not resolve some of these bottlenecks. The organization saw a painfully visible gap between its actual and desired performance levels, which triggered a firm consensus throughout the organization that solutions had to be found.

The subsequent search for solutions generated ideas that had relatively few managerial and identity uncertainties. The benefit created by IOLs clearly legitimated pursuing their introduction in India without getting distracted by naysayers from the global development community. Aravind had the best available surgeons, who could readily adopt the new procedure with little training. The ideas were also grounded in deep knowledge about existing patient needs and demands and their willingness to adopt IOLs. Unintended consequences were unlikely because Aravind IOL-based cataract surgery was a well-understood and established procedure in the medical community; it targeted a need (cataract) that varied little between geographic regions and could therefore be treated with exactly the same surgical procedure.

Aravind's modular structure of operating several smaller hospitals was an additional important element in making its innovations more productive and creating more impact from them. Scaling through exact replication of smaller units reduced complexity and ensured predictable outcomes. This setup allowed Aravind to test a variety of ideas simultaneously at small scales. Because all Aravind hospitals worked in exactly the same way, successful innovations could be easily adopted by other Aravind hospitals. Internal knowledge transfer thus was another important channel for scaling. In contrast, external knowledge transfer was a much less efficient scaling strategy. The effort to implement managed care failed because the partner hospitals differed too much from Aravind's own hospitals. Aravind's ideas and knowledge were outside the partner hospitals' impact-creation logics. Knowledge transfer switched from a green zone activity to a red zone activity. Aravind eventually declared the experiment a failure and stopped it.

The areas of uncertainty that Aravind's innovations focused on were mostly more technical: Could Aravind devise a workable solution, could it get the required resources, could it make the innovation economically self-sustaining? By keeping its innovations close to its scaling efforts and thus its green zone, Aravind loaded the innovation dice in its favor. And Aravind did even more to make its innovations productive. It invested in directly lowering important uncertainties at early stages in their innovations. It actively sought and openly received external input from many experts. Their contributions further improved the quality and legitimacy of ideas. For its explorations into IOL manufacturing, Aravind hired two experts full time to work on reducing technical and market uncertainties before it committed serious resources to implementing potentially bad ideas. This method brought the idea closer to its green zone, where uncertainties are low, and increased the chances of success and productive implementation. For most eye hospitals, because they do not have Aravind's knowledge and experience, evaluating and implementing the same idea—venturing into IOL manufacturing—would be unlikely to succeed. The idea would lie deeply in their red zones.

Being squarely focused on emerging bottlenecks lent Aravind's innovations a particular pace, direction, and rationale. It made innovating more productive than exploring ideas far from Aravind's green zone. These innovations further improved Aravind's scaling efforts and capacity and thus enabled Aravind to create more impact from its previous innovations. A central factor in Aravind's impact-creation logic is its willingness to walk in the footsteps of its founder. Family members are recruited and socialized into this organization to continue the journey. This policy prevents the potential pathology of new management coming in with a desire to leave their own footprint through risky innovations and changes to Aravind's impact-creation logic. At particular times in Aravind's past, it has shown a remarkable capacity to innovate productively. But in between these inflection points remained the hard, dedicated, focused work of creating impact for thousands of patients every day: "In the last three years we have not done anything drastically new." Perhaps innovation is not central to the impact-creation logic of the "most innovative eye hospital in the world."

5 INNOVATING AND SCALING FOR TRANSFORMATIVE IMPACT
The Story of BRAC (Bangladesh)

We didn't innovate because we thought innovation was a good idea. We innovated because we wanted to solve the problem. —Andrew Jenkins, BRAC RED

START OF THE INNOVATION JOURNEY: TRADING AN XL FIRM FOR AN XS SOCIAL ENTERPRISE

In 1954, a young man named Fazle Abed, who grew up in a part of British India that is Bangladesh today, went to Glasgow to study naval architecture.[1] He was eighteen years old and followed his older brother and his uncle, who was Pakistan's trade commissioner in London. Abed soon realized that he had insufficient passion to pursue a career as a naval architect. He joined his uncle in London and began to study accounting. He earned money providing accounting support to various companies during his studies. In 1962 he became a British citizen. He bought a house in London and moved in with his girlfriend, who shared his passion for the arts. The pair frequently visited the London opera and art galleries throughout Europe. He surrounded himself with Marxist friends, always dressed well, and started smoking cigars. This lifestyle, however, left less and less time for his studies. After a breakup with his girlfriend, who—after visiting Dhaka in 1965—did not find the promise of a future life in Pakistan attractive, Abed decided to go home. He was hired by the Shell

Oil Company and returned to Pakistan in 1969. Within two years he was heading the accounting department, living in a large house with servants and a private car and playing tennis with other businessmen at the Chittagong Club.[2]

In November 1970 the Bhola cyclone hit East Pakistan (today's Bangladesh), killing half a million people. Abed and some friends organized a group of relief workers and started helping people in the areas most affected by the cyclone: "The death and destruction of the cyclone affected me tremendously. I questioned whether the life I was leading was worthwhile. So this was the first idea, the seeds of change in my own thinking." Less than half a year later, the Bangladesh Liberation War broke out. Abed was getting sucked into the military machine and knew he had to leave the country. But the chairman of Shell Pakistan informed the secret police of his plans and had him arrested. Abed nevertheless made it to Shell's headquarters in London, where he angrily handed in his resignation. He sold his London house as a substitute for his lost income and joined friends to start Action Bangladesh, an organization lobbying and fund-raising for Bangladeshi independence.

In 1972, after nine months of war, Bangladesh became independent. Abed was devastated by the misery created by the war and the large numbers of victims and refugees.[3] The feelings of doubt about his own life that he had experienced after the cyclone resurfaced:

This type of life is not something that one continues in the face of this extreme human misery, the liberation movement, liberation war, and the cyclone. I decided to change. One could get meaning out of life if one could do something about it, about alleviating human suffering. So that's what motivated me, this poverty in Bangladesh, to start BRAC. At that time I had many options. I could go into politics to serve my people, but then I thought that if I could start at the bottom right with the people, then maybe I could bring about a substantive change in the structure of our society and the way we looked at it, rather than going into politics at the top and then trying to serve them from there.

Abed returned to Bangladesh in early 1972 and gathered friends to found a new organization, the Bangladesh Rehabilitation Assistance Committee (BRAC), to provide immediate support to the victims of the war: "The initial idea was not a long-term idea. The initial idea was to do relief and rehabilitation. Ten million people who went to India during the Liberation War were coming back to Bangladesh, and I thought that they needed support, so I started a relief organization." BRAC organized a survey to understand the problems in the most devastated areas. With a grant from Oxfam, BRAC initially focused on building houses, distributing economic assets for farmers and fishermen, and organizing health and educational services. It quickly made a name for itself for its efficiency:

We built thousands of housing units with bamboo and corrugated iron sheets for families who had lost their houses. We built more houses than we were asked and initially intended to. We built them faster in the sense that the initial plan of work was one year, and we finished houses in ten months. So I wrote back to our donor that I can now send back the money left. The donor said that nobody saved money once a grant was made. They told us to keep the money for the next phase of our work.

Abed envisioned BRAC as a temporary relief organization that he might leave after a year; he would then look for a job. But reflecting on the impact after the first projects made him reconsider his strategy:

After nine months of working with relief for the refugees who came back from India, some evolution was taking place. After seeing the support these people received, they built their houses, they got fishing nets, a boat, and other help. But what happened was they couldn't even retain the resources that were given to them. For example, they sold their houses. They couldn't even retain their fishing boats. Then the question came: "Why? What have we done here?"

This question led BRAC to the realization that it needed to search for ideas for a very different approach: "The realization came that relief is not really development work. It is needed, and it can mitigate immediate sufferings. But we realized that we had to do something more." BRAC changed its strategy and decided to work long-term in community development. The long-term commitment was crucial: "We came to the conclusion that, in order to do poverty eradication, one has to do long-term work and not short-term work." And this required a personal commitment far beyond that of the original BRAC vision: "After a year, I realized that just doing the relief and the rehabilitation, people are going to remain poor unless a long-term development strategy is worked out for them, and so it was not something that I could do in two years or three years. I had to commit my entire life for a slow and definite improvement in the lives of the poor."

INNOVATIONS IN COMMUNITY DEVELOPMENT

In 1973 the Bangladesh Rehabilitation Assistance Committee changed its name to the Bangladesh Rural Advancement Committee (still abbreviated BRAC). With a staff of about ten, the organization started to focus on community development. The model that influenced Abed and his colleagues was a program built on the principles of grassroots cooperative participation that had been piloted in the 1960s by the founder of the Bangladesh Academy for Rural Development. That program, also known as the Comilla Model, framed poverty as an economic problem that can be solved through organized community action. It argued that solutions based on merely providing missing resources were inadequate. Local communities needed to organize productive use, maintenance, and accumulation of their own resources. The inspiration for this model originally came from the credit unions that Friedrich Wilhelm Raiffeisen had developed in the 1870s in rural Germany. These unions were based on the values of self-help, self-governance, and personal responsibility.

At that time, the Comilla Model had the attention and support of the government and the international development community. It was intended to be rolled out nationally as part of Bangladesh's integrated rural development program (IRDP), and one of Comilla's experts was appointed head of IRDP. Because BRAC did not have any development expertise, it made sense to participate in the rollout rather than reinvent the wheel.

Community Development through Functional Education and Empowerment

In response to the high level of illiteracy in Bangladesh, BRAC began providing educational courses for adults. The courses were formulated around the Comilla Model: "They had an adult education program, or an adult leadership program, you could say. We thought that it was appropriate providing literacy and numeracy to the rural poor." As a part of its early educational efforts, BRAC trained teachers and established literacy centers. BRAC also developed microfinance and various income-generating programs.

After a short time, however, BRAC realized that a large number of people were dropping out of its educational activities. The high dropout rate motivated the organization to investigate. Why was its educational program unsuccessful and apparently not aligned with the needs of the poor? "So we went to them; we asked them. They said that, basically, it does not help us, it doesn't say anything about our life. It is only for giving literacy and numeracy. The contents were not designed according to the needs of the people." Subsequently, BRAC designed a new program of functional education focusing on life skills, basic health issues, and other problems that the beneficiaries were encountering in their daily lives: "We called it functional education. It is not adult education. Functional education means that people discuss their daily lives or everyday problems. They discuss these things in a group."

Although dropout rates declined, they were still significant, and the program was deemed a failure. Observers point out the "brutal honesty" with which BRAC acknowledged and reported its lack of progress as a sign of its particular culture and beliefs. BRAC was disappointed by the lack of progress:

It worked in Comilla, because the founder Akhter Hameed Khan was based in Comilla. The government repeated it all over Bangladesh, but it failed. It didn't work in other parts of Bangladesh. Why? The whole approach was a community-based approach. The whole community was involved. But we found in our group that those who are rich guys in the cooperatives exploited others. They went to the city or town, spent all the money of the cooperative, and said: "Your funds all have been exhausted." Then we at BRAC thought: "No, this is not the right approach. Community is not the right way of thinking about poverty alleviation. The better approach is that interest groups should be organized." Nowadays, there's a group; we call it village organization. Cohesiveness is more important than to organize the whole community.

The move from communities to interest groups was the first departure from the model that shaped the government's IRDP. The second was the move from the group to individuals:

I have a very Marxist kind of framework of mind. The collective was important at one point in my life. I was trying to get everybody working together for the common cause. But then there were lots of free riders, people who don't want to work because everybody else is working. If there's no good leadership it doesn't work. In Bangladesh people also tend to be a little more individualistic. So for three or four years I did that, and then I went into individual lending within the group and individual responsibility to repay the loan.

A third change to the established model was to overcome destructive gender-based power structures:

Again there is another learning, from the initial stage there was a mixed group, male and female. We found that males are dominating the females and that males are exploiting the women. Then we founded a separate group for women. Nowadays you will find that most of our group members are women.

Thus the organization changed its approach to focus on village groups that were made up of women under the name of village organizations. They became the basic medium for empowerment and educational activities as well as for providing health services, financial training and support, and income-generating activities.

A New Start

"BRAC then didn't have any experience. It was simply a baby. I'm talking about 1974, born in 1972. That's a two-year baby." BRAC acknowledged that adopting and replicating preconceived notions of development and mainstream approaches did not form a sound basis for development work. Poverty was not what it seemed from a distance. Poverty was a multifaceted set of problems that had to be understood on the ground. Preconceived solutions without a deep understanding of the problem did not generate expected outcomes for BRAC. In particular, it realized that poverty was not primarily an economic or technical problem. BRAC directly experienced the destructive dynamics of relational problems, including abuses of power and exploitation. These problems were difficult to deal with, given the small size of the organization and the limited experience the founders had. The introduction of village organizations enabled progress by minimizing power issues because of the particular way they structured their approach. By working with groups of women who had shared interests and equal economic and social status, BRAC avoided dealing with power issues directly until the members had a better understanding of these dynamics and how to overcome them.

BRAC abandoned the government's IRDP and started from scratch in two different districts. In implementing interventions that were not grounded in an existing green zone, the young organization had experienced all the uncertainties involved in red-zone innovations. The leaders realized that their understanding of problem spaces was not adequate, that their solutions were not effective, that communities did not adopt their innovations in education and other areas, and that the innovations had unintended consequences by reinforcing exploitative power structures or socializing communities to a donor-driven approach and losing their trust.

For the pilots in two new districts, the focus of the intervention design remained the same: education, microfinance, and income generation. But the approach had changed. First, the village organization became the new structural model for all the interventions. Second, they needed to spend much more time talking to the poor directly and listening and learning from them. "Every month, Abed went to the field and spent a lot of time there. Whenever he goes to the field, he doesn't allow anyone to talk. He always speaks directly to the people and listens to them. Most of our ideas came from the people." Third, BRAC realized that it needed to become more donor-independent to make its own long-term decisions:

I like this proverb: "If you keep your hands in a friend's pocket, if that person moves you'll have to move." If you are totally dependent on donors' money, as we were in the seventies, 100 percent dependent on donors' money, our trajectory would have been very different. Many of the NGOs in Bangladesh have not developed this financial capacity.

Donor independence was also important to generate funds that could be invested in training staff and building an efficient organization, things that donors often dismissed as "overhead." BRAC knew that it needed to invest in systematic learning and experimentation to develop interventions that worked more productively. Efficiency and productivity had been hallmarks of BRAC's operation from the beginning. Partly, this was a legacy of the socialization of BRAC's founder in the corporate world, but it was also an insight from its earlier work that donors liked organizations with reliable and efficient implementation. And BRAC still relied on donors to fund its new approach.

ORGANIZATIONAL INNOVATION: BRAC'S RESEARCH AND EVALUATION DIVISION

A common error is to assume that reliable adherence to a plan of action is a desirable characteristic in an agency engaged in rural development. In fact the need is for organizations able to engage in a continuing process of creative adaptation; organizations that have the capacity to deal constructively with error.[4]

BRAC was aware of its lack of practical knowledge for designing better interventions and improving them over time. Uncertainties in all dimensions of Figure 1.1 held it back. But its awareness and open acknowledgment of these uncertainties enabled BRAC to learn fast and to evaluate its solutions in light of an emerging understanding of what the problems of poverty really were. In 1977, BRAC hired a graduate from the University of Dhaka, a statistician, as a one-person research unit that focused on gathering data and feedback from beneficiaries and evaluating BRAC's work. Because this early work was considered beneficial, BRAC in 1978 formally established its Research and Evaluation Division (RED).

The need for research was even more evident when the organization experimented with approaches to community development in three districts with a staff of approximately 200. The organization had to, and also wanted to, pay close attention to the needs of the people and to systematically understand the circumstances that created these needs.

RED launched a number of detailed studies in various villages. BRAC's executive director wrote in 1979 in the foreword to RED's first extensive report on the nature, structure, and dynamics of resources in rural villages:

In the last seven years BRAC has developed certain capacities within the organization and gained some perceptions of the rural scene through experience at the grassroots. It was, however, felt that more systematic investigation and analysis of the structure and dynamics of society were essential for formulating appropriate development strategies. Moreover, insights gained through experience needed to be analyzed and documented if they were to be of use to others. BRAC decided to develop research capabilities. This study is the first of the series of microstudies which was undertaken in the process of training a group of BRAC staff on the basic principles of observational research.[5]

The problem of power came up again and again. It was the subject of a second large study, as we see in a quotation from the preface of that report:

This study gives some indication of the extent of corruption and malpractices that characterises resource distribution in rural Bangladesh and the consequent difficulties of achieving development through conventional approaches. The powerlessness of the poor to withstand the machination of the rural elite appears to be the primary constraint to development and social change. Without the resolution of the problems of power, genuine development in rural Bangladesh will continue to elude us.[6]

Over the next decade, RED grew substantially to become one of the largest NGO research units in the world. In 2014, RED reported that, since its inception, it had produced nearly 1,398 research reports, 372 journal articles, 283 books and book chapters, 24 theses, 60 research monographs, 95 working papers, 51 RED newsletters, 24 volumes of Nirjash (a research compendium in lucid Bangla language), and 187 popular articles in newspapers. BRAC also established a dedicated training and learning center for its staff development because the organization already had clear ambitions to grow. It wanted to implement efficient management practices from the beginning. For BRAC, becoming large was important because it meant extending its social impact. The founder was not afraid to grow his organization to a large size:

The ambition to grow came from my own experience working for Shell Oil Company. Shell was the second-largest company in the world and they were very well managed. I thought there is always a feeling that small is beautiful and big is ugly. But I never had this experience. At Shell, big was not ugly, and I thought I would become big and effective. When you have millions of poor people, how can you remain content with doing the small thing? You have to have impact on the people's lives.

Between 1977 and 1980, BRAC's staff grew from about 200 to about 1,300.

With RED, BRAC gained a medium through which it could professionally and objectively evaluate its work and research the needs of potential beneficiaries more deeply. In addition, the organization gained evidence that its activities brought change and therefore dared to invest in scaling them up: "That generated the confidence and the statistically valid results which led to replication in other places." Evidence provided by RED was also important to demonstrate impact to stakeholders and hence strengthen BRAC's reputation vis-à-vis existing and prospective donors.

Later, RED also became an important support to various BRAC divisions to secure funding for new projects: "People come to RED and say: 'You've got to help us do a study on this pilot.' Because they know that if you don't have a study these days you probably won't get the funding to expand it." And this inquiry-driven approach helped create a particular culture in BRAC: "The question 'Why?' is also very important. 'Why failure?' Or, even if it is success, 'Why? Why are there limits?' or 'Are there limits?' Not just, 'It succeeded.' If you ask these questions, you will get, sometimes, answers."

The 1980s were important formative years for RED. This was the time when the unit engaged in more varied research, not only conducting surveys and baseline studies but also evaluating BRAC's activities and its impact. For example, RED contributed greatly to the design of the Oral Therapy Extension Program of BRAC in 1980.

A CRITICAL INNOVATION: ORAL REHYDRATION THERAPY TO TREAT DIARRHEA

BRAC adopted health services early on to generate livelihood opportunities for the poor, for instance for some microfinance borrowers: "I'm trying to empower poor people to solve their own problems, so the poor woman, who is our microfinance borrower, one of them is chosen to become a health person. So it's not a doctor who's coming from the town to

help them but some of their own. So their basic essential needs are met."
Health was also viewed as crucial for poverty eradication. It justified investments in developing innovative ideas:

We didn't innovate because we thought innovation was a good idea. We innovated because we wanted to solve the problem. 1979 was the International Year of the Child, and under-five mortality was more than 250, and I thought, unless we cut that down, there were no prospects for our poverty to go down. It was visible in many societies that first infant mortality must go down before poverty starts declining.

In 1980 BRAC started its first intervention into child mortality with the Oral Therapy Extension Program. The program was used to combat diarrhea, one of the major causes of morbidity in developing countries. A recipe for a simple and cheap treatment known as oral rehydration therapy (ORT) had just been published; it became popular in development circles. ORT was based on locally available ingredients: water, salt, and sugar that must be combined in a particular ratio.

The program eventually became a tremendous success story for BRAC and Bangladesh. But the innovation was difficult and challenged BRAC's ability to develop an efficient and robust intervention that would also scale well. Large numbers of trained and supervised employees, as well as research and evaluation capabilities, were crucial in enabling BRAC's success in oral rehydration. The latter were used to evaluate various program designs and experiments. In its pilot study, BRAC hired about 700 women, trained them, and sent them to about 30,000 households to teach ORT. Confidence was high, because ORT is extremely easy to prepare from readily available ingredients, and the benefits of ORT had been clearly established in thousands of cases. And then BRAC evaluated the program's impact: "We also sent a group of monitors to check how many actually used ORT in a case of diarrhea. Diarrhea incidence was 27 percent, but ORT use was only 6 percent. This was a big disappointment. We investigated possible barriers and found that not even our ORT workers believed in ORT—they bought drugs instead." BRAC assembled about 300 women at its training center and taught them how to make the ORT solution of salt, water, and sugar. It then had a lab check to see if they did it correctly:

We took health workers twice to the cholera research lab in Dhaka to show them exactly how the rehydration works among children who are dying of diarrhea. We developed a seven-point program, and we explained to them why and how it worked until we felt they were convinced. We started again with 30,000 households. Then we evaluated using the monitors. Uptake had increased to 19 percent, but we were still unhappy.

BRAC sent three RED anthropologists to interview 600 households that did not use ORT during diarrhea episodes:

What we found was that the program ignored the men who were suspicious about ORT. Women told them: "Oh, our menfolk, our brothers, our husbands, they think oral rehydration is secondary. They go and buy medicine from the markets to stop diarrhea." So we organized meetings with men, and we also launched TV and radio spots. Finally, uptake was improved to 40, 50, then eventually 70 percent.

BRAC also came up with the idea of a performance-based payment for health workers administering ORT:

We tested many things. One was paying people for the results. Oral rehydration workers were paid on the basis of the retention of knowledge by the mothers six weeks after they taught them about oral rehydration. They were not given a salary; they were paid on the basis of what the people they taught remembered and whether they could make the rehydration fluid correctly. We had groups of monitors who would go in six weeks after the households were taught oral rehydration and find out what percentage of the seven-point message that we wanted to transmit to them was remembered by the mothers. On this basis we paid our workers.

BRAC monitors also took samples that the households had prepared to a lab to check the concentrations of ingredients. Then BRAC had an additional idea: "How to monitor the monitors? Monitors were required to write down on their evaluation forms the name of the youngest member of the household, which due to insufficient records they could usually only get from the households themselves. A lot of monitors lost their jobs."

The changes helped BRAC to achieve impressive results. Over ten years of the program, 13 million households in Bangladesh learned how to make oral rehydration fluid to combat diarrhea: "We started having great results. So, right now, Bangladesh has the highest rate of oral rehydration usage in the world. Because of that, ultimately, the infant mortality rate went down dramatically." This success strengthened BRAC's reputation among the government and donors in Bangladesh and internationally. It also gave BRAC confidence, know-how, and an infrastructure to embark on solving other health issues in Bangladesh: "Oral therapy extension program was the program that we have run for the country. We covered 13 million households. That really helped BRAC to develop this impression by donors that we can do this, no problem." Subsequently, BRAC started its Tuberculosis Program in 1984, a Child Survival Program in 1986, and a number of other health initiatives after that.

And that became the hallmark of BRAC's approach to productive innovation: surveying the local environment, gaining a deep understanding of problem spaces, careful piloting, constant evaluation, objective critical learning, and scaling up successful pilots to sizes and levels of impact commensurate with the problems it targeted: "I was ambitious to really bring about change and not content with doing small things, and so—even when BRAC was only 500 strong, 500 people in BRAC, I decided to take on the entire country to cut down the child mortality rate."

INNOVATIONS TO ADDRESS
IDEOLOGICAL UNCERTAINTIES

In the early 1980s, while BRAC was developing the ORT program, an ideological divide within its senior staff opened up. Some, including BRAC's founder, were inspired by the idea of conscientization. This idea promoted raising the awareness of the poor about their problems and building their capacity for solving them within their own means:

The way poverty was looked at is that you bring resources and give it to the poor, so the poor are mere objects of your support, they're not subjects of it. They are not empowered to build their own destiny. At that time there was a book from a Brazilian educator. His name was Paulo Freire, and he came up with the idea.

Basically, you don't have to do much; all you have to do is facilitate an interaction between the poor. And the poor know their problems, and many of them can solve their problems.

Out of this inspiration, two different approaches to community development emerged. One group of BRAC staff promoted Paulo Freire's use of critical consciousness and empowerment as a way to fight poverty and inequality. This group focused on providing functional education and development of the poor's own resources. Its work was organized under the term *rural outreach program*. A second group propagated training and financial assistance supported by the provision of external resources and was therefore named the *rural credit and training program*:

BRAC was enjoying two schools of thought. For the poor people to take their destiny in their own hands to change it, you needed to give them the sense of self-worth, and so that's what we started building through our education in the initial part of BRAC. But another school of thought at the same time said no, it will not work. You need to provide them with training; you need to provide them financial support.

So BRAC set up two pilots to test the different ideologies. The outreach program was largely based on organizing people for power and using collective savings, because borrowing money was deemed to reinforce dependency structures. The rural credit and training program was centered on identifying economic opportunities and providing economic resources and training to realize these opportunities.

Community Development through Microfinance
Whereas the conscientization approach followed a more traditional intervention design that BRAC had pioneered earlier, microfinance was the key to the credit and training program. The idea of providing microfinance to the poor had emerged in the mid-seventies in parallel to the educational activities at BRAC. BRAC also used village organizations to formalize and scale up its microfinance activities as it did with its educational programs. But it departed from earlier attempts by relying exclusively on women as receivers of financial support: "The woman will be the one who is re-

sponsible for caring for and feeding the children as well as keeping the relationship with the extended family, despite poverty. So we thought if women could manage poverty, then they could also manage development. Women could be agents of change." Village organizations built solidarity among their members:

It is not like a company, but it's an organization that doesn't have shares. Each individual can do her own thing, but they help each other. For example—you borrowed some money, but one week, you can't repay your installment. So somebody else would say: "All right, I'll help you today and, when I have problems, you help me."

An important question was confronted in parallel in another pilot: "Can women manage other women?" Answers to this question were crucial for BRAC's design of its village organization. And the question finally was answered in the affirmative. Women-led groups of women became a robust element in BRAC's strategy going forward.

The easiest part of microfinance was providing loans. The most difficult but most crucial part was to identify productive opportunities and to enable the poor to take advantage of opportunities for their own benefit and to repay the loans for BRAC's benefit. BRAC's microfinance activities were among the earliest projects that brought income to the organization. Over time, this income made the microfinance unit of BRAC financially independent and enabled the unit to try out many new ideas: "In microfinance they have a certain kind of independence because they are quite self-sufficient on their funding stream. They don't have to write proposals and those kinds of things. They just try it, take the risk, and run with it."

In the mid-eighties BRAC felt that the parallel pilots of conscientization and microfinance should be integrated into a unitary strategy to avoid inefficiencies and unproductive ideological debates. Owing to its pragmatism, BRAC learned to reconcile ideological tensions like this one largely by using pilots, gathering data, and objectively evaluating performance. That way BRAC learned from both pilots to shape its principal approach going forward:

1985 was a period of consolidation and learning from all those experiments that were going on in different areas. The group with the empowerment approach at some point noticed that the poor may not take action because they are without the support of finance. The Rural Credit and Training Program people came out with the idea that yes, the program is working very well, but at the same time they believed they also needed educational support. People were raising these questions. Well, if you just work with education, it will not work. If you just work with credit, it will not work. What should we do? He said if you cannot integrate all services, health, education, development, all those together, you may not have substantial improvement for the people.

And in 1986, elements of both pilots were adopted and formalized in the rural development program (RDP).

BRAC now had a portfolio of initiatives that it could enact as part of its RDP. Although many NGOs and development organizations worked on a number of issues in thousands of villages in BRAC collectively, almost no one was able to work on all the issues in a single village. Poor people got either education or microloans or health care or legal services but rarely more than one of these. BRAC was enacting an impact strategy by providing people and communities with all these services concomitantly. The coincidence of multiple interventions over a long time enabled people to fundamentally change their skills, perspectives on life, and awareness of opportunities.

The impact strategy thus constituted a departure from an undesirable status quo for thousands of villagers:

The Rural Development Program has got several projects. Microfinance is one of the major areas. We have health as another area. We also have capacity development. It was basically decided in such a way that we are going in this particular area, with the health program, with the education program, and also moving into microfinance. At the entry level, we may start with a softer approach. Maybe start with education or health and gradually move into microfinance.

The organizational challenge was to design new interventions as BRAC discovered important needs of the poor that remained unresolved. But its organizational infrastructure allowed BRAC to innovate and scale into areas that completed its impact strategy.

In the nineties, BRAC staff started asking new questions:

In BRAC there are regular meetings all the way up to senior management where programs talk about what they are doing. "Basically," they said, "microfinance is not reaching the poorest." Then RED did a study to find out, "Does microfinance reach the poorest?" and the answer was, "No, it doesn't."

BRAC learned that it needed to think about poverty in an even more sophisticated way than previously. It knew that levels of poverty required careful segmentation and a more nuanced understanding of poor people's lives as a basis for a number of segment-specific intervention designs. This need was the basis for BRAC's graduation model: People whom it supported could slowly climb up a social and economic ladder toward reduced poverty levels and reduced vulnerability.

The RED study demonstrated that targeting the so-called ultra-poor was a challenge that neither BRAC nor the government nor the larger NGO community had tackled. A new program was piloted and further developed over a number of years that involved a transfer of assets, supported by careful training and support services, to the poorest people, who did not own any productive resources themselves: "Some senior people in BRAC sat down and thought: 'What are we going to do?' That's when they thought of the asset transfer. I don't know whose idea it was. I suspect it came from somewhere else." The pilot eventually was adopted as a central program within RDP under the name of Challenging the Frontiers of Poverty Reduction–Targeting the Ultra Poor (CFPR/TUP).

BRAC's green zone expanded into areas of poverty that were close to its existing operations. By keeping its innovations close to its current practices and targeting problems that it understood well, BRAC was able to innovate productively. It was able to test new ideas efficiently and quickly through its ongoing operations—for example, by using as pilot sites villages that had trusted relations with program staff in place. It sourced ideas and attracted relevant expertise from its global network of supporters, which it had built and nurtured over the years:

Invention, most of the time, is a mistake. It usually happens because people don't spend enough time and effort trying to find out what everybody else has been doing. Most development isn't rocket science. Most problems, almost all problems that you find, someone else has already done it somewhere. And there are some problems that you can better solve by incremental improvement. Or there are some problems where you've already got the innovation but you need to implement it on a large scale.

BRAC is now improving its well-weathered survey-pilot-evaluation approach to innovation:

In the past we said: "Is there a problem? Let's design a survey and send out some people and collect some information." Well, before we even think about the methodology or formulate the research question, maybe we should actually read what everyone else has done. We did that for microfinance recently, and it turned out to be very revealing. We did quite a good literature review, and it led us toward some quite interesting conclusions that were not what we were expecting.

BRAC reinforced its approach to problem-driven innovation rather than solution-driven innovation: "Unfortunately, the world is full of experts with their pockets full of their own solutions trying to find a problem to attach their own solutions to."

INNOVATION FOR ECONOMIC OPPORTUNITY: BRAC SOCIAL ENTERPRISES

As early as 1976, BRAC established the Agriculture and Fisheries Programs, which provided training and support to farmers. Later, the organization ventured into more specialized areas of farming. In 1978, BRAC started the Sericulture Program to generate employment for poor women. In 1983, it initiated the Poultry Vaccination Program to help women who raised poultry. In 1977, BRAC established its first social enterprise, BRAC Printers. A year later, the organization started a handicraft marketing outlet, Aarong. Both enterprises had three things in common. First, they provided livelihood opportunities to the poor. Second, they targeted needs that emerged from BRAC's development activities. Third, they supported the organization's ambition to generate income and to become self-sufficient.

In relation to the first point, BRAC social enterprises were used to provide more advanced livelihood opportunities for the people, for example for women:

The basic objective is that the income generation is the key to poverty alleviation. In rural areas there are many women who have traditional handicraft skills, and they are not being able to sell their products. We played that catalytic role of trying to assess the market in the upper middle class and others, what kind of handicrafts that there is a demand for. Then trying to get the best designers from abroad to provide the design and also supply good-quality cloth. Then they organized the production. They do that in between their domestic duties, so that helps in improving their livelihood. But at the same time we collect their products and sell them. We generate a surplus, also subsidizing our education and health programs. That's how we started. This is a typical case of market failure, because the private sector could have done that, but they are not doing it for some reason or other.

Second, BRAC social enterprises were generated out of previous BRAC work. For instance, BRAC opened its printing business because it needed to print materials for its functional education program: "Because I was going into education in a big way, I thought I needed a printing press, so two donors provided the money for the printing press." BRAC's social enterprise Aarong was opened in connection with the BRAC Sericulture Program:

Then I started another business, called Aarong, which is a shop chain to market the products of poor artisans who produce handicrafts. There are a lot of women who do handicrafts to earn money, but they can't market their products; in the village nobody buys them. So I have to bring these products into Dhaka and resell them. This business has become a $50 million business: we sell $50 million worth of artisan products in Bangladesh.

Aarong is now one of Bangladesh's largest retail chains, with eight stores in Dhaka, Chittagong, Khulna, and Sylhet and one in London, UK.

Later, BRAC discovered other needs emerging from its previous activities: "There were about a million women who borrowed from us to buy a cow. So what do we do? I had to sell the milk, purchasing their dairy, so I collect all their milk from all over Bangladesh, chill it, and bring it to the factory in Dhaka, every day." Thus BRAC set up a dairy plant. Other needs followed. For example, women who grew vegetables to provide some income for themselves and their families needed high-quality seeds: "About

400,000 women grew vegetables, but they didn't have good seeds. So I set up a company, BRAC Seed Company, and provide all the vegetable seeds to them. We have high quality, so women can improve the productivity of their vegetable gardens and get more money."

Third, BRAC social enterprises generated income for the organization. BRAC needed income to grow big and become independent of donors:

BRAC wanted to serve as many people as we could as fast as we could. Fast growth and largeness were important for us, and we wanted to grow as fast as possible. But we were held back by donors. We realized that we should not remain donor dependent too much. We must aim for achieving sustainability. For that we need to generate revenue for ourselves.

Impressive results followed. BRAC's dependence on donors declined substantially over the years: "The strength of the organization and the relative financial power helps. It puts profits back in the organization." The organization also gained a large market share in some areas of its activities. For example, at one stage it provided about 30 percent of the milk in the Bangladeshi milk market. On the other hand, BRAC's pragmatism allowed the organization to see the positive aspects of some financial "dependence" as well:

I like to be evaluated by third parties. When we get donor money, they have to evaluate me. So the third-party experts come in and look at BRAC. I like that, because this keeps us on our toes. I would like to keep some amount of money coming from a third party, so that third party has a responsibility to come and look at our program and tell us where we have been wrong.

The accumulation and constant flow of resources also enabled BRAC to allocate more resources to innovation than most other social enterprises can afford to. It could undertake innovations without threatening its ability to generate value and benefits from existing operations. And BRAC had built a powerful organizational capacity to scale any successful innovations efficiently:

Scaling at BRAC just seems to be like adding a layer on the cake. It's not as difficult a process, I think, to some extent, as a new pilot is. In some ways, a pilot is much more energy intensive. Once you've shown the pilot is effective and you want to scale it up, we've got a national infrastructure here. You have staff, you have monitors, you have all these other infrastructures in place, so you can just sort of push it in.

BRAC thus became a popular outlet for donors who knew that its implementation capacity was a safe bet for generating significant impact from their funds—and that it had good data to prove it. Nevertheless, this also had some unproductive consequences. Major funders today often ask BRAC: "Why don't you do this and why don't you try that? Education currently has ten pilots running in parallel because one of our major donors asked them. There is no evaluation if the ideas make sense or if it fits BRAC's strategy. People just do it on top of their normal work."

SCALING: BUILDING AND NURTURING A DEEP GREEN ZONE

Growing big had become BRAC's ambition. The organization deeply believed in growth after changing its initial short-term strategy for development in the early 1970s. Scaling required a willingness to think long term and investing in organizational capabilities. That was a particular quality of BRAC's founder Abed:

I call him a visionary leader. Obviously you should be a visionary leader, otherwise you can't scale it up. You must understand what will happen after twenty years so that you can prepare yourself by that time. For example, Abed Bhai told me: "You should think about five years." I said, "I can't think even five days. How could I think about five years?"

An important part of the long-term vision was building a culture of focused experimentation and quality control during piloting to make sure that the outcomes of its innovations actually achieved their intended outcomes. Bad interventions don't scale well and would use organizational resources inefficiently:

From the very beginning it was Abed's approach that any ideas, maybe even wild ideas, share it with your colleagues, with your supervisors, or with your peers. You will feel that—oh, people will criticize me. Abed said: "Don't hesitate to share your wild ideas. Somebody can fine-tune it, and then you can develop some program from your wild idea." Then don't go for implementing it with the poor people. Go for experimentation instead. You experiment it first. If you get positive results, then go for replication. If it fails, then ask why.

This culture was supported by formal structures such as RED and BRAC's training center that helped with objective learning and evaluations and dissemination of learning internally.

Its careful and objective approach to piloting and learning thus created interventions that could be scaled with few negative surprises and unexpected outcomes. But its pace and ambition to scale were sometimes met with resistance and suspicion: "Most of the donor money goes into education and health care. These are the two areas that we cannot make financially self-sufficient. Some donors would say: 'Don't grow so fast, the quality would suffer and all that.'" BRAC therefore had to keep a close eye on quality issues during scaling.

BRAC's growth unavoidably created communication and supervision challenges. For example, regular meetings with all BRAC employees present were no longer possible:

I used to meet all workers in the field every month for the first ten years of BRAC. I could see workers in my meetings every month, try to go to various places and meet them and talk about what was happening. Then, when we became larger once we went into the oral rehydration program, it was no longer possible.

BRAC in the eighties had to set up more formalized management processes to enable efficient and effective scaling of its programs. In 1988, it set up a dedicated monitoring department. The importance of monitoring had become clear to BRAC during its ORT pilots and during its efforts to scale them up. Monitoring was crucial in observing what was really happening on the ground. And this became the basic mandate of monitoring: to be a feedback mechanism that provided programs regularly with essential data from their operations.

Those who are running the programs can understand operations better from this neutral assessment, because the monitoring department is not reporting to the programs but to the executive director. The programs get data from the MIS [management information system]. But this is my experience, the MIS report is always inflated. Why? Because the workers, most of them are from the middle class, they want to retain their job. And also they want to get some kind of promotion. If they don't inflate, how will they get promotions? That's why they can now crosscheck MIS data with the monitoring department. For example, they said that we have 4 million mulberry trees. But we monitored, and we found that they have only 2 million. Then management asked them: "Why is it in your MIS you report 4 million?" The responsible person replied that those trees died. But they didn't subtract them from the MIS.

And so monitoring started to complement RED on the operations side, making sure that BRAC's ongoing scaling work is validated and that performance data are in line with its targets and quality standards.

But monitoring had only an advisory role to program directors. It was left up to them to respond to any feedback:

There is a debate in BRAC, the point is obviously, you should be target oriented, undoubtedly; otherwise, if you don't give any direction or any target, you will find that there is a tendency for your workers just to do the minimum; they will be low performers. But you should follow the consultative process. As I mentioned, regarding developing the program, this was the guideline also of Paulo Freire.

BRAC did not replace personal responsibility and empowerment by formal processes and sanctions. It worked its people hard, but it also wanted to help them develop themselves.

Apart from the formal units that enabled productive scaling, BRAC built a culture of achievement and constant improvement. "BRAC is very target driven. Every program is given a target, and then everybody goes all out to meet that target. So it understands numbers very well. It's part of the culture, the founder's culture, which has trickled down." BRAC had a person in charge of all of RDP. Everyone called him Amin, the field marshal:

His legacy is everywhere within BRAC because he was the hard-core taskmaster. He was in the field a lot. He was also very passionately involved. A lot of ideas came from the chairperson as well as other directors, and staff, various places, but in terms of getting them done, and for prioritizing them, he was the person.

From 1974 until 2010, Amin made sure that no problem could hide from his scrutiny and that solutions were speedily devised and implemented, bottlenecks removed, and opportunities realized.[7] His expertise grew to cover all of BRAC's programs, and he could look across various interventions and identify potential synergies and common problems.

BRAC also implemented a tight achievement-based payment system and kept raising targets to force people to invest in improvements:

The expectation is that as soon as you get 100 percent, the denominator gets bigger, so now you're getting tested out of 110 and then 120. You can keep increasing the expectations, and, even if you're succeeding, that just keeps on being a race against expectations.

And success with new plans or existing programs and achieving targets was the expected norm:

The culture is such that if you're not perceived to be impactful enough, that is quite visible. Automatically you know that something's got to change, and then you do it. Success is pretty much expected. If you are at BRAC, then it's expected. That was a shock for me when I joined. I did a nationwide project. . . . It was a very, very complex three-month process. We defined it, and the results came in. I thought we did a very good job in terms of getting it done because it had never been done in BRAC before, and I was expecting some pat in the back. Nothing of that sort came. That's taken for granted. That's how BRAC operates. Don't expect anything. Anything short of success, for example when we missed a deadline, my God—it was brutal. People were commenting left and right.

BRAC does not consider itself a particularly innovative organization:

Hearing new ideas and evaluating them: We're not very good at that. BRAC is very target driven. For meeting targets, people are going to come up with a lot of ideas and change the programs and stuff. So when they have limited resources and they have to do it better, there was this constant push to make it better, more impactful. Then they had to come up with innovative ways to do that, so the innovations were happening like that. But something completely different from what we are working on right now, there's no space. There's no way to pitch them.

And innovation has never been a priority at BRAC: "You don't see prolif-eration of a lot of innovation in BRAC, but whatever we do, scale is very important. If it's not scalable, then they don't want to even do the pilot."

BRAC's culture is built around efficiency, serving more poor people better and pushing its green zone. All of this comes from a willingness to invest in its organization and building deep organizational capabilities:

A lot of NGOs that I see are, in a sense, very much wherever the donor money is. They position themselves that way because there is no seed funding available. So they have to survive that way as opposed to having a theory of change, or kind of "this is how we operate, this is the model. This is our core expertise."

RADICAL INNOVATIONS:
ADVENTURES IN THE RED ZONE

BRAC has taken on more radical innovations by pursuing ideas outside its green zone. These ideas were usually triggered by an articulation of important needs that no one was trying to meet:

I think the radical innovations are how we say there's a need that exists that we're not addressing at all. An older example would be the targeting the ultra-poor program. There's a population that's not qualified for microfinance, and we're not doing anything for them. Let's design a whole program for them. More recently, one would be the human rights and legal services program; BRAC had deliberately chosen not to work on property rights at all just because of their long, energy intensive, expensive cases. But then, when they looked to see what takes up the majority of cases in the courts, it's like 90 percent land cases, so they decided they have to do something. But we've never done anything around that before, so what should we do around land issues, property rights? And so, let's design an entirely new pilot around that.

BRAC is usually very considerate when evaluating new ideas and de-ciding whether or not to adopt pilots:

Actually, when we pilot, we basically look into three areas. The first level, whether it is relevant, whether it is relevant for the people for which it has been designed. The number two, you always look into whether this program was effec-tive in terms of reaching our objectives. And number three, whether it is efficient in terms of cost. If the three things are satisfied, then we go for replication. And so during the piloting phase, we always try to understand whether it's relevant, whether it is effective and efficient.

And BRAC is clear about what not to do: "When you go for innovation, ask yourself: 'Is this really your mandate, or is this someone else's mandate?' For example, we never went into transportation, which was always an important topic."

Occasionally, more radical innovations are not motivated by their own recognition of needs but are reactions to external requests or suggestions. An example is a request by Afghanistan in about 2001 that asked BRAC to replicate its programs in their country. The decision was highly contested within BRAC. Some called the decision an "accident" rather than a strategy. Others opined that for an organization of BRAC's caliber it was difficult to say no to such a high-level request.

This turned out to be a very challenging experiment for BRAC. It was a stretch to BRAC's resources because it relied on many of its most experienced staff to enact replications, and they were consequently not available to support important ongoing projects in Bangladesh. Its entry into Afghanistan in 2002 exposed BRAC to violence and aggression for which it was unprepared. Staff members were killed, and operational realities turned out very different from those in Bangladesh:

We're closing our microfinance program in Afghanistan. one of our experiences initially when we went abroad. We started with microfinance because microfinance allows you to have associations. With frequent meetings you identify their other needs. Then you try to mobilize resources in order to organize programs for that. But we saw that in many African countries: That's not the way because the level of economic activity is so low that the microfinance doesn't work. Microfinance works when there is a vibrant economy and there is a need for that.

But BRAC does not give up easily. It has tremendous implementation power, ability to experiment intelligently, and ability to mobilize large amounts of resources. Undeterred by the difficulties in Afghanistan, it entered Sri Lanka in 2005, Tanzania and Uganda in 2006, Pakistan and

South Sudan in 2007, Sierra Leone and Liberia in 2008, Haiti in 2010, the Philippines in 2012, and Myanmar in 2013.

INNOVATION AND SCALING AT MATURITY

In 2012, BRAC celebrated its fortieth anniversary. A quick glance at BRAC's 2013 annual report illustrates the enormous scale and scope to which BRAC had grown. It was among the largest NGOs in the world. Its staff of more than 106,000, plus more than 105,000 community health workers, were serving 135 million people worldwide. There was a strong sense of expectation from external stakeholders, particularly donors, that BRAC needed to continue to innovate. And there was also a strong drive from its top management to innovate to keep the organization relevant:

There is this constant in-built expectation from the very top that's thrown to the programs. "OK, great, you have done a good job in sanitation in the rest of the country, but what have you done in the urban space?" "Fine, you're running the largest ever sanitation program, but you have done nothing for the slums." It's always like, "OK, what next, what next, what next?" That has been his thing. That is very, very much the founder's culture. He's basically saying that BRAC has to evolve. The nature of the society changes, problems of the society change, so BRAC has to evolve with the changes as well, to come up with the solutions.

BRAC's reputation attracted significant donor funds despite its continuous efforts to reach financial self-sufficiency: "For the first time in its history, BRAC actually now has the scope to reassign quite large amounts of money and resources to different sectors if it decided to do that." Its reputation and implementation capacity make it a tremendously attractive outlet for donor funds:

As BRAC is becoming more visible, saying it can deliver projects efficiently, we are getting resources. We have now contracted core funding with two of our major donors. The benefit from their side is that the transaction cost will be substantially reduced compared to project-based and donor/recipient relationships to a core fund. For us, it covers nearly 60 to 65 percent of our funding needs for the next five years. That has tremendously reduced the burden on us to organize institutional funding.

The combination of BRAC's implementation power, operational scope and scale, and resource endowment attracted a lot of talent. The organization had a constant inflow of experts from all areas who wanted to make a contribution and who brought new ideas and perspectives into the organization.

BRAC was continuously bringing fresh blood into the organization. The senior leaders never felt threatened bringing new people over here. I think one of the reasons why people work in BRAC is because you get a lot of opportunity to do things you want to do. If you've really got something you want to do you've probably got a fair chance that someone within BRAC will give you some funding or you can go outside and get some funding or you can convince somebody to do it. That's what attracts people, particularly at the higher levels. People come in with much lower salaries than they would get elsewhere.

BRAC has also been able to retain a number of senior managers from the beginning who accumulated tremendous know-how and experience. They personally championed innovative efforts and ensured consistency in BRAC's strategy and approaches.

But on BRAC's fortieth anniversary, a reflection on its organization also revealed important gaps. Some felt that with the death of its field marshal in 2010, an important force that used to connect programs with each other and fieldworkers with headquarters got lost. "As a result, there was also this idea that nobody really knew, from an organizational perspective, if there were new ideas, new things happening. It kind of stayed within the programs."

And senior BRAC managers and program directors started to spend a lot more time at headquarters offices than in the field:

It used to be before that senior people would spend fifteen days at a stretch in the field and meet the program directors, participants, and hear about things that didn't work. So they would make instant decisions right there. Right now, you're depending a lot on your middle managers for that, because there are all these tiers that came in between the top management decision makers and the fieldworkers. Today, directors basically are bogged down with so many activities that they don't get much time to give their input in the field.

Synergies between programs, innovations across program areas, and getting ideas from the field up the hierarchy were becoming increasingly difficult: "The typical problems of a bigger organization where it risks being very, very 'siloed,' and communication, information, became difficult to go up from the field." These perceived maturity effects thus created some serious difficulties. Filling its pipeline of middle managers, who connected its large cadre of field staff and its top management, became an important organizational task. BRAC also needed to nurture future leaders from within the organization because many of its managers, including its founder, were nearing retirement age. And BRAC realized that it needed to diffuse a willingness and capability for innovation more deeply into the organization:

I think the big issue is, can we empower people at lower levels more, not just to innovate but to actually take initiative? So innovation will be part of a broader empowerment. It's about: Can we encourage meaningful initiative at lower levels and in people outside this building [BRAC headquarter in Dhaka] as well? That's the big question. And I think that will determine BRAC's success in the future.

BRAC is dealing with these problems by redefining and reemphasizing its core values as part of its forty-year celebrations:

We engaged in a rebranding process where we had to define four core values of BRAC in 2010. One of them was innovation. The four values of BRAC now are inclusiveness, innovation, integrity, and effectiveness. We started the first year to promote it. I think it already has started generating a lot of conversation: "What is innovation; what are new ideas; where do we pitch the ideas?"

BRAC felt that it needed to identify and give voice to ideas from the field or risk becoming too much of a process-driven organization.

But the focus on "innovation" did not immediately create the expected effects:

People struggled because they weren't clear what was "innovation." There wasn't a proper Bengali word for innovation. I mean there's something in Bengali for invention, but nothing for innovation. And we didn't think it was invention. I think innovation is something more integral, so we called it somehow "creativity." So people did not even know they were innovating; they were just doing their program delivery better.

In 2014, the Social Innovation Lab (SIL) was set up to build momentum. One of its first initiatives, installing idea boxes at several BRAC branches, did not work well. It became mainly a complaint box; people voiced their problems instead of providing ideas for solving them. The SIL had to operate in a hands-on mode, proactively engaging with staff throughout BRAC, identifying and connecting ideas. In 2015 the SIL was still working hard to define legitimacy and a clearer strategy for its unit.

In 2008, BRAC had established a Young Professionals Program (YPP) to counteract some of the maturity effects that it had identified. Before the YPP, BRAC never had an explicit HR (human resources) strategy that focused on identifying and nurturing talent. The YPP tried to attract the best and brightest graduates from Bangladesh's universities, who would traditionally go into private industry or the public sector but not join an NGO. Starting a career at BRAC is challenging. People are really respected and heard only after they have earned their laurels in the field, working from the bottom up:

Having shown commitment to BRAC is important. People will judge you: "Are you only here for a year to use BRAC as a platform, or are you here because you really, really care?" The most important thing that worked for me was that I really spent a lot of time in the field, as much as possible out of my office in the field. And that stems from a deep belief that that's where the answers really are—which is how a lot of people at BRAC think.

YPP members are expected to spend a lot of time operating in several difficult field programs. BRAC also needed to break with tradition and give them higher salaries than its traditional entry-level salaries. And it needed to carve out a credible career path within the organization.

Still, the prospect that one's knowledge and formal education do not make much of a difference within BRAC is hard to swallow for those young graduates:

I can give you so many failed examples of BRAC, why BRAC failed, and BRAC learned more from failures than its successes. That's why I feel that nowadays, there is a tendency in BRAC that: "You see I have a very good education from different universities. Should I really go to the field for learning from the people?" Maybe you are a Harvard graduate, but Harvard did not teach you how the Bangladeshi people behave, or react, in a particular situation. My approach to the young generation is that: "Yes, you have a very good education, from a reputed institution, but now you are going to that real university—the rural areas of Bangladesh." This is one of the best universities in the world. There, there is no particular content, or fixed syllabus, or curriculum, or your library, laboratory, but the people can teach you a lot. You will have to interact with the people; then they will teach you. But you should accept it, that "Yes, I'm learning from the people. They are my teachers." And you will have to unlearn a lot. That is the hardest part.

BRAC'S INNOVATION ARCHETYPE

We call BRAC's unique innovation archetype "innovation for transformative impact." BRAC enacted multiple innovations to target several needs of individuals and communities concomitantly. This strategy enabled a fundamental transformation of the people and communities it served.

BRAC, like Gram Vikas, started out without any real green zone and thus struggled to create impact in its early years. But unlike Gram Vikas, BRAC was not seeking to serve the most disadvantaged and to solve the hardest problems in the beginning. It pragmatically targeted poverty-related problems that it could feasibly take on, rather than—like Gram Vikas— pursuing the loftier but vaguer ideal of lowering inequality. Like Aravind, BRAC put the principle of organizing up front. Its founder knew how to operate a large, efficient organization. He set up dedicated organizational processes and structures from the beginning. At a very early stage, BRAC committed to an explicit strategy of building organizational capacity to reach national scale, as the tremendous growth in staff within its first ten years of operations illustrates.

A critical challenge for BRAC was its broad and only loosely defined strategic scope. With every poverty-associated problem that BRAC tackled, it observed additional problems that held individuals and communities back. BRAC's management spent a significant time in the field and visibly nurtured a culture of listening to the poor. Careful problem understanding and problem formulation preceded the development of ideas for solutions. This focused knowledge accumulation lowered problem-frame and adoption uncertainties, which reduced solution uncertainties as well. Its critical evaluation of its own performance prevented a "stop too early" innovation pathology, as the innovation of its oral rehydration therapy illustrates. Instead of scaling an immature innovation too early and thus running into all kinds of problems, it stayed in piloting mode until it had sufficient evidence to adopt the innovation as a new program for scaling.

A hallmark of BRAC's innovation trajectory is its focus on clustering several innovations around individuals within a larger community. Thousands of NGOs in Bangladesh cater to almost any need of the poor, but individuals are often served by only one or two. Poor people have access either to microfinance or to health or to education or to human rights training, but not all at once. This approach creates benefits for the poor in very specific areas. But it rarely transforms their lives or communities in a more fundamental way. BRAC provides poor people with a multitude of economic (microfinance, creation of opportunities, better health), cognitive (kindergartens, schools, adult training), and normative/political (human rights training, empowerment of women, legal) support interventions. The concurrence of several interventions for an individual often has significant consequences for that person. She does not change one aspect of her life temporarily—as is the case with single interventions—but instead she has a real opportunity to reinvent herself and fundamentally change her life path. BRAC does not just create short-term benefits for individuals; it transforms what people can and will do in their lives. Because BRAC targets a critical mass within communities, it sees a real opportunity for community-level transformation as well.

Transformative impact required building a unique ability to innovate around a number of different needs. To this end, BRAC invested in building a dedicated organizational infrastructure for learning and for sharing and disseminating accumulated knowledge. Because BRAC decided to become as financially independent as possible, it could afford to (and had the freedom to) make investments that were crucial for productive innovation and for efficient scaling:

Many NGOs remain primarily donor supported. BRAC earned its own money. You get good staff and capacity. Funding is not a problem; the problem is good leadership, how to use the funds. There are not enough good managers. So we develop them ourselves. Our many pilots create many good managers.

BRAC also developed formal processes for innovating. It evaluated ideas using explicit criteria to decide whether or not to pilot them. It pursued innovations that: (1) were relevant to its strategic priorities and mission, (2) could be delivered in a cost-efficient manner and preferably could become financially self-sufficient, and (3) could be scaled to a significant size in relation to the problems they hoped to solve. This explicit perspective of directly integrating innovation and scaling is illustrative of our overall innovation process in Chapter 2.

BRAC systematically used survey methods to gather as much information as possible about a problem area for innovation. It also used RED's research facilities to reduce uncertainties before investing in pilots. It accumulated deep organizational capabilities for managing pilots productively. Senior managers had direct oversight and championed pilots, which limited the pathology of "stopping too early" due to premature removal of vital resources from ongoing pilots. RED often helped to evaluate pilots and to establish rigorously *why* something worked and not just *that* it worked. Understanding the causality of an innovation—why it worked—in turn led to much more efficient scaling decisions.

BRAC's culture of constant monitoring and evaluation enabled objective learning to avoid investments in bad ideas or in pilots that did not work. The organization also nurtured a culture of constant improvement that created tremendous impact from scaling its innovations. Thus BRAC dramatically expanded its scope through a number of innovations. At the same time, it nurtured an organizational culture and infrastructure that forcefully and efficiently scaled its innovations. This is an extremely tricky balancing act that few organizations are able to pursue.

The case study of BRAC is also a reminder that organizations that grow by innovating and scaling in many areas require constant critical monitoring and adaptation. For example, BRAC's reliance on senior management to champion innovations while organizing most of its staff into an extremely productive implementation machinery has now created a management gap that may generate a number of innovation pathologies. Senior managers cannot be in the field as much as they used to. Ideas now come less from deep listening and more from requests by external parties, particularly funders for whom BRAC has become a favorite outlet for implementing ideas. "Too many bad ideas" may get piloted, and too many of them may "stop too early" owing to a lack of commitment and ownership of the ideas by BRAC staff. These pilots may also underinvest in building scaling capacities because they may not fit BRAC's strategies and priorities. BRAC has therefore started to rebuild more organic innovation capabilities to achieve at least two crucial objectives: (1) to stay relevant and create innovations that are grounded in its own expertise and strategic priorities, and (2) to build and nurture its management pipeline. It now has a dedicated innovation team that works across units, and it has a dedicated young professionals program to fill the emerging gap of middle management that brokers between senior management and operations in the field.

In comparison, for Gram Vikas, the management gap has been a great challenge. Because of the nature of its work and the remoteness of its operations, it struggled to build a strong management pipeline that could carry on its work beyond the founding team that is now retiring. Gram Vikas could not use pilots to nurture management talent. Aravind, on the other hand, has built a strong management cadre in a different way. It has systematically used strong and—fortunately—abundant family ties to build management capacity and to maintain and further expand its accumulated knowledge through deep relational mechanisms. The fourth generation is currently starting to shape the future of Aravind.

6 INNOVATION THAT ENABLES DIFFUSION OF PROVEN IDEAS
The Story of Waste Concern (Bangladesh)

In social innovation, there is a problem with the project-based approach. You have a specific target and a tick mark that we have achieved what we wanted. For example, there was this sanitation team from the Gates Foundation. It came to Dhaka, to our office, two years back. "We have got some money, and we want you to do research on sanitation. We'll give you the money. Do it in ten towns." We said, "No." And that is what I'm a little bit afraid of. That is the project-based approach. For social innovation, you have to look into a program-based approach. A program is different. I believe that for social enterprise in the long run, they have to look into a program-based approach.

—Iftekhar Enayetullah, founder of Waste Concern

START OF THE INNOVATION JOURNEY:
AN IDEA NOT WASTED

The world is smothering in solid waste. More than 5 million tons of disposable diapers, tin cans, plastic bags, food scraps, rotted lumber, and human excrement pile up every day, about three-quarters of it in developing countries.[1] Two young men from Dhaka, the capital of Bangladesh, Iftekhar Enayetullah and Abu Hasnat Md. Maqsood Sinha, independently developed an academic interest in the very visible problem that was piling up everywhere in the city. The contrast with much cleaner cities that they knew from their international travels was painful. Creating awareness for the waste problem and collecting objective data motivated their research. Little did they know that their paths would soon cross and that one day they would be known as the "garbage men."

The World Bank estimates that global annual waste management costs will increase from a current estimate of $205 billion to about $375 billion within the next decade.[2] This increase will create an overwhelming financial burden on developing countries because waste management costs as a fraction of income are several times higher than in developed, high-income countries. Even though municipalities in developing countries spend a relatively large proportion of their budgets on waste collection, actual collection rates are low. Not dealing with waste effectively threatens people, municipalities, countries, and global society. Uncollected and improperly processed waste generates large amounts of greenhouse gases, mainly by the decomposition of organic matter. These gases contribute to accelerating human-induced climate change. Waste also pollutes air, soil, and freshwater resources and is a serious public health hazard.

In the 1990s, Dhaka was among the fastest-growing megacities in the world. The Dhaka City Corporation (DCC), the administrative body that governs Dhaka's 7 million residents, was struggling with 4,300 tons of waste generated every day. Despite spending a significant amount of its budget on waste disposal, it was collecting less than half of the waste. Iftekhar, trained as a civil engineer and urban planner, was doing research on urban waste for his master's degree in urban and regional planning and environmental management from Bangladesh University of Engineering and Technology. Maqsood, after earning a degree in architecture, pursued a master's degree in urban planning from the Asian Institute of Technology in Bangkok, Thailand. He was also researching links between the formal and informal sector engaged with waste management and recycling activities in urban centers. Maqsood's research brought him back to Dhaka, where he was introduced to Iftekhar. The two discovered a strong shared vision for alternative models of waste management and started collaborating on action research projects in Dhaka.

They observed the ways in which an informal sector had emerged to recycle a number of different waste materials for income. A whole value chain was informally organized by more than 100,000 poor scavengers, who collected reusable materials such as plastics, glass, metals, paper, and textiles. They sold their finds to brokers, who marketed them to various recycling factories. Maqsood and Iftekhar's observations triggered a number of ideas about how waste management could be organized in a decentralized, community-led model as a market-driven alternative to the budget-driven, centralized DCC model. The duo also noticed that only a relatively small amount of material waste was recovered. More than 70 percent of Dhaka's waste consisted of organic matter, primarily remains of fruits and vegetables, which the scavengers did not collect.

As part of the two young men's postgraduate research, they designed a model of waste management whereby organic waste would be collected at the household level before reaching landfill sites. The waste would then naturally compost in specially designed compost barrels or in facilities where it could be processed into compost on a larger scale and in a controlled manner. The compost could provide income and thus incentives for waste collection because it could be sold to farmers to improve soil quality and agricultural yield. The pair believed that the concept could be put into practice; they articulated the main advantages of their innovative idea to the DCC:[3]

- A decentralized composting system is labor intensive and less costly than a centralized one.
- It is well suited for our waste stream, climate, and social and economic conditions.
- Low-cost, easily available local materials and low technology can be used with our technique.
- Our method improves community participation in source separation and reduces the volume of solid waste at the source.
- We can significantly improve collection rates of solid waste.
- Costs incurred for the collection, transportation, and disposal of waste by the municipal authority will decline.
- Income and job opportunities will increase for poor, socially deprived informal workers and small entrepreneurs.

Initially, the DCC did not favor the idea despite the desperate state of its current waste management performance and the burden on its budget. The new plan would have required a radical departure from current practices, and the DCC perceived too many uncertainties in implementing the idea: "In 1994, we tried hard to convince different government agencies to initiate the project by offering free consultancy services, but they were all skeptical. . . . Eventually, a high-ranking official told us: "If the idea is so good, why don't you do it yourself?'"

WASTE CONCERN, EXPERIMENTING
WITH IDEAS ON A SMALL SCALE

In 1995, Maqsood and Iftekhar decided to establish a small research-based NGO called Waste Concern to pilot converting waste into resource and to demonstrate its benefits in a more tangible way. Besides the skepticism in the government, the duo faced other barriers as well. They did not have access to appropriate waste treatment technology, nor did they have any land for building a small-scale composting plant to launch their pilot project. The pair sought seed money and financing but were unsuccessful for a year. Eventually, they convinced the Lions Club Dhaka North to spare 1,000 square meters of unused land. Although the president of the club was a close relative of one of the founders, initially they got the land for only three months to see if the facility would create any waste-related nuisances: "When we first approached them, the Lions Club was very hesitant to give us land. They were concerned about the waste and in particular about the potential smell this might create."

The pilot explored a number of uncertainties: technical and operational issues, for example the ability to minimize odor during composting, as well as economic issues such as the willingness of households to adopt the collection scheme and pay for it and the willingness of farmers to buy compost:

We did some R&D, research with different technologies for waste recycling. We used several technologies, and we are continuously updating it. Initially we experimented with a composting method from Indonesia. Later we developed a different system of aerobic composting, which was very suitable and a new idea for the Bangladesh context. But when the new idea came, it was a technology demonstration. How you bring it for societal benefit that is the point of innovation—use of technology or use of invention for benefit.

They started with collection of household waste in a small area in Dhaka, using simple rickshaw vans to transport it to Waste Concern's pilot composting facility on the land donated by the Lions Club.

"In the beginning, people were skeptical. We became known as the garbage men." Several fortunate factors collided to build momentum for the project. The Lions Club extended its support because Waste Concern implemented a composting technology that generated little odor. It also discovered that a majority of households in their pilot community were concerned about the problem of waste and were willing to pay a small amount for frequent garbage collection. On the other end of the value chain from waste to compost, a survey of farmers indicated a sufficient level of demand for the end product.

The small-scale collection model worked well, with immediate and visible benefits for households: no more piles of waste in front of their houses, less irritating odor and fewer insects, the ability to reclaim spaces for recreational activities, particularly for children, and fewer problems with obstructions to road traffic. Other effects that were not immediately visible were better health and increased property values. Consequently, households encouraged others to join the program and used social sanctions to punish those who continued to litter. Soon almost 100 percent of households in the pilot community were on board. After three years, the model was relatively robust and self-financing. The visible benefits triggered high adoption rates. In 1999 Waste Concern collected 2 tons of waste daily from 600 households; these two tons would generate half a ton of final pure compost fifty-five days later.[3] And Waste Concern had increased the capacity of its composting facility to 3 tons per day. The firm reached this capacity in 2001, serving more than 1,400 households. Most important, Waste Concern, owing to the academic background of its founders, had documented every step of the process and provided transparent and objective data on all aspects of cost as well as financial and other benefits. An obsession with data and documentation would become a hallmark of Waste Concern that greatly facilitated support and adoption by many stakeholders.

INCREASING SCALE BY ENGAGING THE PRIVATE SECTOR

With the growth in compost supply, Waste Concern ran into an important bottleneck in its model. The founders had no capacity, expertise, or motivation to market and sell the compost to end consumers. To convince farmers of the benefits, they bought a small piece of land for a demonstration farm growing organic vegetables using their own compost. In parallel, they engaged with several large companies that sold chemical fertilizer to their networks of farmers. But no one was interested:

> People's mind-set was, "I pay taxes. It's the responsibility of the government." So there was no participation from the private sector. But we created a clear opportunity for investors and companies. Now you see a lot of entrepreneurs entering all aspects of our model of waste management, collecting waste, transporting waste, selling compost, and so on.

MAP Agro, a large fertilizer retailer in Dhaka, was as skeptical as many of its competitors: "Then we sent a basket of our vegetables to the house of the chairman of a large retailer [MAP Agro]. He liked the taste so much that he was immediately interested to discuss a potential collaboration."

MAP Agro started to package and market branded compost: "Produced by Waste Concern; Marketed by MAP Agro." This was a big push, not just for removing the bottleneck on the sales side of the composting model but also for growing brand awareness for Waste Concern. Owing to attractive margins and sales growth, MAP Agro soon invested in a dedicated enrichment facility to add nutrients to Waste Concern's compost. Waste Concern also made studies on its own farm and those of early adopters of compost to provide plausible data showing that compost increased yield and quality of produce. They also did a study that demonstrated the benefits of replacing chemical fertilizer with compost by building up soil quality and requiring less irrigation because of the high moisture-holding capacity of compost. The results increased farmers' willingness to adopt compost and helped MAP Agro's business.

To meet the additional demand, Waste Concern also started experimenting with new models in Dhaka's slums. It put perforated waste storage bins everywhere. Households put their waste in the bins, where it started to compost. Waste Concern then bought the compost from them. But despite all these early successes, scale that made a tangible difference for the problem of waste was not achieved.

In 2008, Waste Concern launched compost using the brand name "Waste Concern Organic Fertilizer." It is the first compost approved and registered by the Ministry of Agriculture under the Fertilizer Act 2006 of the Government of Bangladesh. Since 2008 ACI, a private company, has been marketing the compost throughout Bangladesh. In 2015, Waste Concern signed an agreement with a private company to export 10,000 tons of organic fertilizer to a neighboring country.

INCREASING SCALE THROUGH REPLICATION
A serious bottleneck of Waste Concern's solution was the cost of land required for high-volume composting facilities. Land is an extremely scarce asset in Bangladesh, particularly in cities because of their high population density. And any composting plant below a capacity of three, or even better five, tons per day was hardly financially sustainable:

The single biggest obstacle for the model of a community-based decentralized composting project was availability of land in the city for such facilities. Public-private-community partnership and the concept of the 4 Rs (reduce, reuse, recycle, and recover waste) were absent in Bangladesh before our intervention.[4]

The availability of land thus limited Waste Concern's ability to create more impact from its innovative waste collection model. In 1999, the enterprise was still constrained by the three-ton capacity of the pilot plant on donated land. Waste Concern used the pilot project as a demonstration site and showed it extensively to government officials, private companies, journalists, delegates from other countries, communities, and international development agencies.

The success with reframing waste as a resource rather than a problem was noticed by the public sector and international agencies. Under the traditional DCC waste management paradigm, waste was a stubborn, complex, and costly problem that could be tackled only by large-scale centralized public intervention. In the Waste Concern model, waste was an opportunity to create environmental and economic benefits for communities and farmers. In the late 1990s, the Ministry of Environment and Forests collaborated with the United Nations Development Program (UNDP) under the Sustainable Environmental Management Program. In 1998, both organizations decided that Waste Concern could be an ideal subimplementing agency and requested a rollout of community waste collection and composting to four additional communities within Dhaka. After identifying suitable land, Waste Concern contacted the Public Works Department (PWD), which owned the land. Several demonstration visits and meetings were needed to overcome PWD's skepticism and hesitation to engage. Waste Concern also provided data that resonated with the public sector. Its staff calculated that the pilot project alone, at a scale of three tons per day, reduced municipal waste transportation and landfill costs by more than US$18,000 per year.[5] At last, in 1999, the PWD provided suitable plots of land for an initial period of one year. Soon after, when the positive outcomes of the project became visible, the contract was extended to 2005.

All of a sudden, a small NGO found itself in a major coordinating role between several public ministries and departments, local communities, international donor agencies, and the private sector. Representatives from other cities approached Waste Concern to see if the concept could be rolled out to more sites: "We thought originally that we would be able to roll out the decentralized model and replicate it ourselves on other sites. But it was not possible to do from a manpower perspective. If we had tried to do it all ourselves, it would have resulted in major delays in implementing it."

The potential to create more impact by scaling their innovative model was still constrained by resources. This limitation triggered a search for ideas in two main directions: (1) finding ways of making the waste collection and composting model ever more productive and resource efficient and (2) thinking about ways to remove bottlenecks. Waste Concern constantly tinkered, systematically documented its activities, and reflected deeply on what works and what does not. The founders' training as scientists gave them a keen eye for objective evaluation of data instead of subjective learning that could have created a number of innovation pathologies. The rapid accumulation of knowledge enabled them to innovate in line with clearly articulated priorities:

The government was giving us land, but land is a very scarce resource in Bangladesh. So we needed to reduce the amount of land. We first tried different technologies and increased efficiencies. Then, we saw that even in medium-sized towns, not only in Dhaka, land was becoming an issue. So we asked: "How can we reduce the time of composting so that with the same land we can process more waste?" The idea came up: If we use mechanically blown air during the composting, would this reduce the time? The answer was, "Yes." Improvement is a continuous process for us.

Removing resource bottlenecks was another high priority: "Innovation for us is where we use that technology in partnership with others to implement it on the ground, and you do different partnerships for getting land, getting financing, for marketing, and so on." Waste Concern invested a lot of thought in enabling others to create more impact from its innovations. Transferring knowledge through proper documentation and standardization of interventions, training other stakeholders, and influencing donors and national policies became central scaling strategies for Waste Concern:

We are not trying to become an organization like BRAC or Grameen Bank, where you do everything. We want to grow our idea. Our model is to create multiple partnerships, and then you solve the problem. There are many things that are beyond our control. As Waste Concern, we wanted to be an organization that is creating an invention and then supports governments in Bangladesh and beyond Bangladesh with policy reform on waste management. Waste Concern's mandate is to solve waste problems, to demonstrate technology, not so much to scale it up: product demonstration, getting good data, working with the government, disseminating information, and giving training.

One of Waste Concern's beliefs is that interventions need to be standardized to some extent:

I think at some stage you need to standardize and formalize. For example, if you look at the microcredit model, what are the basic features that are required to make it a success? That kind of study has to be done. That kind of knowledge has to be there. It is not there. Social innovation is not so easy. It's a time-tested, long process. You have to understand the process and document it well. Often what you find is a documentation of the story but not a process documentation.

Waste Concern developed four standardized models and process documentation that provide options for others and help them to replicate the model. Three models are based on ownership of the land by a municipality and operations by the municipality, community, or private sector. And one is full ownership and operation by the private sector.

ORGANIZATIONAL INNOVATION: MISSION-ENABLING PRAGMATISM

In parallel to the successful replications in four districts as part of the UNDP-sponsored project, Waste Concern also replicated its model in an additional district with financing from a Swiss development agency. All projects were handed over to local community owners, freeing up Waste Concern to pursue additional projects and R&D for other initiatives. Waste Concern extended its work to additional cities in Bangladesh. By 2005, thirty-eight successful replications had been achieved in Bangladesh. Replication also defined the longer-term innovation strategy of Waste Concern:

We wanted to be an organization that is doing inventions, creating and developing new ideas. Innovation is where we use that technology in partnership with others to implement it on the ground. Whatever invention we made in technology, implementation and scaling of the invention using UNESCAP, UNDP, FMO, Triodos Bank, or others, is the innovation.

And the organization also developed the use of patents for its inventions: "You can develop a patent. If you keep it within yourself, I would not call it innovation. When the patent or the technology is accepted and used for societal needs or societal environmental problems, then I believe it's innovation."

In 2000, Waste Concern began international replications in Sri Lanka and Vietnam in collaboration with the United Nations Economic and Social Commission for Asia and the Pacific (UNESCAP):

UNESCAP came to us saying they wanted to try our ideas in new jurisdictions. One is Sri Lanka; one is Vietnam. They wanted to see whether and how these new ideas could be replicated. But then we said: "OK, if you bring the mayors of the municipalities of those countries to Bangladesh, they should stay here for seven days and see the operation. If they feel it works in their country, only then will we step in."

This idea proved successful, although a number of local adaptations were needed. For example, Vietnam was too hilly for rickshaw-based transport of waste. But a solution with motorized vehicles was found. And in Sri Lanka the operators needed to adapt the model to much higher levels of rainfall. "You need to adapt about 20 percent of your model. Local adaptation requires creativity and innovation capacity, which are our strength."

Later, replication was continued in several additional Asian and African countries in collaboration with UNESCAP and the Bill & Melinda Gates Foundation (BMGF). In 2002 Waste Concern assumed the role of technical partner/consultant for the United Nations Children's Emergency Fund (UNICEF) and the governmental Department of Public Health Engineering. Through this work, the organization gained valuable expertise and experience in composting. It also earned acceptance and reputation among governmental officials and donors: "Policy makers, leaders—they accepted the idea." International recognition for Waste Concern followed, and the founders received the Ashoka Fellowship in 2000.[6]

Enthusiasm about the novel waste management approach triggered more and more requests from various stakeholders for Waste Concern's involvement in projects. It also created a perceived dependence on external funds that might reduce degrees of freedom for Waste Concern: "Financing was coming either from UN agencies or government. That was the area where we again thought that we are having impact, but we are dependent too much on financing from the public sector." The organization was not able to generate its own income or apply for a bank loan. During meetings with potential lenders, it became clear that Waste Concern was not considered bankable, mainly because lenders were concerned that it might not be able to repay a loan. Traditional equity instruments were also not feasible. Investors were attracted by the environmental and social benefits created, but they were concerned about insufficient economic rates of return. Development organizations supported similar projects for piloting purposes only.

The problem of funding created a need to think about organizational innovation.

We thought that, in 2000, people are requesting us to give advisory services to different projects, like the Asian Development Bank, World Bank, or developmental organizations. But it was not possible to do this through Waste Concern. If we did it, at one point in time, there would be a question mark within the board, and with the government: "Why are you doing it?" This has happened with many nonprofit organizations in Bangladesh. So we created Waste Concern Consultants with the focus that we will do a few consulting services, and we pay tax for them. But Waste Concern will not take part in this. It's an independent organization. We decided as the founders of Waste Concern Consultants—and that is in our constitution in writing—"OK, whatever profit comes to Waste Concern Consultants, 30 percent will go to Waste Concern to do its own R&D projects."

Explicitly, the goal of Waste Concern Consultants was formalized in such a way that it would enable and maintain the mission and mandate of Waste Concern.

This decision turned out to enable tremendous progress. With time, Waste Concern Consultants became more and more successful in securing consulting assignments from the government and development organizations. They used their newfound comfort with involvement in different organizational forms to start a number of new companies and initiatives over the next years. As a result, Waste Concern's networks grew, and its access to ideas, technologies, and resources increased. The founders were also able to strengthen their reputation as waste management experts. And by using organizational vehicles and partner organizations to run day-to-day operations, they freed up time for R&D. They now spend about 50 percent of their time on implementing innovation processes. Their motivation levels stay up, and they make the best use of their particular skills and growing subject expertise and reputation. During this phase of organizational development, Fast Company recognized Waste Concern's founders as the Fast 50 Social Entrepreneurs in 2001. In 2002 the organization was awarded the UNDP "Race against Poverty" prize. In 2003 Maqsood and Iftekhar were recognized by the Schwab Foundation as "Outstanding Social Entrepreneurs" and received the "Global Tech Museum Award." In 2008, the Department of Environment of the Government of Bangladesh awarded Waste Concern its "Environment Award."

SCALING WINDFALL: THE CLEAN DEVELOPMENT MECHANISM

In 2002, Waste Concern was approached by the UNDP and the Ministry of Environment and Forests of Bangladesh. The organization was asked to identify the starting points for projects in Bangladesh under the Clean Development Mechanism (CDM) that allows organizations to earn tradable certificates called Certified Emission Reductions (CERs). Under the CDM, nations were able to buy and sell CERs to hit their specific Kyoto Protocol emission reduction targets. Waste Concern produced a baseline study and a business plan of the first CDM projects in the country.

After completing this assignment, Waste Concern was concerned about the lack of efforts to implement any of these projects: "Nobody at the government public sector level knew what CDM or carbon trading was. We had to inform every level of the bureaucracy and the banks, what is CDM, why it is important, how it works." Perhaps Waste Concern once again needed to be a catalyzing agent for building momentum on CDM, as it had done with its original community-based waste management and composting models. At the same time, Waste Concern was seeking ideas to increase the scale of its three-ton composting plant:

Small is beautiful, but you need to have scale. The small-scale decentralized three-ton composting plant is great for small and medium-sized cities. In Dhaka, however, it's probably best to have a larger centralized composting site. And, with a larger site, you have a real opportunity with tradable certificates. Without trading certificates, the opportunity of creating a centralized 700-ton-per-day composting site would not be feasible. Also, with large centralized sites, you can transfer the learning to smaller decentralized locations.

In addition to the idea of building a 700-ton composting site, Waste Concern started to evaluate an idea to use the existing landfill site in Matuail, an area seven kilometres from Dhaka, to recover methane gas from the five-meter-high landfill pile.

Waste Concern also engaged in the policy-making process around CDM and helped to create and develop the Designated National Authority for CDM projects in Bangladesh. As a result of its early CDM work, Waste Concern acquired knowledge of carbon trading as well as a foot in the door of agencies interested in promoting CDM. In 2004, Waste Concern began discussing these ideas with the Dutch company World Wide Recycling BV (WWR). WWR was a for-profit company that acted as an investor and operator, partnering with private and public enterprises to create decentralized recycling centers. In September 2004, WWR and Waste Concern signed a memorandum of understanding to form a special purpose company and put forward a proposal for consideration by the United Nations CDM Executive Board. WWR would provide all of the financing; Waste Concern would supply the local knowledge and technology and seek Bangladeshi government approval.

On September 17, 2005, both the landfill gas recovery project and the composting plant were registered with the United Nations Framework Convention on Climate Change (UNFCCC). In the landfill recovery zone, methane gas that was emitted naturally by the decomposing landfill would be captured and turned into electricity through a gas-powered engine. The electricity would then be used by local power utilities. The 700-ton composting plant would be designed to reduce methane gas by avoiding landfill and performing aerobic composting. Waste Concern and WWR developed a new method to calculate the reduction of methane emissions by composting, which was approved by the UNFCCC. The compost would be turned into organic fertilizer.

By that time, the government of Bangladesh was actively encouraging farmers to increase their use of organic compost. Compost was cheaper than chemical fertilizer, and most agreed that it produced superior crops. The acceptance of organic fertilizer encouraged three companies in addition to MAP Agro to include organic fertilizers as part of their product portfolios: "The demand for organic fertilizer is growing, and there's currently a problem with supply. Now, with four companies all offering organic fertilizers, this is good for fair competition."

Waste Concern also got a green light by the CDM Board of the Government of Bangladesh in 2004. But in September 2005 it was still waiting for approval from the municipal DCC, which owned and operated the Matuail landfill site:

We were authorized to go ahead with the project by the national government, but then the municipality did not give their authorization. They were a little concerned that they were handing over control of the landfill site to us. That was the point where we said, "Maybe we can separate the landfill site from the composting activity and change our approach." It's not necessary to keep the landfill and composting site together. We would just have to think of another plan.

Waste Concern and WWR set up a dedicated company, Mutual Power Ltd., to manage the landfill project. The decision about how best to implement the 700-ton composting project was more complicated. The project partners decided that they wanted to remain independent of the public sector and thus had to modify the traditional governance model. Instead of the government lending the land, the new company would buy and own the land. The project partners brokered a fifteen-year concession contract with the government to collect large quantities of waste, mainly from the large vegetable markets in Dhaka. The funding and income of the project would come from foreign direct investment, the sale of compost, and selling carbon credits.

Unfortunately, however, the government was suspicious of foreign direct investment, fearing that profits would accrue not to Bangladesh but to foreign partners. At that time there were long waiting times for licenses. For example, foreign telephone providers had to wait about five years for a license:

Fifty-six permissions were required to get started. This was the first CDM project in Dhaka. We had to educate all levels of government about CDM projects. For a normal person it takes at least one month for each permission. But we had built a lot of goodwill with the government over the years. So we got the license and all permissions within 2.5 years.

What also helped Waste Concern to get the agreement of the government was the impeccable and creative use of data, which resonated with public sector officials. Not only did Waste Concern produce a detailed study that quantified the amount of money the government saved in waste management costs, it also linked composting to Bangladesh's balance of payments. The organization argued that locally produced compost replaced a significant amount of imported chemical fertilizer, which was subsidized by the government. A transparent calculation of these costs suggested that more than US$1 million would be saved annually by reducing imports of chemical fertilizer and that this number could go up to more than US$8 million if more compost became available. These savings provided additional motivation for the public sector to support the CDM project: "We know that we need to make our models a win-win or they do not get adopted."

In 2006, WWR put in the seed money for a joint company, WWR Bio Fertilizer Bangladesh, Ltd., created as an implementation and management facility. At the same time, two other organizations, FMO, a Dutch development bank, and Triodos, a Dutch bank that promotes sustainable investments, got interested and signed up as co-investors: "The companies were interested in the CERs, which also had to do with supporting their corporate social responsibility strategies. We priced in five euros per CER, but already in 2008 it was twenty-five euros per CER. So we had a very short payback time of the loans." The first of three planned composting sites at a capacity of 130 tons per day opened in November 2008 as the largest CDM project in Bangladesh and the largest-ever composting-based CDM project globally. Additional plants would be built in the coming years.

Unfortunately, the carbon markets became extremely volatile, and the value of CERs plummeted, at one point close to zero. Although Waste Concern had estimated relatively low prices in the original plan, nobody envisaged that the carbon market would be close to crashing within a few years. But the organization managed to deal with this challenge, pointing out that "when there is a problem, there is also an opportunity." It signed the agreement with the Asian Development Bank to sell its carbon credits at the lowest price predicted in its original business plan for a number of years. Waste Concern also found new ways to finance its CDM projects. For example, the organization developed a technology for turning waste rejects from the compost plant into fuel or liquid compost. It also found new opportunities to sell compost outside of Bangladesh. These changes offset the low prices for carbon CERs and increased cash flow for Waste Concern's CDM companies.

Unintended Beneficial Consequences and Diffusion of CDM Projects

Waste Concern points out that CDM has an important effect on improving governance:

Data are required to get the credits. Everything you do needs to be documented, quantified, and verified by a third party. We record everything electronically so we can look at the data at any time. Governments don't always like that transparency, and that is a general problem in developing countries. We think that CDM is a great tool to promote governance and transparency in public sector projects.

In 2010, Bangladesh published its national 3R (reduce, reuse, recycle) Strategy, which was highly influenced by Waste Concern's input. As part of this strategy, the government is replicating Waste Concern's composting models in sixty-four districts in Bangladesh. Waste Concern is supporting this work through ongoing technology transfer, training of the public sector, and coordinating a number of stakeholders. The CDM process has come a long way from the initial hesitation of the public sector:

We created a CDM project in Dhaka. Why did we create it? Because the government did not understand it. A high government official told us: "What are you talking about? How can you sell greenhouse gas emission using certificates with containerizing it? You must be out of your mind." Then we sold the CERs to the Asian Development Bank. Now the government is doing the CDM projects itself in many cities of Bangladesh. We just created the model, and then it can be done by someone else. We are there to provide technology, to help them with adopting it. That is the way of our operation.

To diffuse their model even further, Waste Concern opened a dedicated training center: "We thought that we needed to bring more people into this, so we established a training center in Dhaka. We tried to create an entity so that at one point it raises awareness and creates manpower." In 2009, Waste Concern was approached by the Bill & Melinda Gates Foundation to extend waste recycling training to other countries in Asia and Africa. The organization started to provide training for interested organizations from abroad. It also opened a new training center in Sri Lanka and developed manuals for composting plants to enable efficient replication. Waste Concern convinced the Gates Foundation to create a special fund that "invests in pro-poor and sustainable solid waste management projects that reduce greenhouse gases in developing countries."[7] For quality control, in 2003 Waste Concern established a state-of-the-art laboratory with support from UNDP and the Ministry of Environment and Forests of Bangladesh.

Through this work, Waste Concern wanted to offer technical know-how for waste recycling but at the same time to avoid being directly involved in actual operations. The founders compared their model to other established social enterprises in Bangladesh: "Models of Grameen Bank or BRAC are different. They have projects in different countries but under their name, for example Grameen Afghanistan or BRAC in Africa. But at Waste Concern, we don't do Waste Concern Sri Lanka." They also patented some of their technology. But the purpose of the patents was different from that in the for-profit sector, where patents minimize imitation and diffusion and maximize the ability to capture profits. With so many requests for replicating and adopting Waste Concern's models, the organization wanted to ensure that adopters would have sufficient expertise to be able to scale their models and create impact from Waste Concern's innovations: "If they want to use our models, they need to come to Dhaka and spend some time at our training centers so that they understand all aspects. Only then will we give them a license." In their experience, the main bottleneck for local adoption and diffusion of their model is local talent: "The key is to find a local organization that has implementation competence. Technology and financing are readily available on a global scale. But if there is no 'orgware,' it will not work." Waste Concern found that people and organizations who just studied its model and tried to replicate it usually ran into serious problems. But people who attended the training center and worked with Waste Concern's staff performed much better: "We need to invest much more money into 'orgware' issues and not just into putting technology in a developing country." As a result of its work in training and capacity development of waste organizations in Bangladesh and abroad,

Waste Concern succeeded in passing its waste recycling solutions to local implementers in ten cities in the Asia Pacific region and ten cities in Africa. Diffusion is taking place through other mechanisms as well: "In Vietnam we trained one engineer in a city. She learned how to prepare a baseline study. We helped them, and now she's training other cities."

Today, a number of private companies have entered the opportunity space of compost-based organic fertilizers. And Waste Concern continues to find ways to accelerate diffusion of its innovations:

We worked with the government to create a policy for organic fertilizer, how it will be used, and how licenses will be provided. Waste Concern was the first organization to get a license. Now there are forty private companies doing composting in Bangladesh. So what we have done is to create more enterprises rather than keeping it to ourselves. Our growth model is that we don't want to do everything by ourselves. The forty companies include for-profit and not-for-profit, and there are more than twenty companies in the pipeline for registration. What is happening is that organic waste is becoming a sector that was not there. We also work with the government to give a tax break for any company that is operating in big cities to have a five-year tax holiday—outside Dhaka, seven years. Then we work with the government to promote that this is an environmental project, so don't impose value added tax. Government agreed to that also."

Waste to Resource Fund

In partnership with UNESCAP and the Bill & Melinda Gates Foundation, Waste Concern established the Waste to Resource Fund (W2RF) in 2012. The idea of W2RF was to provide a vehicle for further replication and scaling of Waste Concern's methods in Asia and Africa. The fund was registered in 2011 as a Company Limited by Guarantee with charitable status in London, UK. It has three trustees nominated by BMGF, Waste Concern, and ESCAP.

W2RF is a nonbanking financial institution that provides equity, soft loans, grants, or a combination of all three to finance resource recovery from urban waste in developing countries. The projects link with carbon financing opportunities and can be of various sizes, stand-alone or programmatic. W2RF's comparative advantage is that it will provide not only project financing but also technical support and capacity building to enable project partners to operate the projects. Once the investment cost of W2RF is recovered, the project partners in the country will also benefit from the remaining carbon credits.

W2RF is now exploring the opportunity to work closely with UNCCC and KfW (a German bank) to harness cobenefits from waste sector projects using the vehicle of Nationally Appropriate Mitigation Actions in the least developed countries. Waste Concern expanded its study of positive spillover effects of mitigation actions by quantifying factors such as green job creation, improved health, improved waste collection, cost savings from reduced need for landfilling, and improved crop yields through the use of compost, among others. They calculated the economic value of these "cobenefits" as amounting to US$184 per ton of CO_2 emissions reduced in developing countries in Asia-Pacific.[8]

Waste Concern Baraka

An unforeseen challenge was the dramatic increase in available compost as a result of scaling up Waste Concern's models by many stakeholders. In 2006 Waste Concern established yet another company, Waste Concern Baraka Agro Products Ltd. The company aimed to promote organic food and sustainable agriculture and create green jobs in Bangladesh. It partnered with the Ahmed Amin Group, which provided land for organic farms.

A Waste Concern study demonstrated that using compost would reduce irrigation volume in agriculture while increasing yield. This was a strong motivation for farmers who had to use expensive and unstable fuel-driven pumps for irrigation. The company also tried to supply solar-powered irrigation pumps. But the costs involved in sourcing the pumps were high.

Waste Concern also observed the negative outcomes of a new policy by the government to promote cotton cultivation in Bangladesh to provide farmers with better incomes. The government targets were not met, mainly because the government paid the farmers only a low price for the cotton. Waste Concern thought that if it promoted organic cotton farming using its compost, farmers could achieve higher yields and much higher prices.

Through its networks, Waste Concern managed to convince a British-based organic clothing company, People Tree, to preorder its first organic cotton yield. In 2007 Waste Concern Baraka Agro planted a small plot and found that the cotton had the right fiber length and strength. The company succeeded in growing the first organic cotton in Bangladesh. But shortly afterward, it experienced some problems with its seeds, which had to be imported from India. It decided to stop producing organic cotton and instead focused its efforts on other organic produce as well as securing organic certification.

Fortunately, the demand for compost was picking up in other areas, including tea gardens in Bangladesh, and a new market for organic tea emerged. And a number of foreign countries wanted to buy compost for landscaping:

If you get the demonstration project right, a new market emerges. We got calls from companies in China and Malaysia who wanted to buy bulk compost. They use it for landscaping, not just tea gardens. They are more developed, so the organic content in their waste is lower, and perhaps the farmers there already use up all the available compost. And also companies from the Middle East. There is regional competition for growth. To attract people you need to grow food, build gardens for hotels and golf courses, and so on. These are desert countries, so they need a lot of compost.

CURRENT INNOVATIONS TRIGGERED BY SIDE EFFECTS OF ECONOMIC DEVELOPMENT

A number of new challenges are created by economic development that generates more waste and changes the composition of waste. Waste Concern thinks that it has a window of opportunity for composting that is less than fifteen years: "For Bangladesh that means that we have maybe fifteen years left to capture this market. Once you cross about $1,100 per capita, your organic content will be drastically down to about 50 percent, according to global data from other countries."

A big new project is tackling plastic waste. In the mid-2000s, Bangladesh's plastic industry was increasingly afraid that the government would limit them to avoid a further accumulation of plastic waste:

The government attitude was: "All plastic is bad." So they came to us and said, "Help us, we want to be seen as a responsible industry." The plastic industry started working with the municipalities on source separation. They sponsored collection bins and promised to buy the collected plastic waste. We were helping them to design this project so that they can recover more plastic. This means less plastic is going to the landfill. And that was a huge incentive to the Ministry of Environment and the Dhaka City Corporation because less land is required.

That work triggered a search for additional ways to generate value from more or less clean plastic waste. A company in the Netherlands had experience with converting plastic into fuel with a relatively high caloric content. The product was known as refuse-derived fuel (RDF): "We thought, this could create another whole new market. If the plastic is clean, it can be reused for new products. If it is more contaminated, we can use it for RDF."

As usual, there was skepticism about adopting this idea:

The Minister of Environment wanted to stop plastic. But we did a calculation that showed the benefits of using RDF instead of coal in the thousands of brick factories in Bangladesh. First, because coal is imported, we reduce import costs. But it also reduces greenhouse gas emissions from coal burning. RDF has a higher caloric content than coal. So this becomes a CDM project, and that is money for the government. We showed the numbers to the Minister of Finance. And this created strong support for our proposal.

The idea was to do all the R&D and pilot work and then share the outcome of the innovation with various companies that would scale it up. The approach highlights Waste Concern's pragmatism and its willingness to use multiple organizational vehicles to create impact from innovations:

With the economic growth of Bangladesh, the nature of waste and the problems are changing for the government. We must create new solutions that are a win-win for them. So we are promoting what we call environmental business that will make the city clean and creates some profit. If we don't make a little bit of profit, we cannot grow and expand. If the R&D is done and the RDF pilot is successful and profitable, we can give it to our for-profit power company and to other companies to scale it up. And now other industries are coming to us besides plastics.

Maqsood and Iftekhar continue spending 50 percent of their time on innovations using the NGO Waste Concern as the organizational vehicle.

They are currently taking on a number of new challenges, such as biomedical waste, batteries, and energy-efficient buildings. They get many requests for other initiatives but often decline: "We say no a lot." In particular, they are wary of the persistent "project focus" of many development actors:

If it is just a project, there's a problem. The problem is that the project is always time bound, and the project has specific goals. You have a specific target and a tick mark that we have achieved what we wanted. They never look beyond their nose for long-term sustainability.

And they were concerned that the project focus prevented building their capacity for scaling: "In the project which the UNDP has developed, they only wanted to pilot the idea in five areas. But what next?"

Waste Concern's strategy always follows what the founders call a "program-based approach." It starts with innovative ideas but constantly asks, "So what? What do we need to do to scale this?" A strong sense of mission is a clear thread through Waste Concern's innovation journey: "Many people are surprised about all the things we are doing. On our web page you find this and that. If you boil it down to one single language: We convert waste to resource. We have never diverted from that." And the organization has clear evaluation criteria:

When we look into a sector, we always look to see whether there has been any work done. If there is a private sector operating there, if there are legal instruments in place, then there is no market failure. If there is a market failure, then we step in. So in the waste sector there was a market failure with the solid waste. We stepped in. Now we have forty companies operating there. But even if there is a market failure, we look at whether there is a policy in place. If there is a policy vacuum, then we step in. We work with the government to create policies, like the biomedical policies, the solid-waste policies. We collect data and provide models for a green strategy. All that work is done by us. We have influenced twenty-seven policies in Bangladesh. The third thing we look for is: What are the incentives? For example, we are never going to go into the textile sector, because the government is already giving incentives. No need for us to step in.

In 2010, the government of Bangladesh published the National 3R Strategy for Waste Management. Reading the document makes it clear how much influence Waste Concern had. It quotes heavily from Waste Concern studies and publications and refers to the organization's work throughout. A quote from the introduction by a ministry representative illustrates the dramatic changes in framing the problem of waste management: "Waste is unrecovered wealth. Waste should, therefore, not be wasted. Waste needs to be recovered and 3R strategy is the most accepted way to recover wealth from waste sources." Clearly the public sector has adopted Waste Concern's language at least, and we hope also its way of thinking and acting.

WASTE CONCERN'S INNOVATION ARCHETYPE

We refer to Waste Concern's unique innovation archetype as "innovation for diffusion." Waste Concern is not motivated to operate large, productive organizations that could create sufficient impact from its investment in innovation. Instead, it enables other organizations to scale its innovation assets.

As with Aravind, the founders of Waste Concern built an organization to further develop an existing set of ideas, knowledge, and activities. In particular, they operated with an explicit identity and sense of mission from the beginning. Their motto of "waste to resource" provided direction and focus throughout their journey. They also had a clear strategy that helped them evaluate ideas. They would explore only the development of innovations in areas of clear policy or market failure. Waste Concern also used internally clear and consistent terminology around innovation and scaling that worked for them. They used the term *invention* for what we would call *innovation* in Chapter 1. And their use of the term *innovation* resembles our term *scaling*.

Waste Concern also had a clear perspective on coupling innovation and scaling for impact. The founders were less motivated to build a large and efficient implementing organization to scale their innovations. Instead, their impact-creation logic revolved around developing evidence and demonstration projects to convince others to adopt Waste Concern's solutions to environmental and social problems. This choice created a dual challenge: (1) Waste Concern needed to learn how to improve its R&D activities and reduce uncertainties in its own innovation projects, and

(2) it also needed to remove uncertainties in the perceptions of others about whether adopting its ideas was beneficial or not. In other words, Waste Concern's challenge was to design innovations in such a way that they would diffuse to other stakeholders efficiently. That way, the founders did not need to do most of the scaling themselves but ensured that others would create impact from their innovations.

In 1962 the sociologist Everett Rogers published an influential book that proposed a number of ways in which an innovator could facilitate the diffusion of innovations.[9] It helps us to understand the logic of Waste Concern's approach. Rogers listed five characteristics of innovations that matter in important ways for their likelihood of being adopted by others. We have slightly modified his list:

1. *Relative advantage.* Adoption of an innovation is more likely if it is perceived as better than the one it supersedes. Waste Concern cleverly and creatively documented its innovations and calculated data that communicated its benefits in objective and credible terms. It published its data and findings together with other experts, which provided additional credibility.

2. *Compatibility.* Adoption is more likely if the innovation fits the prevailing values and priorities of the adopting organization, is compatible with existing knowledge and practices, and fits the needs of important stakeholders such as customers, funders, or voters. Waste Concern emphasized generally accepted values and priorities, such as cost savings, efficiency, environmental protection, profits, and jobs, that were attractive to private sector and public sector stakeholders.

3. *Complexity.* Adoption is more likely if an innovation has relatively low technical and social complexity (that is, if it can be understood and used easily). Waste Concern used simplicity and functional robustness as design criteria for its innovations. Close interactions with stakeholders that adopted their innovations allowed further improvements.

4. *Observability.* Adoption is more likely if an innovation is visible to potential adopters. Waste Concern invested in scaling its

demonstration projects so that visitors could observe all aspects of its operations. Transparency and availability of process documents and data on social, environmental, and financial aspects further supported the observability of innovations and the benefits of scaling them.

5. *Trialability.* Adoption is more likely if important elements of an innovation can be tried, for example, in the form of prototypes that require less investment or if peers have already tried the innovation successfully. The demonstration plants and a dedicated training facility were investments to give others hands-on experience with the innovations. Waste Concern even used patents for this purpose. Patents in the business sector protect and increase the private benefits of the innovator. Waste Concern used them for a different purpose. If stakeholders wanted to use the patented innovations, they got a license only if they came for training to Waste Concern's facilities. That way Waste Concern ensured that replications were successful and efficient and that more impact was created from its investments in innovations.

Not everyone can or aspires to build an efficient implementing organization. Waste Concern demonstrates that this potential weakness can be overcome by its particular innovation archetype, "innovation for diffusion." In this archetype, impact creation from innovations is maximized by enabling diffusion, the adoption of innovations by others. And the ability of Waste Concern to innovate productively is an important asset in helping local adoptions of their models that may require additional innovations due to contextual variance.

Nevertheless, scaling work is still required. Waste Concern does its own scaling through demonstration plants and jointly with other private sector parties who provide resources and management capacity. The scaling work has two main objectives: First, it provides income and financial support for R&D activities; second, it explores ways of making scaling simpler and more robust to demonstrate feasibility, which leads to adoption by others. Both founders are closely involved in all of Waste Concern's innovation work. The accumulated knowledge and experience of the founders and their clarity of strategy and mission make innovations very productive. But this dependence of the organization on its founders is a great problem for succession planning. The founders are struggling to find and nurture talent that could replace them. They quote a lack of commitment and inflated expectations of salaries as primary reasons.

PART III

Recommendations for Organizations and Their Supporters

The following three chapters provide a comparative analysis of innovation archetypes to expand and to generalize our findings from the four case studies. We will explore the dynamics of green zones more deeply and reflect on the ways in which green zones enable more productive innovations at lower levels of uncertainty. Next, we expand these organizational perspectives with a focus on problem spaces. Problem spaces define the context that creates and sustains the needs of people and communities. They are a central dimension of an organization's impact-creation logic. A diagnostic framework for mapping problem spaces alerts us to the importance of distinguishing between technical and relational problems for making decisions about innovation and scaling. Finally, we translate our findings into a practical guide that puts you on a productive journey to innovate and scale for impact.

7 INNOVATION ARCHETYPES
Balancing Innovation and Scaling over Time

The preceding four chapters demonstrated the roles of innovation and scaling in four social enterprises. At first glance, the histories of these organizations seem to be strikingly different from each other. They challenged us to compare and to distill insights that would help answer questions we raised in Part I: How do innovations relate to the long-term impact-creation logics of organizations? Do green and red zone characteristics change in organizations over time, and what are the consequences? How can we think about balancing resource allocations to innovation and scaling over time? How do organizations overcome or deal with their innovation pathologies? In this chapter, we summarize our findings from comparing the trajectories of our four organizations. We emphasize important distinctions around innovation and scaling that illustrate and extend those we have discussed in Chapters 1 and 2.

The experiences of Gram Vikas and BRAC in their earlier years vividly illustrate our claim that innovating sounds much easier than it actually is. Despite much enthusiasm and motivation to "do good," both organizations initially failed to create the expected benefits from their innovations for a number of years. Their success was limited because of significant uncertainties about framing the problems they were trying to solve, as well as uncertainties about resources and capabilities required for devising effective solutions.

The organizations were also challenged to define more clearly and more explicitly who they wanted to be and what their missions should be. BRAC needed to clarify ideological tensions within its staff that prescribed different solutions to problems of poverty. Gram Vikas needed to clarify whether they wanted to solve the problems of tribes or of more heterogeneous village communities. Innovations provided important opportunities to explore these questions and to get answers. As a result, both organizations accumulated knowledge in all the dimensions of uncertainty displayed in Figure 1.1. The principal role of innovation in these organizations was to enable learning, not to create tangible and measurable benefits.

The early trajectories of Gram Vikas and BRAC were very different from those of Aravind and Waste Concern. Both of the latter organizations were founded on existing knowledge and deep expertise in the domains of their work. Aravind's founder had a lifetime of experience working in rural India and had already invested in the surgical innovations that became the basis of Aravind's operating model. Waste Concern's founders were academics with years of action-research experience as a basis for their innovation efforts. Consequently, Aravind and Waste Concern started out with much lower levels of uncertainty and thus stronger impact-creation logics. They were able to create tangible benefits very soon.

IF YOU CAN'T LEARN, DON'T INNOVATE!

Both Gram Vikas and BRAC in their early years benefited from acknowledging failures as soon as they became apparent. They could avoid falling into the trap of the "stop too late" innovation pathology. They paid close attention to the communities they served. They critically evaluated progress against expectations. It was important that the criteria for evaluation came largely from their own values and identities, their experiences and ambitions, rather than merely from seeking external approval or reporting to standardized impact metrics. Both Gram Vikas with its farmer cooperatives and BRAC with its housing and educational activities could have reported sufficiently positive project data to please some funders.

BRAC could easily have adopted a national rollout of the Comilla Model, which created some benefits for poor communities. As a loyal implementer of the rollout, BRAC could have won funds and legitimacy. Instead, the organization developed a critical, evidence-based perspective on its own desired performance. It was not interested in reporting short-term achievements and treating development work as a tick-the-box exercise. The senior managers spent much more time in the field than in the office. This hands-on approach strongly supported real-time evaluation and objective learning. They could directly observe problems, opportunities, and the consequences of their work for communities. Their observations triggered relevant and timely ideas for subsequent innovations grounded in real local problems and opportunities rather than in predefined assumptions and standard solutions. This direct engagement with communities and problems prevented other innovation pathologies, such as wasting resources on "too many bad ideas" or scaling immature projects that did not really work.

BRAC's pragmatism and its investments in developing an efficient organizational infrastructure seemed to make it more capable of fast and objective learning than Gram Vikas. BRAC developed a green zone and a capacity for scaling workable solutions at a much earlier stage in its history. But Gram Vikas had a unique impact-creation logic that limits comparisons of the two organizations. Fighting inequality is a formidable objective. Integrating this particular mission into an impact-creation logic was difficult. Many facets led to inequality in rural India. The founding team's lack of organizational and environmental experience created unique challenges and a drawn-out learning curve. And therefore the two organizations developed in very different ways.

In retrospect, the lack of knowledge that challenged Gram Vikas and BRAC in their early years may—counterintuitively—have been an advantage. Albert Hirschman shed light on this subject when he introduced the principle of the hiding hand.[1] In a nutshell, the principle of the hiding hand states that ignorance about the real complexity and all the difficulties of development work is often beneficial or even a necessary "evil." Lacking ignorance, a rational person would never get started because the complexity of dealing with all the difficulties would seem overwhelming. But once you are in action, the full complexity of the situation reveals itself, and you are forced to be creative, to learn and adapt, and to innovate. The chances increase that you will find an approach that works. Addressing this complexity based on preconceived strategies and solutions might lower an organization's ability and willingness to learn. Thus the hiding hand coupled with a lack of prior experience might have been crucial factors in enabling productive learning required to develop better impact-creation logics by both Gram Vikas and BRAC. The resulting knowledge accumulation transformed their nascent impact-creation logics into green zones capable of creating significant impact.

In general, the hiding hand works only if an organization is able and willing to learn objectively and to commit to an idea without giving up too early or too easily. It doesn't work if innovations are judged merely by the expectation of beneficial outcomes. Rather, the crucial question that organizations should ask is: Do we make progress along an important learning curve, and does this knowledge accumulation reduce uncertainty in central areas of concern? Because only then can organizations build a green zone and start creating impact. If you can't learn productively, don't innovate!

The previous discussions of the link between innovation and learning have two implications. First, the less developed an organization's green zone is, the greater is its need to be able to learn. Many new and inexperienced organizations fail not just because they take too much risk but also because they are not good at productive learning that reduces important uncertainties. Second, ideas that are farther away from an organization's green zone require stronger and more focused learning capabilities. As we discuss in the following pages, the ways in which Aravind tended to innovate—by keeping its innovations close to its green zone—are productive because the innovations had lower degrees of uncertainty. Aravind could therefore translate more of its innovation efforts into real impact rather than into "just" learning.

IF YOU CAN'T SCALE, DON'T INNOVATE!

In the case study of BRAC, a manager expressed his concern that too many NGOs tended to jump from one project to another and therefore never built vital organizational capabilities as a basis for a distinct and focused impact-creation logic. Capabilities accrue from repetitive work, constant improvements, and commitment, not from constant changes of an organization's focus, priorities, and activities. In our terminology, the BRAC manager's statement would mean that many organizations never develop much of a green zone and thus do not have a basis for significant scaling of a proven intervention. These organizations are often small, surviving grant by grant, or they are large, becoming bureaucracies with little transparency and accountability. Such organizations are unlikely to generate impact from investments in innovation. They suffer from a number of innovation pathologies that are usually not acknowledged or reflected on.

When we evaluate social enterprises, the absence of a distinct green zone is a warning signal. It implies a lack of implementation and scaling capacity. This deficiency leads to an additional simple but important conclusion: If you can't scale, don't innovate! Two reasons support our admonition. First, scaling creates impact from investment in innovations: no scaling, no benefits. Second, scaling has tremendous positive feedback effects on innovation. Organizations with high scaling capacity tend to create better ideas and better ability to evaluate ideas. Both of these advantages result from the accumulated knowledge that defines their green zones. They have enough relevant ideas that are close to their green zones, permitting innovation with less uncertainty and thus a higher chance of success. Knowledge accumulation from focused scaling sharpens the lens for "knowing what you don't know" and promotes a realistic assessment of uncertainties. And as we have learned from Gram Vikas, BRAC, and Aravind, ongoing scaling work lets organizations test ideas much more efficiently in current programs and in communities where basic trust exists. This ability makes innovation processes much more productive. Gram Vikas's transition out of biogas shows what we mean: The goodwill and trust its people had built in villages from scaling their biogas projects enabled the organization to choose appropriate pilot villages for the subsequent MANTRA innovation. Organizations that scale well tend to have more valuable resources to facilitate productive piloting as part of their innovations.

In the next sections, we lay out a more systematic set of arguments for these conclusions. We will show how they help us to evaluate the impact-creation capacity of organizations systematically and to make better decisions about innovation and scaling within organizations.

INNOVATION ARCHETYPES

Each of our featured organizations has a distinct innovation archetype. We use the term *innovation archetypes* to refer to the dynamic balancing of innovation and scaling that creates and strengthens the impact-creation logic of an organization over time. Archetypes give funders and managers a realistic and practical lens for evaluating the roles of innovation and scaling in supporting an organization's objectives and aspirations and the capacity of organizations to create impact.

As we have seen, our featured organizations all started their journeys with very different capabilities for generating and implementing relevant ideas and creating impact. But they all ended up building significant green zones. This fact alone is not surprising because we selected the organizations for this characteristic as part of our research design. All four organizations are recognized as leading social enterprises for their ability to create tremendous impact for the constituencies that they serve. This is just another way of saying that they have effective and efficient green zones.

We have estimated the relative allocations of each organization's resources (1) to activities of scaling, driven by their green zones and (2) to innovations, activities in their red zones. We compared these relative allocations at the start of each organization's trajectory with its allocations now, roughly twenty years later. Figure 7.1 shows this comparison.

What we notice in Figure 7.1 is the prominent role of scaling in all the organizations today. Today, they either allocate almost no resources to innovation (Gram Vikas) or pursue relatively few innovations (Aravind and BRAC) when compared to how most resources in these organizations are used on a daily basis. Waste Concern is an exception. The founders continue to allocate about 50 percent of their time to research and development activities exploring innovative ideas.

The organizations employed interesting organizational strategies to support their particular innovation archetypes and to nurture their green zones. They used a number of different organizational vehicles to build

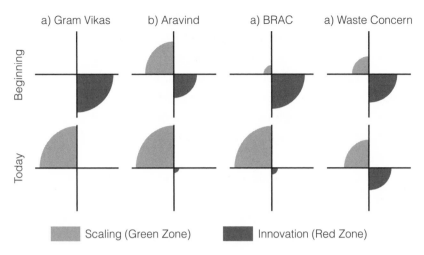

FIGURE 7.1
Relative allocations of organizational resources to innovation and scaling at the time of an organization's beginning and today.

an infrastructure that facilitated different aspects of innovation and scaling. Aravind established a manufacturing company, Aurolab. Although Aurolab is owned by a nonprofit trust, it is run like a business. Aurolab directly supports Aravind's scaling strategy by producing resources such as lenses and surgical material cheaply and at high quality. Aurolab innovations support Aravind by targeting important bottlenecks that limit its scaling efforts.

BRAC employs a wide variety of for-profit and nonprofit organizations. This organizational ecosystem enables large scope for innovations by increasing the variety of ideas that it generates and pilots. BRAC also ensures sufficient scale by separating its activity areas, such as microfinance, education, health, and its various enterprises, into dedicated and focused organizational units that are independently managed.

Waste Concern is somewhat in between Aravind and BRAC. Its scope is larger than Aravind's but smaller than BRAC's. It operates a number of smaller nonprofit and for-profit organizations and participates in some larger organizations that are primarily managed by external partner organizations. This setup addresses a number of operational needs in its unique innovation archetype, as we have discussed in Part II.

Gram Vikas is an exception in that it does not operate different types of organizations in parallel. But it has changed its organizational structure several times, from a loose student organization to a more formal NGO to a technical implementation organization and finally back to an NGO. Because it has enacted a focused impact-creation logic in scaling its MANTRA approach over the last decade, it has not seen the need to operate different organizational structures in parallel. Furthermore, because Gram Vikas is strongly driven by its unique values and sense of mission, running a for-profit organization that could generate funds was not part of its identity.

All four organizations arrived at their green zones in different ways. And the roles that innovation and scaling played, and the pace and types of innovations that shaped their trajectories, were unique for each organization. We briefly sketch the similarities and differences of their innovation archetypes.

Four Innovation Archetypes

In all four organizations, innovations presented opportunities for learning that reduced uncertainties and increased knowledge. Knowledge accumulation enabled each organization to develop a distinct impact-creation logic. As their impact-creation logics became clearer and more robust, they resembled green zones, which enabled efficient scaling and impact creation. Green zones provided subsequent innovations with a particular purpose, pace, and sense of direction. The organizations found better decision criteria to determine whether and when to allocate resources to innovation or scaling.

Figure 7.2 is a high-level abstraction of our previous discussions about the roles of innovation and scaling in shaping the trajectories of our featured organizations. It makes visual the particular roles and the dynamics of innovation and scaling as a distinct archetype.

How can archetypes be used for decision making? The innovation archetypes remind us that innovation serves different purposes in organizations and thus has different characteristics. Figure 7.2 shows the central distinctions we made in the case-study chapters. Archetypes may serve as guiding templates and sources of inspiration for other organizations. For

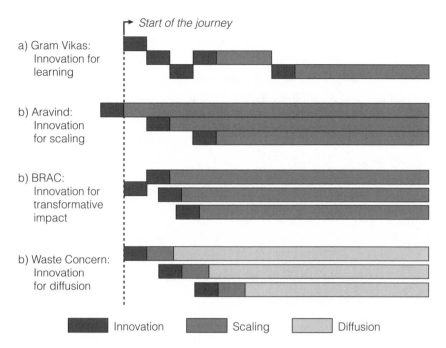

FIGURE 7.2
Four innovation archetypes.

example, entrepreneurs who care about innovation but not so much about running an efficient organization may find inspiration from Waste Concern. Not that anyone could do what Waste Concern does. Every organization is unique! But adopting a plan of innovation for diffusion might lead to more realistic decisions about organizational structures, design parameters for innovation, and encouraging diffusion of innovations. The case study on Waste Concern provides ample detail to support strategizing by other organizations.

Innovation archetypes facilitate a realistic assessment of how to create impact from innovation and scaling. The innovation archetype of Aravind is an example that shows funders and organizations what it takes to create impact from innovations in a particular environment. Aravind chose innovations that create a product or service for which demand is potentially large (cataract surgery) but economic realities are challenging (acquiring sufficient supplies). Aravind prioritized its investments and generated an efficient, dedicated organization that is committed to long-term impact creation and does not jump from one innovation to the next.

The particular innovation archetype of Gram Vikas reminds us of the fallacy of seeing value only in successful innovations. Organizations that target tough and complex relational problems grounded in stifling norms, abuse of power, and politics, need adequate support for the often painful and drawn-out learning journey required for eventual success. Expecting funds to generate short-term impact rather than learning would harm their efforts.

Archetypes and Innovation Pathologies

Choice of an innovation archetype also enabled our four organizations to prevent or to overcome innovation pathologies. For example, the case study of Gram Vikas indicated a number of innovation pathologies, caused by factors such as a lack of resources and the resistance of a busy organization to evaluating new ideas. This situation makes idea generation, communication, and implementation difficult. It would also be hard for Gram Vikas to organize itself to take its innovations to a large scale. The organization decided to keep its staff focused on the extremely difficult work of transforming village after village one at a time. Over the years, it built a powerful green zone for this scaling work that resulted from focus and constant improvements. Gram Vikas creates impact by restricting innovations and focusing on scaling. Most of its innovation pathologies are therefore irrelevant.

Aravind's homogeneous organization and its use of behavioral control to achieve consistency and predictable success also indicate that it might be liable to a number of innovation pathologies, including "never get started" and "stop too early." Aravind's innovation pathologies are caused by organizational factors that define its identity. Aravind is not willing to compromise or change them. But its unique innovation archetype prevents it from being stifled by these innovation pathologies. Aravind innovates close to its top strategic and operational priorities and capabilities to eliminate scaling bottlenecks. By keeping innovations close to its green zone, Aravind avoids exposure to risk that it is unable to bear. Perhaps the notion of "innovating safely," which we dismissed in Chapter 1, starts to make more sense from Aravind's unique perspective.

Waste Concern had to find ways to overcome the potential innovation pathology of insufficient exploitation, which was a consequence of its founders' lack of willingness to manage a large and efficient organization. Its innovation archetype neutralizes this pathology. Waste Concern creates impact from its innovations by enabling others to scale them.

BRAC, on the other hand, was built around dealing with novelty and the challenges of systematically creating transformative impact from innovation. Its broad scope potentially exposes it to the threat of losing focus and suffering from innovation pathologies such as "innovate again too soon" and "insufficient exploitation." BRAC avoids investing too many resources in exciting new ideas by building an extremely outcome-oriented "delivery machinery." It nurtures a culture of focus, constant improvement, and delivery on stretch targets, ensuring that insufficient impact creation from scaling is not an issue limiting BRAC's impact. And its impressive size and resource endowment mean that it can afford to allocate resources to innovation without threatening current performance. It also does not suffer much if a few things go wrong from time to time, because it creates tremendous impact from its established routine program activities.

Table 7.1 summarizes some general ways in which the four organizations reduce or eliminate potential innovation pathologies.

THE DYNAMICS OF GREEN ZONES

Is the dominance of green zone activities in the current state of our featured organizations only a matter of the criteria by which we have selected them? No, there are more interesting and important explanations for that observation. Understanding them requires that we look at the dynamics by which green zones evolve. The sizes of the green zone and red zone segments in Figure 7.1 depict allocations relative to all available resources within an organization. They are not a comparative measure across organizations. For example, BRAC pursues a number of innovations at any given time. But because it is a huge organization, its relative allocation of resources to innovation is still low. BRAC's balance between innovation

TABLE 7.1
How four organizations reduced innovation pathologies.

	Gram Vikas	Aravind	BRAC	Waste Concern
Never get started	Focus on scaling reduced the need to create innovative ideas.	Senior managers are close to patients; they have total visibility of problems and bottlenecks in all areas of operations.	High levels of ambition and a constant reflection on BRAC's relevance, stimulate ideas. Some programs have small discretionary budgets for innovation. BRAC's size, reputation, and scope of work attract a constant inflow of people, ideas, and resources (also true for Aravind).	Because the founders limit their involvement in scaling and routine management, they can allocate significant time to identifying and evaluating ideas. Their reputation for productive innovation exposes them to many ideas and requests from big donors and governments.
Too many bad ideas	The staff knows from experience why most new ideas would not work in their context (for example, deviating from the 100 percent rule). Memories of many failed innovations act as a reminder of innovation risk.	Clarity of its impact-creation logic prevents a loss of focus. The culture is risk averse. Obsession with scaling in a narrow domain creates bottlenecks that trigger searches for ideas close to its green zone (which tend to be better ideas). Tremendous accumulated experience of management and staff improves quality and evaluation of ideas.	BRAC uses explicit rules to evaluate ideas. RED provides objective input into idea creation and evaluation. A deep green zone allows experienced leaders who tend to stay with BRAC for long times to evaluate ideas productively (knowing what likely will not work). Listening to communities and observing needs in the field by senior management improves problem frames and thus reduces uncertainties.	The organization has clear rules for evaluating ideas. Accumulated expertise in its field of innovations improves quality of idea creation and evaluation. Focus on the long-term program rather than project thinking lowers risk of unintended negative consequences, as does saying "no" a lot to external ideas.

Stop too early		Decision makers who are connected by strong family ties are able to reach consensus for innovations that target high priority problems. Aravind is able to attract resources from a wide network of supporters.	Innovations are championed by decision makers who command resources. BRAC has been able to attract significant dedicated innovation funds for particular topics from donors.	Founders are directly involved in all R&D. Resources are available and protected by direct founder supervision.
Stop too late		Resources are incredibly stretched, and thus the opportunity cost of innovating is high. Everyone is constantly evaluated on how his or her actions make a real difference for patients.	Research and monitoring units as well as program directors keep a close eye on progress. BRAC is willing and able to evaluate progress critically and to learn objectively.	Scarcity of founder capacity and specialized resources limits unproductive innovation efforts. Founders directly monitor progress.
Insufficient exploitation	A deep commitment to scaling a proven intervention has created a deep green zone as a basis for generating tremendous impact for the communities it serves.	A high-performance culture continuously monitors and improves progress. Everyone is expected to report on ways of improving performance through error correction and efficiency. Data displays allow live monitoring of all operational areas.	A high-performance culture continuously monitors and improves progress. A dedicated monitoring unit evaluates progress objectively. A large amount of available resources is allocated to green-zone activities. Stretch targets are routinely employed.	Scalability is a design criterion for innovations. The founders explicitly innovate to enable others to adopt and scale their innovations. A training center, patent mechanisms, and hands-on field visits maximize the impact others can create from Waste Concern's innovations.
Innovate again too soon	Large demand for its services creates a deep commitment to continue scaling the main intervention. Leaders are aware that they do not have the organizational resources to invest in innovation.	Positive demand, coupled with observable continuous impact creation from existing solutions, limits tendencies to overinvest in innovations.	Size and resource endowments reduce negative effects of allocating resources to innovation (Figure 1.3b). BRAC's delivery machine ensures continuous performance in main program areas.	Limited capacity of the small founding team prevents too many parallel innovation efforts.

and scaling is strongly tilted toward scaling. Why? One explanation is that social enterprises, like all organizations, tend to become more conservative and risk averse over time. Creating predictable positive impact from scaling thus naturally becomes more dominant. But risk aversion may not be the main explanation for the relative dominance of green zone activities. In truly effective organizations, another important mechanism is the key: Everything they do, whether it is innovation or scaling, eventually feeds into and improves their green zones.

To appreciate this point, let's look at the evolution of green zones over time. In our featured organizations we have identified four mechanisms that drive the development and strengthening of green zones. First, scaling increases the level and quality of knowledge in an organization. Let's recall that we have defined green zones as the required conditions necessary for scaling and thus predictable impact creation. But green zones don't just enable scaling; they also benefit from it. Scaling over time creates many small improvements and additional knowledge. This is another way of saying that organizations repeatedly doing the same thing get better at it over time. Scaling creates knowledge in all three dimensions of an organization's impact-creation logic and this knowledge accumulation improves an organization's green zone.

Second, scaling improves consistency and continuity. Experiencing beneficial outcomes tends to make the fit between the three dimensions of an impact-creation logic more robust and explicit. The positive experience of success and accomplishment strengthens motivation and commitment to a current direction and to investing in further improvements. Aravind's and Gram Vikas's innovation archetypes clearly illustrate the power of these two mechanisms.

Third, scaling increases the resources available to an organization. Positive achievements from scaling strengthen an organization's reputation. A good reputation increases access to resources that improve an organization's capacity for creating more impact. A noteworthy example of this mechanism is the change in Gram Vikas's reputation after it had scaled its biogas program for a decade. The influx of talent, funds, and ideas in all four organizations today is an enduring effect of this mechanism. The financial surplus that Aravind's and BRAC's productive scaling generate enable the organizations to acquire resources and to invest in training and skill development.

Through these three mechanisms, scaling further strengthens an organization's green zone. These mechanisms increase an organization's impact-creation potential (through knowledge accumulation) and impact-creation capacity (through resource accumulation). But there is a fourth crucial mechanism: productive innovation. If an innovation fails, an organization that innovates productively is able to extract important lessons from the failure, improving its knowledge base. Our case studies remind us that green zones also improve in the direction of knowing "what not to do." Failing without learning would constitute an unproductive innovation effort, a sign of innovation pathologies. If an innovation succeeds, an effective organization will enact and build a new green zone. Or—as is most explicitly the case in Aravind's innovation archetype—innovation directly targets and strengthens an existing green zone by removing a stubborn bottleneck in its operations. Thus both innovation and scaling potentially build and strengthen green zones. We have observed this phenomenon in almost all the organizations we have studied that were able to generate tremendous benefits for their constituencies over time.

Thin, Deep, Narrow, and Broad Green Zones: Implications for Productive Innovation

An important additional distinction for this dynamic lies in what we call thin versus deep green zones and narrow versus broad green zones. A thin green zone is an impact-creation logic that enables steady or only slowly growing scaling and impact. It often results from a lack of ambition more than from a lack of competence. Competence can be acquired. Ambition is more difficult. The difference between a thin and a deep green zone is best illustrated by Aravind. Aravind focuses on a small set of needs. In this case the organization focuses on the need of patients for efficient cataract surgeries to regain sight. Aravind has refined and optimized its interventions over more than twenty years. It has thus become the most efficient eye care center in the world. Its impact is growing significantly every year. This is a deep green zone. The deep levels of knowledge and the reinforcing fit of the dimensions of its impact-creation logic enable Aravind to create a lot of impact for a particular set of needs. Gram Vikas is another example of an organization with a deep green zone. It has tremendously invested in refining its community engagement approach over a decade.

Organizations with deep green zones are very good at creating relevant ideas that fit their current missions and priorities. They are very good at enacting these ideas given their refined organizational capabilities. Because they understand a particular set of needs well, they encounter few uncertainties in enacting these ideas. But it would be a mistake to consider these organizations "innovative." They do a few things exceptionally well. Their green zones are deep but narrow. Many ideas—particularly those suggested to them by external stakeholders or funders—potentially lie outside their green zones. These organizations are thus usually not well prepared for adopting external "innovative" ideas.

Organizations with deep and narrow green zones tend to have very particular innovation pathologies. Frequently, they are used to success and thus become less capable of dealing productively with failures inherent in innovative efforts. The episode in the Aravind case study about the managed care program illustrates this observation. Also, these organizations tend to hire not for creativity but for organizational fit. They socialize new hires very quickly into expected behavior and performance consistent with their impact-creation logics and the cultures and processes that reflect them. Organizations with deep and narrow green zones often have homogeneous cultures. Their staffs are used to dealing with routine problems but not with novelty. The fact that these organizations are efficient means that they do not have underutilized resources. Enacting innovations may thus lower their current performance in their green zone activities, as indicated in Figure 1.3b. One of the authors recently did an innovation workshop with Aravind that was attended by ten of their eye doctors. We calculated that each doctor could easily perform about twenty-five surgeries a day. The opportunity cost of participating in a two-day innovation workshop is thus 500 patients regaining their eyesight. Scary!

These focused and productive organizations have very specific capabilities and motivations. Even if innovations succeeded, they may not be willing or able to scale them effectively if the innovations depart too far from their green zones. But they can innovate very productively around bottlenecks to their focused scaling work, as we have seen in the case study of Aravind.

Organizations with thin and narrow green zones are best advised to focus on scaling and marginal improvements to deepen and to stabilize their green zones. They will then be in a much better position to create impact and to innovate productively within or close to their green zones. The trajectory of Gram Vikas's MANTRA intervention illustrates the value of resisting innovations and focusing on scaling to stabilize and deepen a green zone over many years.

Sometimes, organizations with thin green zones have access to abundant resources, usually in the form of funds. In these cases, they can afford to innovate in the direction of learning about important areas of uncertainties in their green zones without necessarily lowering current performance (see Figure 1.3b). However, they need to resist the temptation to prioritize innovations over the difficult routine work of scaling and strengthening their green zones, or they risk never really developing deep competencies. For these organizations, having access to fewer funds is usually healthier and reinforces a search for ideas that increase efficiency and effectiveness rather than merely novelty. We wished that big funders who are required to spend significant amounts of funds annually would reflect more explicitly on this dynamic. Generosity may sometimes create more harm than good.

A broad green zone means that organizations are prepared to deal with a range of problems and needs. BRAC is an illustrative example. It is organized to systematically take on a broad range of ideas. The diversity of its staff is higher than in the other three organizations. At any given time, it has a range of external visitors working in various positions who might have relevant expertise to take on an idea. It has vast resources that enable it to plug most ideas into ongoing operations with little distraction or decline in current performance. And BRAC has a dedicated learning, evaluation, and monitoring infrastructure. This infrastructure creates capabilities for reducing innovation uncertainty, for example through custom research and accessing relevant knowledge and expertise. It is set up to deal efficiently with a broad range of ideas that would be risky challenges for most other organizations.

BRAC is unique in that it has both a broad and a deep green zone. We have seen from the case study how BRAC has invested in organizational infrastructure for concomitant capacity of productive innovation and productive scaling. However, building this capacity poses a substantial managerial challenge for any organization. Organizations with broad green zones often have relatively thin green zones. They are average or good at many things, but they are not excellent at anything. These organizations are well advised to focus on fewer problem spaces and to radically prioritize scaling over innovations at least in some areas of their work. Investing in nurturing management talent internally and finding ways in keeping talent in the organization may make the biggest impact for these organizations. The broader an organization's green zone, the more investment in "overhead" matters.

We believe that managers, funders, and supporters are well advised to keep these distinctions between thin, deep, narrow, and broad green zones in mind when they evaluate the potential of organizations to innovate or explore particular ideas and evaluate how to generally improve the impact potential of these organizations.

A "Comparative Advantage" for Innovative Ideas

An important but counterintuitive consequence of a broad green zone is that it allows organizations to enact many "innovations" within their green zones. This seems like a contradiction of our green and red zone distinction. But the framework in Figure 1.2 was only a static display. We now add a temporal dimension.

Consider BRAC's early years: Everything the founders did was a red zone activity due to limited experience. But what used to be a red zone idea in the beginning is today likely to be just a standard green zone idea. The strength of BRAC's understanding of the problem spaces it targeted, clarity about its mission and strategy, and levels of organizational resources and capabilities have grown dramatically over the past decades.

The terms *red zone* and *green zone* therefore imply an important relative meaning. An idea that would have been innovative with major uncertainties in an inexperienced organization may—because of accumulated

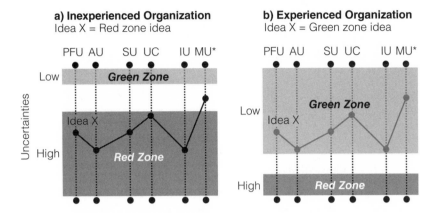

FIGURE 7.3

An organization's green zone broadens with experience.

NOTE: See Figure 1.2 for abbreviations.

knowledge derived from its failures and successes—become just a standard idea with much lower uncertainty. Figure 7.3 illustrates this argument.

In Figure 7.3a, the evaluation and development of a hypothetical Idea *X* is associated with a number of uncertainties. It is thus a red zone idea, and significant risk is associated with its pursuit. Outcomes are uncertain and may take a lot of time and effort to realize. In Figure 7.3b, the same idea is now a green zone idea. The organization has accumulated significant knowledge and experience to evaluate and enact this idea efficiently, with predictable positive outcomes. Alternatively, even though Idea *X* now has few associated uncertainties, the organization may conclude that the idea is unlikely to work, a conclusion based on its knowledge about problem spaces or its own capabilities. It would then not waste time and effort in pursuing the idea.

Thus whether an idea is innovative or not depends on the organization. This is a crucial distinction that is often forgotten in discussions of innovation. What is a standard idea for BRAC may be an innovative idea with high degrees of uncertainty for most other organizations. It may also have been an innovative idea with uncertain prospects for BRAC twenty years ago. *Innovative* is thus a relative term within an organization over time, and it is a relative term across organizations. The term *innovative* refers less to particular characteristics of ideas than to the relation of ideas to a given organization and its particular level of knowledge.

We believe that this crucial point is often overlooked by funders who require and reward the generous use of the term *innovative* to legitimate and strengthen grant proposals. Our discussions indicate that organizations have a comparative advantage for certain ideas but not for others. Funders might find it productive to invest in a deeper understanding of the particular characteristics of an organization's green zone instead of just funding "innovative proposals." For example, they could ask, "Which types of ideas best fit an organization's particular green zone so that not all dimensions of an idea are uncertain?" Our innovation frameworks in Figures 1.2 and 7.3 might help them map ideas and make better decisions. Other questions might be, "Does an organization have a broad or a narrow green zone?" and "What are its likely innovation pathologies?" Systematic inquiries into these questions enable much better decisions about the prospects of ideas for new projects and innovations enacted by a given organization.

A related implication is that established organizations that do not have recognizable green zones are—in general—not good outlets for funds for innovative projects, for two reasons: (1) The project idea is risky because it does not lie in or close to a green zone, and (2) the lack of a green zone means that the organization does not have implementation and thus scaling capacities. Even if the innovation succeeds, the organization is unlikely to create much impact from it.

The dynamics of green zones have several implications for productive innovation. The best way to deal with innovative ideas more productively is to strengthen an organization's green zone (and to be clear where that green zone ends) so that it does not become a victim of the illusion of competence. Not every idea can be enacted within an organization's green zone. Often, uncertainties in some dimensions remain. Having a deep green zone enables an organization to create more relevant ideas, to evaluate them more objectively and realistically, and to pilot them using resources and capabilities at its disposal. Thus innovating close to an organization's green zone can load the innovation dice in its favor. The organization over time will create impact much more powerfully and predictably. Organizations with deep green zones stop wasting time with bad ideas just to be "innovative." A manager from BRAC's social innovation lab described this dynamic:

Some group gave us an [electronic] tablet that had lots of information. It teaches people about basic literacy, how to write basic characters. They are very proud of it. They have come here four or five times wanting to work with BRAC. BRAC is a little skeptical about technology. And their technology was also more for self-learning, not for groups. Pretty much all that BRAC does is through groups. But they pushed, and so we thought about a few places that could work, and we have taken them to the field. In the process we have actually learned a lot. We have learned which kind of technologies probably won't work for BRAC. And I think it has helped me appreciate that BRAC directors have very good instincts about what works and what won't work. If a BRAC director tells me this won't work, even if they can't fully explain why it won't work, they are probably right. So it's interesting from some of these "nos" how much you learn about "Why did they say no, what's wrong with it?"

8   MAPPING PROBLEM SPACES

Those people, the so-called evangelists of innovation, will always be small [in numbers]. They need to be small. If you had 300 people, and all 300 would run around with 900 ideas of innovation [laughs], it might not work. In Google, you can do that. I think you will be able to do that in a technical way. With Google or Apple you have a machine, you have a program, and it will act in a particular way. You give the 300 people one problem, and say: "All right, I want a solution within a year. You spend what you want; resources are no problem." Yes, you will get this for a technical problem. But you come to a village where you are taking each one's action, reaction, response, et cetera. Working with people, especially in innovation and development, is a completely different cup of soup or tea, is a different cup altogether than a technical problem.

—*Joe Madiath, founder of Gram Vikas*

In the previous chapter we had a deep look inside an organization's impact-creation logic. We saw how both innovation and scaling potentially contribute to transforming a weak impact-creation logic into a powerful green zone that generates significant impact. And we realized how the strength of a green zone in turn enables productive innovation and scaling. We have also discussed how the dynamics of innovation and scaling depend on particular characteristics of the three dimensions that define an organization's unique impact-creation logic. Our four featured organizations have very different missions and strategies, and thus innovation played different roles in their long-term trajectories. They also built very different organizational resources and capabilities. The two dimensions of mission/strategy and resources/capabilities are thus associated with very different innovation archetypes. But what is the role of problem spaces, the third dimension of an organization's impact-creation logic? What are the unique implications of different problem spaces for innovation and scaling? And can we map problem spaces systematically to improve our decisions about funding or enacting innovations?

Joe Madiath hints at the importance of seriously considering the particular characteristics of the problems and needs that an organization addresses. Only then can we understand and effectively decide on the roles and specifics of innovation for creating impact. The organizational trajectories of Aravind and Gram Vikas vividly illustrate this point. Preventing needless blindness by conducting cataract surgeries represents a drastically different problem space from confronting inequality or reversing tribal villagers' dependence on powerful moneylenders in rural Orissa. The two have vastly different implications for organizations.

Social enterprises and their supporters need to understand the nature of these problem spaces and how they are embedded in local realities. In our research we have found that the characteristics of problem spaces are important determinants of the options for impact creation available for social enterprises.[1]

In this chapter we draw from our case studies and introduce an analytical framework for mapping problem spaces. It captures important aspects of local realities and distinguishes between two broad categories of problems, technical and relational. The framework also captures the economic, cognitive, normative, and political barriers that organizations need to overcome if they want to create impact. Our objective here is to construct a framework that allows us to analyze and compare different problem spaces and to think more systematically about their implications for innovation and scaling.

Unfortunately, organizations in the development sector rarely consider the implications of the environmental characteristics—the local problem spaces—in a systematic way. This oversight can have detrimental effects. It can also lead to a bias toward technical innovations and implementing best practices. But these innovations and best practice solutions often remind us of Maslow's famous hammer: All poverty-related problems start looking like nails.

Microfinance is an example of such a "hammer." In the mid-2000s, it almost reached the status of a panacea for global poverty. The year 2005 was designated by the UN General Assembly as the International Year of Microcredit. In 2006, Muhammad Yunus and the Grameen Bank received the Nobel Peace Prize for their leadership in pioneering microfinance for development work. But critical assessments of outcomes show a very mixed picture.[2,3] Microfinance works differently in various environments: Sometimes it creates positive outcomes, but often it has negative unintended consequences. Clearly, these results are not due just to variance in microfinance implementations. They require consideration of environmental variance as well.

Unfortunately, the bias toward technical solutions has spread to university campuses too. At entrepreneurship centers around the world, young, motivated entrepreneurs design new poverty-targeting technologies typically after spending anytime up to three weeks in a developing country. "Disruptive solutions" are the new mantra! Solutions are sexy, and problems are mere annoyances that stand in the way of all these wonderful solutions. During recent discussions about solutions to stubborn problems of poverty a young student at a business school remarked: "Let's just do a hackathon!" Yet, poverty and poverty-associated problems persist.

We believe that people can make better investment and operational decisions by prioritizing a deep understanding of problem spaces instead of prioritizing solutions. To begin, we propose a diagnostic framework as a starting point for productive decisions on innovation and scaling.

FOUR DIMENSIONS SHAPE PROBLEM SPACES

Effective social enterprises invest significant time and effort in exploring and learning about the true nature of people's problems and needs. All four of our case study organizations have accumulated deep knowledge of the problem spaces they target. They all invested time and effort in examining and documenting factors that capture how problems manifest in people's lives on the ground. The studies of BRAC's research and evaluation division in the many aspects of village life in the 1970s and 1980s and Gram Vikas's studies of power dynamics in tribal villages in the 1980s are illustrative examples. Many of their decisions about innovation and scaling seem to have arisen from their accumulated knowledge of the factors that constitute the problem space of poverty in the communities that the organizations served.

In particular, they ask a crucial question that goes beyond merely identifying a problem or need as an opportunity for action: Why is this problem or need so persistent? Answers to this question produce better ideas for the development of effective interventions and solutions. The "mapping problem spaces" framework identifies a constellation of barriers that sustain poverty-associated problems and needs. Effective interventions must overcome these barriers to make progress and have any impact. Decisions about innovation and scaling thus need to target the barriers explicitly. In working with organizations more directly, we found it tremendously useful to separate the barriers that characterize problem spaces into four dimensions: economic, cognitive, normative, and political.

Economic Barriers

Economic barriers range from a lack of savings, disposable income, or insurance at the level of individuals to community-level barriers, including missing infrastructure and lack of access to markets. Economic factors are the most frequent characteristic of poverty that the development sector measures and uses as a defining criterion. Gross domestic production (GDP) per capita at the country level and income per person at the individual level are examples. Economic barriers prevent people from satisfying urgent needs, even if postponement has dramatically negative consequences. The inability to feed children adequately and to get essential health care are examples. Some barriers, such as a lack of savings or insurance, prevent people from allocating resources across time. These barriers make it difficult to act on temporary opportunities or to protect people during crises.

Aravind is a good example of working in a problem space in which economic factors are important barriers for effective solutions. Most poor people in Indian towns and particularly in rural villages cannot afford adequate health services even for life-threatening conditions. Lowering or eliminating economic barriers through efficiency, productivity, and cross-subsidization thus were hallmarks of Aravind's impact-creation logic.

Economic barriers may also sometimes mask other problems at a deeper level. For instance, the indebtedness of the tribal villages that Gram Vikas worked with in the 1980s seemed to be just economic problems. But—as the case study showed—bad economic outcomes were caused by power relations that kept the tribal villagers dependent on moneylenders. Focusing solely on economic factors would not solve the underlying relational problem, the asymmetric power dynamics between moneylenders and tribal villagers. Microfinance represents another solution that sometimes suffers from false problem specification and little systematic engagement with the problem space. Providing loans targets only the economic dimension of the problems of the poor. BRAC has learned how important it is to support a loan by proper training, creation of opportunities, and using social processes to prevent borrowers from making bad decisions. All these additional program areas target cognitive barriers. The mere provision of a loan ignores a crucial set of barriers that constitute the local problem space of poverty. The result is failed interventions.

Cognitive Barriers

Cognitive barriers refer to human reasoning and knowledge. They include a particular outlook on oneself and one's life. The permanence of poverty-associated problems is often taken for granted by poor communities. They may find workarounds for some problems but do not question their situation or perceive an opportunity for fundamental change. BRAC's efforts at conscientization targeted cognitive barriers. Based on ideas introduced by Paulo Freire, conscientization strives to enable people to realize and critically reflect on their situation and to devise ways to improve their lives. We would say it helps people diagnose their own problem spaces and the barriers that prevent them from making progress. This knowledge empowers them to act instead of just reacting.

TABLE 8.1
The architecture of problem spaces.

Technical problems/needs		Relational problems/needs	
Economic barriers	Cognitive barriers	Normative barriers	Political barriers
• Limited assets or savings • Lack of infrastructure • No access to markets • Inefficient intermediaries • Lack of essential products and services	• Low problem awareness • Opportunities not perceived • Unproductive habits • Superstition • Lack of skills • Lack of trust	• Traditions that reinforce and legitimize the status quo • Stifling class, status, and gender distinctions • Unsettling customs (for example, forced marriage, female genital mutilation)	• Private objectives of powerful actors • Inefficient or discriminatory policies • Corruption • Tribal disputes or violence

Cognitive barriers also include a lack of skills, trust, and hope that generates a state of lethargy. An inability to learn objectively prevents communities from accumulating valid knowledge that could support progress and lead to smarter decisions over time. Superstitious explanations of events often justify and sustain the old ways. All of these barriers sustain an undesirable status quo.

Economic and cognitive barriers have closely related implications for innovation and scaling, as we will see in the next section. We find it useful to group problems and needs that are sustained by predominantly economic or cognitive barriers as technical problems (see Table 8.1).

Normative Barriers

Normative barriers refer to what are seen as appropriate roles and behavior in a society or in a local community. They are deeply grounded in societal and community values, norms, and traditions. Religious beliefs, ancient traditions, and social habits are powerful structural forces that prescribe how members of a community behave and relate to each other. Normative barriers are an important factor to understand the problem space in which Gram Vikas operates in India: inequality in villages in rural Orissa. Norms and traditions anchored in religion, as well as local systems of patriarchy and kinship, shape the daily lives of both advantaged and disadvantaged people in a community. What makes these barriers particularly challenging is that the norms and customs at their core are taken for granted and deeply entrenched in the daily lives of the inhabitants.

Equally, BRAC in Bangladesh faces important normative barriers in its home territory. Each intervention BRAC designs has to factor in how the solution resonates with local communities and local customs. Often the solutions proactively integrate local customs. For example, in its human rights initiatives, BRAC builds on local and historical traditions of theater play to communicate and implement its programs.[4] It also encountered a series of normative barriers in the early days of microfinance. Bangladeshis did not think it was appropriate for women to engage in transactional activities involving money, to participate in market-based activities, and to earn income. Each program and intervention related to microfinance had to factor in such local normative proscriptions.

Political Barriers

A fourth type of barrier is political. Political barriers include power asymmetries as well as the ambiguity, absence, or weakness of formal rules and regulatory arrangements. Poor people are the most vulnerable. They often lack actual or formal rights and are liable to abuses by powerful actors. The aggression and violence that BRAC staff experienced in some of their international operations outside of Bangladesh are examples of this dimension of problem spaces.

The abuse of tribespeople by liquor sellers and the designated roles of lower-caste people in rural villages were crucial barriers that Gram Vikas had to overcome. They severely challenged the organization's innovations and efforts to achieve scale.

Persistent problems that are primarily due to normative or political barriers often provide similar challenges for innovation and scaling. We thus group them into the broad category of relational problems. Table 8.1 summarizes characteristics of technical and relational problems and needs and the barriers that sustain them.

Identifying the essential barriers that define a problem is a prerequisite for designing adequate and efficient solutions. It should also be a start-

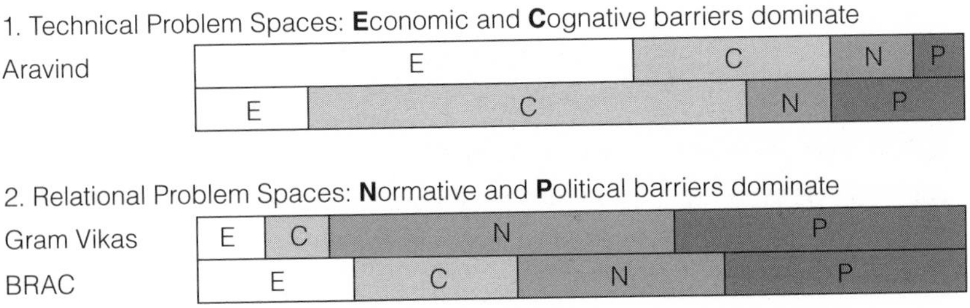

1. Technical Problem Spaces: **E**conomic and **C**ognative barriers dominate

2. Relational Problem Spaces: **N**ormative and **P**olitical barriers dominate

FIGURE 8.1
Maps of problem spaces of our featured organizations.

ing point for evaluating interventions, particularly when we are comparing the performance of different innovations or organizations. Perceived performance is a function of organizational and environmental factors. Performance should be evaluated for the efficiency and effectiveness of a particular social enterprise and—perhaps even more—for the particular type of need an organization caters to and in which environment. We often underestimate how different the particular barriers for seemingly similar problems actually are.[5] Figure 8.1 illustrates what a rough high-level map of the problem spaces targeted by the four organizations featured in this book might look like.

The purpose of the mapping exercise is not to simplify complex needs into purely technical or relational categories. Rather, mapping is intended to illustrate the overall pattern of barriers that generate and sustain particular needs in people and communities. BRAC, for instance, has a much wider scope than the other organizations and does not serve needs only where relational barriers dominate. It also serves more technical needs, particularly with its social enterprise programs. BRAC's innovation archetype "innovation for transformative impact" requires that the organization target all dimensions that shape problem spaces concomitantly. Transformative impact results from this broad set of interventions across technical and relational barriers.

The problem space maps in Figure 8.1 show what the output of an internal exercise at the organizational level or program level might look like. Discussions that unearth rich detail about the four barriers then enable an organization to reach a shared and transparent understanding about the distinct nature of the needs that it targets.

HOW DOES A PROBLEM SPACE MAP INFORM DECISIONS ABOUT INNOVATION AND SCALING?

The distinction between technical and relational problems matters for social enterprises because the two categories of problems are associated with different levels of resistance to change. Let's start by looking at a technical problem with dominant economic barriers that could be effectively and quickly solved by providing economic resources, at least in principle. For example, Aravind's extremely efficient health service model dramatically reduced economic barriers. But doing so was insufficient. Poor rural patients were skeptical and did not demand surgery even if it was free. Cognitive barriers prevented them from adequately assessing the opportunity to restore their eyesight. Four crucial mechanisms enabled Aravind to overcome cognitive and economic barriers and to achieve rapid adoption by patients:

1. There was no ambiguity about positive outcomes. Regaining eyesight was an objectively positive outcome. The technical superiority of Aravind's approach generated low variance in outcomes. Consequently, all eye surgeries had the same positive outcome for all patients.

2. Success was observable within twenty-four hours after surgery. Speed made it easier for patients to connect the two events causally. There was no doubt that the positive outcome was an effect of the surgery and not of some other mysterious cause. Aravind thus accrued the trust and goodwill of poor patients.

3. Cataract surgery works the same on the eyes of Indian, African, and European patients. It makes no difference what religion a patient follows, whether she is rich or poor, or what caste she belongs to. If the right procedure is followed, a beneficial outcome for her is ensured.

4. Investment in scaling and deepening its green zone enabled Aravind to significantly widen the gap between the impact it created for pay-

ing and nonpaying patients and the costs of delivering this impact. Aravind could thus capture a part of the large gap as profits that allowed investment in both scaling and delivering free high-quality surgery within the same business model.

It may not always be possible to design such "ideal" conditions for targeting economic and cognitive barriers. In general, technical problems permit faster scaling because barriers are observable and can be lowered rapidly, demand can often be generated quickly, and scaling—in the sense of doing more of the same—produces positive feedback on the quality and economics of the solution through learning and efficiency effects. Because outcomes—both positive and negative—can be directly observed, errors can be identified and corrected, often immediately. New ideas can be rapidly tested and evaluated. Scaling is easier because the effects of incremental changes and improvements from ongoing error correction or introduction of small new ideas are all observable and positive. Small changes accumulate and positively affect the economic and quality aspects of solutions and thus their potential scale and impact. Aravind owes much of its tremendous success to focusing on technical problems. Its leaders are extremely hesitant to collaborate with the public and corporate sectors, both of which could introduce normative and political barriers beyond their control. The failure of Aravind's managed care program illustrates the uncertainty created by a departure from this strategy.

Relational problems have very different implications for innovation and scaling, as Gram Vikas illustrates. The barriers to change for an issue such as inequality based on gender and social status are persistent. Values, norms, and traditions do not change overnight. In addition, change is not perceived as good by powerful stakeholders who have an interest in maintaining the status quo. Positive outcomes may not be visible for a long time. To target relational problems, social enterprises need to engage much more deeply, much more directly, and over much longer time with people and communities than for technical problems. Even with its optimized program, which has absorbed decades of experience, Gram Vikas faces three years of deep engagement with a village before visible and enduring changes take place in the ways people relate to each other.

Relational problems thus stand in stark contrast to technical problems. In general, innovation is much more difficult for relational problems. Positive outcomes may not be visible for a long time, and therefore real-time error correction is not possible. Furthermore, any innovation errors or failures might damage the trust and legitimacy that are essential for enacting change. These negative consequences of failures dramatically increase the overall risk of innovation. Slow feedback between actions and outcomes limits explicit and fast learning and knowledge accumulation. Scaling dynamics are therefore generally much slower for relational problems. The difficulties of codifying interventions based on deep hands-on engagement and of observing how they work also limit their replicability. Because deep environmental knowledge and the accumulation of intangibles such as trust are essential, innovations may not work in other environments or require the same difficult approach to slow and careful learning about the particularities of a new environment. Table 8.2 summarizes some implications of problem spaces for innovation and scaling.

The case studies of BRAC and Gram Vikas offer potentially fruitful options for strategizing about dealing with relational problems. Their experiences imply that it may not be effective to target relational problems directly if your organization is inexperienced and lacks a substantial green zone. Engagement with communities about relational problems requires knowledge about the barriers that generate and sustain an undesired status quo. Gram Vikas's tribal work demonstrated the importance of earning a community's trust to facilitate this learning. The organization has also learned that, for communities to open their minds and hearts for relational issues, Gram Vikas needed to meet more fundamental personal needs, such as health or water, first. Fortunately, these needs have stronger technical characteristics. Following are some pointers for organizations that target relational problems.

FIND AN ACCESS POINT TO PEOPLE AND COMMUNITIES THAT SOLVES A TECHNICAL PROBLEM. This creates quick benefits and earns trust and legitimacy. Gram Vikas's biogas innovation is a good example. It required that the organization temporarily define an impact-creation logic

TABLE 8.2

How technical and relational problems matter for innovation and scaling.

Technical problems/needs	Relational problems/needs
Economic and cognitive barriers dominate.	Normative and political barriers dominate.
Barriers are malleable.	Barriers are persistent.
Status quo is taken for granted.	Status quo is desirable to powerful actors.
Change is likely to be perceived as beneficial.	Change is likely to be perceived as threat.
Change can be quickly enacted by demonstration effects, training, or resource provision.	Change is slow because of enduring power structures or deep-rooted norms and traditions.
Benefits tend to materialize quickly.	Benefits may not be perceived for a long time.
Errors can be observed and corrected, thus facilitating fast learning and improvement.	Errors may quickly destroy relational assets such as trust and legitimacy that are built over a long time; learning is difficult and slow.
Innovation is less risky and requires less direct interaction with the poor.	Innovation is risky and requires hands-on, relational interventions over a long time.
Technical solutions are easy to codify to enable replication.	Relational solutions are difficult to codify, context-specific, and hard to replicate.
Scaling is likely to be fast and mainly limited by resources.	Scaling may be slow and remain local; resources may not be the limiting factor.
Replication is facilitated by the possibility of ongoing error correction, observation of outcomes, and fast learning and adaptation.	Replication is difficult because of unclear causality, the potential of any errors to destroy trust, and drawn-out learning curves.

that departed from its original sense of mission. Even its final MANTRA innovation was "sold" to villages as a technical problem concerning water and toilets. Gram Vikas focused the attention of communities on the desirable technical solution and thus lowered their awareness of the subtle relational changes that took place in the background. Over time, solving relational problems was eased by the momentum and attractiveness of the ongoing technical work. Organizations with a more pragmatic identity and set of values are in a better position to enact this logic.

USE THE DELIVERY OF TECHNICAL SOLUTIONS TO LEARN ABOUT
BARRIERS AND TO BUILD SCALING CAPABILITIES. Delivery of objective
benefits that are acceptable to most of the people in a community is required
before you can engage with them on a relational level. Development workers
often underestimate the distrust of foreigners who come with promises of
help. The distrust may be a result of accumulated abuse by powerful people
or groups. It may also be the result of failed and abandoned projects by
development organizations or the public sector. Thousands of abandoned
and unusable toilets in rural India that remained from large-scale public
sanitation programs bear witness to that. Distrust and lack of hope are
among the most severe unintended consequences of innovation failures in
development work. Because technical innovations allow faster learning and
scaling, they help with building relations and learning about the complex
set of barriers that determine people's lives. Technical innovations, which
can generally be adopted at lower levels of uncertainty than relational
innovations, are a necessary route to acquiring vital resources—trust and
goodwill, lower uncertainty about the types and relative importance of
barriers, and even income—that permit subsequent work on relational
issues, which is often slow to generate positive results and difficult to
sustain financially. Technical innovations and fast scaling generate goodwill,
objective data for impact reports, and a good reputation among funders.
Reputation may be a crucial asset required to take on difficult relational
problems, whose slower dynamics may stretch the motivation of social
enterprises and funders to keep supporting your efforts.

ISOLATE TECHNICAL BARRIERS FROM RELATIONAL BARRIERS. Even
if your organization already understands relational barriers, it must build
up its resources before it can start targeting them. BRAC isolated technical
dimensions of community problems when its research division was already
aware of the importance of power dynamics in the villages its leaders targeted.
But BRAC had neither the trust, legitimacy, nor organizational capabilities
to take on political barriers. To build momentum and resources, BRAC
started working exclusively with groups of women with similar status and
backgrounds on issues of microfinance, health, and education. Separating
technical from relational barriers helped BRAC innovate a new program

around property rights: "According to Islamic law the daughter gets only half of what her brothers get. We think it is wrong, but we accepted that. We don't do advocacy. For me this was very hard to accept, but at BRAC we are pragmatic about these things." Thus BRAC's innovation design revolved around helping women secure the little property that they were entitled to. Once this plan succeeds, at a later stage BRAC might slowly target the relational aspects that treat women unfairly.

By pragmatically focusing on technical problem aspects, your organization can build momentum and generate measurable benefits, which can motivate both internal and external stakeholders. Gram Vikas's focus on relational problems during the first ten years illustrates the challenge of building and sustaining an organization and preventing people from leaving. The work is hard, and the many setbacks easily frustrate even the most committed staff.

Bad decisions about innovation and scaling often arise from the misperception of a relational problem as a technical problem or vice versa. Funders put pressure on Gram Vikas to scale faster and to innovate more:

Gram Vikas can go for heady numbers—by building toilets and bathing rooms only for those who can afford them and who want them—or it can go through the painful process of getting 100 percent participation from every family in the village and thus transform the lives of everyone in the community. With our process, every person—from the first to the last woman in line—gets the same type of toilet, bathing room, and three taps [kitchen, toilet, and bathing room] with around-the-clock supply of potable drinking water. All this is accomplished mostly through the people's efforts with some financial assistance from the government and Gram Vikas. For this to happen, however, a lot of facilitation, hand-holding, and patience are required in great measure.

Knowledge about the general implications of mapping problem spaces for innovation and scaling, combined with deep environmental knowledge about particular problems or needs, lets organizations make much better decisions about intervention design, expected outcomes, measures, and realistic time scales. We suggest that our framework has great potential for funders as well. Understanding the nature of problem spaces that an organization targets permits better appreciation of how best to support an organization and what types of results may be reasonably expected. This mapping also leads to much more systematic learning by organizations because it explicitly relates the particular problem spaces that they target to the other two dimensions of their impact-creation logic in a way that encourages continuous learning and strategizing.

CONCLUSION

A Guide to Productive Innovation
and Scaling for Impact

We have come a long way since we started our inquiry. We took a probing look into several of the most successful and enduring social enterprises to understand how they integrated innovation and scaling in their organizational trajectories. Did we find a smoking gun? No. What the case studies indicate is that we should have no illusions about easy recipes.

Productive innovation, scaling, and creating positive impact are complicated and difficult. Deriving useful insights requires investing time and effort to deeply understand organizations and their environments. Quick fixes for making organizations more "innovative" are not helpful. "Boring" organizations may not innovate much, but if they execute well-weathered routine work to deliver mature, reliable, and predictable solutions to people's problems, they will create significant impact. Unfortunately, routine work doesn't make for exciting stories. As a result, optimistic accounts of these organizations tend to blank out their day-to-day activities. Often, they focus only on the characteristics of the leaders of these organizations or casually assume that they are indeed innovative. Either way, such accounts draw biased conclusions about how impact is created in the social sector.

We have tried to paint a realistic picture of innovation as an organizational process with distinct characteristics. We took a deep dive into the real world of organizations and their environment to find opportunities for relevant learning. We strongly believe that pragmatic, unidealized knowledge improves decisions about innovation and scaling and creates more positive impact. Fantasies about innovation as a magic pill against poverty do not solve any problems. Rather, they may create new problems by allocating funds to the wrong organizations or the wrong types of activities.

Important change and fundamental improvements often result from individually unremarkable small steps over long periods of time. We wonder how much rapid change organizations and communities can absorb. Perhaps small changes are easier to integrate into the lives of poor communities and organizations than big ones. This is a particularly important consideration for organizations that focus on nontechnical needs and problems. We have shown that these problems are created and sustained by strong relational mechanisms. Productive interventions thus require building trust, rapport, and influence. All of these need to be carefully and patiently built. Small steps can be enacted within an organization's green zone to generate steady, reliable progress. Achieving pronounced change does not necessarily require innovation, as is sometimes falsely assumed. Often, all that you need is patience, focus, and commitment.

RECOMMENDATIONS FOR ORGANIZATIONS AND THEIR SUPPORTERS

In this final chapter we summarize insights from our own learning journey and translate them into concrete recommendations for organizations and their funders, partners, consultants, and other supporters and observers. The most important insight is that every organization operates from some form of implicit impact-creation logic. Unfortunately, very few have a impact-creation logic that is clearly articulated with deep accumulation of knowledge in all three dimensions, as illustrated in Figure 1.1. Few social enterprises have a green zone that drives generating impact through scaling. Pouring effort and resources into innovation makes little sense for most of them. As we said in Chapter 7: "If you don't know how to scale, don't innovate!"

Seriously considering our first three recommendations will help you establish an impact-creation logic and nurture it into a powerful green zone. This is the right basis for considering our subsequent recommendations for beginning a journey toward productive innovation and scaling for impact. As discussed in Chapter 2, productive innovation primarily means three things: (1) to objectively and explicitly learn from innovation failures, because this knowledge reduces the uncertainties of subsequent innovations and informs an organization's impact-creation logic; (2) to efficiently build well-developed innovation assets, because these generate more impact and fewer problems in subsequent scaling efforts; and (3) to create more impact from innovation assets through a strong focus on scaling and building and nurturing a green zone.

1. Don't Try to Be Innovative; Create Impact.

We recommend that organizations push back against funders and other stakeholders who press them to innovate more. And we recommend that funders and other supporters replace their ideology of innovation with a keen sense of how organizations create impact. How can they do it? By keeping an eye on the long-term journeys of organizations and the many trials and tribulations they go through to build and operate from a successful impact-creation logic and by valuing the unique individuality of organizations, their specific trajectories, and the idiosyncrasies of their impact-creation logics.

Most social enterprises are not good at innovation. Perhaps they should focus less on it. Innovation may not deliver what communities really need. In developing countries, the poorest communities often operate in a mode of day-to-day survival. Decisions are short term and opportunistic, revolving around satisfying basic needs and desires. In such an environment, organizational characteristics such as trust, reliability, predictability, and long-term commitment may be much more aligned with the needs and realities of a community than innovation, novelty, and change.

Instead of building an artificial and unauthentic perception of "innovativeness," we propose that social enterprises invest serious work in three domains: (1) realistically reflecting on and establishing who they really are and what they aspire to (mission and strategy), (2) critically assessing what they can and cannot do well (resources and capabilities) and where they need to improve, and (3) evaluating and strengthening their understanding of the problems that they hope to solve (problem spaces).

In other words, organizations need to clearly define and strengthen the three dimensions of their impact-creation logic. And they need to make sure that this logic is shared within the organization. Creating perceptions of innovativeness to get grants and gain visibility does little to build and strengthen an impact-creation logic.

Organizations have shared with us their hopes that funders and supporters will invest more time and effort in learning about them and their environments. The usual transactional relations of grants for impact reports do little beyond nurturing unrealistic assumptions and expectations. Perhaps it makes more sense if funders learn to justify their investments not so much by impact reports but instead by the quality of their assessments of the organizations that they fund. As we pointed out in Chapter 7, organizations have comparative advantages for particular ideas, needs, or environments. Better investment decisions require a better understanding of these links. Funders and supporters often have relationships with many organizations. They are in a privileged position to learn systematically and to generate and aggregate insights across their portfolios. They also need to consider the particular challenges and consequences for organizations that attack technical or relational problems.

2. Embrace "Overhead," Invest in Organizational Infrastructure.

We recommend increasing investments in organizational infrastructure and viewing "overhead" more seriously and positively. We are concerned about the attitudes of funders who demand more "impact for their bucks" and thus reduce overhead expenses to a minimum. Only organizations can build impact-creation logics and shape them into productive green zones. Enacting this potential requires investing in efficient organizational infrastructure. That takes time and dedicated effort.

In the social sector, too many hopes rest on the shoulders of a heroic individual as innovator and leader. But impact requires organizations, not individuals. Many organizations rely on charismatic leaders instead of building structures and processes that complement them and also function without them. And too many social enterprises seem to be (at most) just the sum of their individual parts. They are stuck with weak impact-creation logics that create little impact and never improve. We recommend investing less in individuals with innovative ideas and more in building the organizational infrastructure required for developing and nurturing green zones. The potential of past innovations has to be translated into real impact through focused scaling. And green zones ensure that ideas for improvements or innovations are generated when the time is right and then productively developed and executed.

Many effective social enterprises demonstrate surprising creativity in establishing organizational infrastructure. They integrate and operate a variety of organizational structures and substructures. Among our featured organizations, BRAC, Waste Concern, and Aravind have adopted multiple organizational elements. These include typical specialized departments for research, monitoring and evaluation, and training. But they also include businesses and business-like entities such as BRAC's and Waste Concern's social enterprises or Aravind's manufacturing company Aurolab. They enable the coexistence of different organizational cultures and areas of specialization in support of an overall shared mission. They span for-profit and not-for-profit ideologies and enable access to a variety of capital and nonfinancial resources. They comprise legal structures that range from formal NGOs to companies under a single roof. What keeps the parts aligned is a shared sense of identity, focus and direction, and an understanding of its particular role within the larger organization. Organizational infrastructure is an essential mechanism for developing and strengthening green zones to allow more efficient scaling.

3. Organize for Impact: Constructive Dissatisfaction and Constructive Suspicion.

We recommend that social enterprises nurture two useful attitudes, constructive dissatisfaction and constructive suspicion. These attitudes provide the necessary fuel for pushing an organization to develop and deepen or broaden its green zone. They seem to be a hallmark of impactful organizations. We also recommend that funders and organizations go beyond impact reports and integrate *lack-of-impact* reports in their communications that reflect these two attitudes.

Our featured organizations paid close attention to organizing. By *organizing*, we refer to the way an organization is governed and the central values and beliefs from which it operates. Impactful organizations constantly raise their ambitions and compare them with objective data of current performance. Because they share an attitude of constructive dissatisfaction, our featured organizations never seem to exaggerate the status quo or their current levels of performance, even though all of them have created substantial impact. Rather, they constantly raise the bar and then focus on the gap between ambition and status quo. They keep searching for ideas to do more and to get better.

BRAC used its famous "field marshal" to keep raising targets in all its program areas. Aravind in its strategy retreats sets ambitious growth targets and tasks the organization to find creative ways of meeting them. Gram Vikas spends almost all of its time and effort in direct relations with villages. It is painfully aware of both its positive impact in the villages where it succeeded and the thousands of villages that are still waiting to be served. Waste Concern, with its researcher's lens, is closely engaged with communities and with the private and public sectors. It constantly seeks to identify social and environmental problems that are not being solved by market mechanisms or public sector efforts. This search fuels a motivation to keep investing in new R&D projects. Waste Concern's founders are also networked on a global scale and push themselves to find more opportunities to diffuse their innovations outside Bangladesh.

All the managers and staff in our featured organizations spend significant time directly experiencing the realities of the people and communities they serve. Their emotional engagement seems to be the primary fuel behind the motivation to keep raising the bar. The attitude of constructive dissatisfaction creates a self-reinforcing dynamic. On one hand, it enables efficient scaling by pushing an organization toward serving more people better. On the other hand, the knowledge accumulation that comes from focused scaling further strengthens an organization's green zone.

The second attitude we recommend that social enterprises nurture is constructive suspicion: keeping a close eye on actual performance, not just in light of formal targets and objectives but asking questions such as: "What is not working? Do we really create impact? What do we not know?" BRAC uses its research unit to explore questions such as: "Do our microfinance services really reach the poorest?" Aravind regularly asks, "How many people in our region actually have access to eye care?"

In a way, these organizations seem to wear a prototyping lens even when they scale. They never assume that their products and services are fully developed. They divide attention equally between two areas: (1) a focus on success, knowing how enacting existing knowledge creates impact, and (2) a focus on failure, assuming that something is missing, or something is not yet really working as well as it could.

Constructive suspicion is a great impetus for gathering objective and more complete data—not just the data that demonstrate success but those that indicate gaps and problems with current efforts. We therefore recommend that organizations and funders go beyond exchanging data in the form of impact reports. Experienced organizations that nurture the attitudes of constructive dissatisfaction and constructive suspicion seem to create significant value through lack-of-impact reports. All of our featured organizations have used such reports in a number of formats: white papers, formal internal reports, reports to funders, or even papers published in scholarly journals. This is where crucial learning for organizations, funders, and policy makers comes from. It generates ideas for improvements and triggers focused searches for innovative ideas that are grounded in solid problem frames. BRAC's design of specialized programs targeting the ultra-poor is an example. Waste Concern's explorations into areas that are ignored by the public sector and by markets also illustrate this attitude.

4. Don't Just Innovate, Innovate Productively.

Is there a more general pathway to productive innovation for established organizations? We recommend that organizations start with a serious effort to overcome their illusion of understanding by realistically defining what innovation is and what roles they expect innovation to play for strengthening their impact-creation logics. Then they can dispel their illusion of competence by identifying and targeting their innovation pathologies.

Productive innovation in established organizations requires that people can develop innovative ideas without being stifled by derailing forces of their organization's immune system that give rise to innovation pathologies. It also requires that an organization be able to create impact from successful innovations by building and deepening their capabilities for scaling. Innovation and scaling thus form an important bond: they are part of a continuous overall innovation process (see Figure 2.1), and they depend and influence each other in important ways.

Diagnosing innovation pathologies (see Chapter 2) is the best way to ensure that fewer organizational resources are wasted on innovation failures that do not create benefits for an organization and its constituencies. Productive innovation also makes learning from failure and success more cumulative and relevant. Our insights about how productive innovation expands the green zone, in Chapter 7, offer a route to less risky innovation because knowledge accumulation enables organizations to create better ideas, to evaluate ideas more accurately, and to pilot and scale ideas within a potent organizational infrastructure. All of these characteristics of green zones enable organizations to create more value from past innovations and also enable new productive innovations.

Here are some potential milestones and tips for your journey toward productive innovation:

1. Start by removing the illusion of understanding. Ask some unusual and uncomfortable questions, such as: "What exactly is our impact-creation logic?" "Do we have a green zone?" "How do we know?" "How does innovation help achieve our mission?" Our frameworks in Chapter 1 and Chapter 7 will support your inquiry. Aim to clarify and align the language and mental models within your organization about the nature of innovation and scaling and how they link to impact-creation. Don't just assume that innovation is a better way to create impact. Both green and red zones offer opportunities for progress and impact but with very different potentials and challenges for organizations.

2. As a next step, we suggest removing the illusion of competence. Map your organization's innovation pathologies. Make sure to have board-level commitment and external support in moderating the mapping exercise. The presence of a respected and neutral external moderator helps to avoid senior managers' domination of the discussions or stifling open conversations during the workshop. An

innovation pathology workshop generates an atmosphere of constructive dissatisfaction with the status quo. As discussed before, this attitude is crucial for raising the bar and generating ideas when business as usual is not sufficient to achieve objectives. Understand which pathologies define who you are and are thus integral parts of your impact-creation logic as we have discussed in Chapter 7. Avoid breaking an organization's sense of mission by targeting these defining pathologies directly. The current efforts by the new management of Gram Vikas to make the organization more "innovative" may illustrate this mistake. Only time will tell.

3. Efforts to overcome the illusions of understanding and competence create a new realism about innovation and your organization. It can help you clarify the purpose of innovation and scaling in relation to your long-term ambitions. The objective at this stage is to start a more strategic inquiry and adopt an innovation archetype that clarifies how innovation and scaling build and nurture a green zone over time. Your innovation archetype depends on where you are starting from.

If you are an inexperienced organization, you don't really have a distinct and deep green zone. Building one should be your primary objective. You may, for example, adopt an "innovation as learning" archetype to generate knowledge in critical dimensions of your impact-creation logic. Avoid starting too many innovations. You may not have the resources to develop several innovations in parallel or within a short time frame. You are also unlikely to absorb all the potential knowledge they could provide. Trying to scale immature innovations that have not been carefully piloted and developed generates severe downstream problems.

Instead, make an effort to convert one innovation into a green zone. Focus on a more technical problem (see Chapter 8), for example biogas in the case of Gram Vikas or microfinance and education in the case of BRAC. Targeting technical problems helps to build momentum. It sharpens focus and leads to a faster realization of benefits. Scaling builds organizational capabilities and creates impact. The story of Gram Vikas illustrates the transformative effect of scaling on organizations. Scaling affects organizations internally, by increasing self-confidence and motivation. And it also transforms how an organization is perceived by external stakeholders. Building a reputation as an organization that can deliver generates trust with local communities and a deeper insight into the local problem spaces that characterize poverty. The resulting improved problem frames help create more relevant ideas for subsequent innovations aimed at deepening or broadening a green zone (see Chapter 7).

If you are an experienced organization, you already have a green zone. Adopting an innovation archetype depends on how you want to shape your green zone going forward. Our case studies offer us three options.

NARROW AND DEEP GREEN ZONES   Gram Vikas and Aravind focus on getting good at one or a few interventions by catering to a distinct problem or need. Scaling capabilities are the key, and innovation is driven by the need to make a green zone deeper. Limited organizational resources and problems that are grounded in tough economics (for example, patients who cannot pay) are particularly suited for this type of green zone. Similarly, problems that require organizations to build trust and a positive reputation fit this category.

BROAD AND DEEP GREEN ZONES   BRAC focuses on increasing the organization's scope to target a broader set of needs. It requires more innovation and innovation in different areas. This archetype necessitates expanded organizational resources. Otherwise, innovations might reduce performance by reallocating scarce resources employed in green zone activities. Building an effective organizational infrastructure is the key. It reduces innovation uncertainties quickly and systematically, maximizes learning effects, and ensures that resources and capabilities are available for scaling multiple innovations.

BROAD AND RELATIVELY THIN GREEN ZONES   Waste Concern focuses on increasing scope by adopting multiple innovations. The absence of scaling capacities requires reliance on other organizations to create impact from these innovations. This archetype supports small organizations with few resources that are motivated by creating the potential for impact and less by creating impact directly themselves.

4. Create an awareness of the types of ideas for which your organization has a comparative advantage (see Chapter 7). You will reduce risk and create impact by filtering out ideas that are unlikely to work. Knowing when to say "no" is the key, because the innovation pathology of "too many bad ideas" has severe negative consequences for resource-constrained organizations. Saying "no" is not always easy for organizations that face a myriad of important needs and problems of poor communities. Recognizing an explicit innovation archetype helps your organization decide whether it can productively take on scale-expanding ideas, those that deepen and strengthen green zones, or scope-expanding ideas, those that broaden green zones.

5. Organizations, funders, and supporters need to keep an eye on the "too many bad ideas" pathology. Organizations with strong green zones are very clear about which ideas fit their needs. This clarity often reduces the use of objective and formal idea evaluation processes. As a consequence, bad ideas, perhaps suggested by external partners and funders who do not understand the nature of an organization's green zone, may have an easier entry channel into organizations. It is much easier to say *no* to internal ideas than to those from influential external partners. Examples of this pathology in action are Aravind's adoption of managed care and BRAC's move into international markets. (Because the latter "innovation" is still ongoing, we cannot conclude that it indeed was a bad idea.) Taking more risk and thus occasionally adopting bad ideas is okay if you can live with the consequences of failure or if you have the capacity, experience, and staying power to make it work. A large organization with abundant resources, such as BRAC, can take more risk than a smaller, resource-constrained organization such as Aravind or Gram Vikas.

6. Before you consider creating innovative ideas for tackling particular problems, deeply engage with the communities you intend to serve. They may have ideas of their own that inform your decisions in very productive and sometimes unexpected ways. Look

around and search for instances where similar problems have been addressed by other organizations. Carefully evaluate whether you could adopt their solution rather than developing an innovative idea from scratch. Reflect deeply on the differences between their impact-creation logic and that of your organization. Is the problem they are solving the same one you are facing? Mapping problem spaces carefully using the framework in Chapter 8 helps to answer that question. Do you have or can you build the required capabilities to adopt their solution and to scale it? Is their solution compatible with your value system and sense of identity? Even if the answer to some of these questions is negative, it will pay off to have a deep conversation with organizations that have solved or attempted to solve a problem related to your innovation challenge. Some of their experience might help to reduce uncertainties and load the innovation dice in your favor.

LET'S GIVE ORGANIZATIONS AN INNOVATION BREAK! We hope that our bias is clear by now: We suggest that organizations and their supporters focus much more on green zones than on red zones. Scaling, not innovation, is the key to impact for the organizations we have studied: mature social enterprises that provide products, services, or interventions to poor communities in developing countries. Scaling may be even harder and more demanding for organizations than innovating. Finding enough people who are willing and able to create productive, committed, enduring organizations seems to be a critical bottleneck for development. We reiterate our previous statement: All organizations have an impact-creation logic, but too few have a green zone. We suggest deemphasizing demands on social enterprises to be more "innovative"—let's give them a break from innovation and help them to focus on the tough work of organizing for impact.

The "innovation break" also refers to another viewpoint. We ought to move away from thinking of innovation as a tool for better and faster impact and reducing social enterprises to mere instruments for solving societies' problems. It may be more productive to value innovations for other things than their potential to create impact.

Two important alternative angles come to mind. First, in the social sector we tend to undervalue the importance of failed innovation. Gram Vikas illustrates this pitfall. If we measure innovation only by positive impact, we risk dismissing the crucial learnings of Gram Vikas from failed innovations. From this experience, the organization eventually found a solution that worked. If we measure progress only by positive impact reports, we risk undersupplying the difficult and slow work of targeting relational problems. In many ways, relational problems may be the ultimate frontier of development work.

And second, some level of innovation in organizations is important for what we call organizational hygiene. Innovation can create a feeling of being alive, inspiration, motivation, and opportunities for personal growth and development for the members of an organization. These benefits are valuable, independent of innovation's potential for impact. This perspective on innovation is important for balancing and fine-tuning green zones. A prolonged focus on scaling risks reducing an organization's staff to productivity factors. The green zone risks turning into an iron cage. The danger is that the organization will become uninspiring, exhausting, and rigid, unable to change and renew itself. The Aravind eye hospital works its staff extremely hard by focusing on relentlessly scaling its health services. Recently, it held a workshop entitled "Innovation as Rejuvenation" to consider this dynamic. Although it may not be ready to provide space for an "innovation playground," at least it is aware of the problem. We strongly feel that a certain level of innovation is required to keep an organization "young" and effective, independent of its concrete outcomes.

An Invitation

We began our learning journey by asking, "How, under what circumstances, and with what consequences do social enterprises pursue innovation and scaling?" Our review of the literature found little systematic research on this particular topic. To find answers, we went into the field and studied the current operations and past trajectories of several social enterprises. We also tapped into the organizational innovation literature that focused on the business sector for inspiration.

Perhaps the principal weakness of our research design was to study successful organizations. Our choice somewhat limits the usefulness of our findings because no one can really do what these organizations do. Impact-creation logics are always unique constellations of "soft" and "hard" organizational elements. They are shaped over time through hard and smart work and cannot be set up by design. To continue our research journey, we feel that fruitful progress may come from studying organizations that are not considered particularly successful, organizations that cannot change and innovate or scale efficiently and thus keep underperforming. What are the prevailing patterns of specific pathologies that hold them back? How can we change them productively? If we can't, can we find ways to allocate more resources explicitly to organizations that have fewer pathologies, in the same way we withdraw resources in competitive markets from firms that don't perform?

This book summarizes our current understanding of the links among innovation, scaling, and impact. We see it as a temporary knowledge plateau on our learning journey. We invite you to help develop our knowledge on these issues. Much exciting future work will correct, contextualize, and expand our insights and make them more useful for practice.

NOTES

INTRODUCTION

1. Ashoka. "What is a social entrepreneur?" Retrieved on February 3, 2015, from www.ashoka.org/social_entrepreneur.

2. *The Economist*. "Social innovation: Let's hear those ideas." August 12, 2010.

3. PBS. "The new heroes." Retrieved on July 25, 2015, from www.pbs.org/opb/thenewheroes.

4. *Christian Science Monitor*. "Bill Drayton sees a world where 'everyone is a changemaker.'" Retrieved on July 20, 2015, from www.csmonitor.com/World/Making-a-difference/Change-Agent/2011/0516/Bill-Drayton-sees-a-world-where-everyone-is-a-changemaker.

5. Christian Seelos and Johanna Mair. 2012. "What determines the capacity for continuous innovation in social sector organizations?" *PACS Report to the Rockefeller Foundation*. Stanford, CA: Stanford University.

6. Eric Schmidt and Jonathan Rosenberg. 2014. *How Google Works*. New York: Grand Central Publishing.

CHAPTER 1

1. Leonid Rozenblit and Frank Keil. 2002. "The misunderstood limits of folk science: an illusion of explanatory depth." *Cognitive Science* 26(5): 521–562.

2. Candice M. Mills and Frank C. Keil. 2004. "Knowing the limits of one's understanding: The development of an awareness of an illusion of explanatory depth." *Journal of Experimental Child Psychology* 87(1): 1–32.

3. Richard A. Wolfe. 1994. "Organizational innovation: Review, critique and suggested research directions." *The Journal of Management Studies* 31(3): 405–431.

4. Neil Anderson, Carsten K. W. De Dreu, and Bernard A. Nijstad. 2004. "The routinization of innovation research: a constructively critical review of the state-of-the-science." *Journal of Organizational Behavior* 25(2): 147–173.

5. Mary M. Crossan and Marina Apaydin. 2010. "A multi-dimensional framework of organizational innovation: A systematic review of the literature." *Journal of Management Studies* 47(6): 1154–1191.

6. Christian Seelos and Johanna Mair. 2012. "What determines the capacity for continuous innovation in social sector organizations?" *PACS Report to the Rockefeller Foundation*. Stanford, CA: Stanford University.

7. Peter F. Drucker. 1994. "The theory of the business." *Harvard Business Review* 72(5): 95-104.

8. Stephen J. Kline and Nathan Rosenberg. 1986. "An overview of innovation." In *The Positive Sum Strategy: Harnessing Technology for Economic Growth*, edited by Ralph Landau and Nathan Rosenberg, 275–305. Washington, DC: National Academies Press.

9. Mary O'Sullivan. 2000. "The innovative enterprise and corporate governance." *Cambridge Journal of Economics* 24(4): 393–416.

10. Sue Desmond-Hellmann. 2015. :View from the top." Stanford University, January 9, 2015.

11. Christian Seelos and Johanna Mair. 2013. "Innovate and scale: A tough balancing act." *Stanford Social Innovation Review* 11(3): 12–14.

12. James G. March. 1991. "Exploration and exploitation in organizational learning." *Organization Science* 2(1): 71–87.

13. Julian Birkinshaw and Jonas Ridderstrale. 1999. "Fighting the corporate immune system: A process study of subsidiary initiatives in multinational corporations." *International Business Review* 8(2): 149–180.

14. Jan Schilling and Annette Kluge. 2009. "Barriers to organizational learning: An integration of theory and research." *International Journal of Management Reviews* 11(3): 337–360.

CHAPTER 2

1. Tom Northup. 2008. *Five Hidden Mistakes CEOs Make: How to Unlock the Secrets that Drive Growth and Profitability*. Brisbane: Solutions Press.

2. Mark Simon and Susan M. Houghton. 2003. "The relationship between overconfidence and the Introduction of Risky Products: Evidence from a Field Study." *Academy of Management Journal* 46 (2):139-49.

3. Christian Seelos and Johanna Mair. 2012. "Innovation is not the holy grail." *Stanford Social Innovation Review* 10(4): 45–49.

4. Christian Seelos and Johanna Mair. 2013. "Innovate and scale: A tough balancing act." *Stanford Social Innovation Review* 11(3): 12–14.

5. Jennifer M. George. 2008. *Creativity in Organizations: The Academy of Management Annals*. New York: Taylor & Francis Group/Lawrence Erlbaum Associates.

6. Christian Seelos and Johanna Mair. 2012. "What determines the capacity for continuous innovation in social sector organizations?" *PACS Report to the Rockefeller Foundation.* Stanford, CA: Stanford University.

7. James G. March. 1991. "Exploration and exploitation in organizational learning." *Organization Science* 2(1): 71–87.

8. Christian Seelos and Johanna Mair. 2014. "Organizational closure competencies and scaling: A realist approach to theorizing social enterprise." In *Social Entrepreneurship and Research Methods,* edited by Jeremy Short, 147–187. Bingley, UK: Emerald Group Publishing Limited.

9. Wesley M. Cohen and Daniel A. Levinthal. 1990. "Absorptive capacity: A new perspective on learning and innovation." *Administrative Science Quarterly* 35(1): 128–152.

10. Shaker A. Zahra and Gerard George. 2002. "Absorptive capacity: A review, reconceptualization, and extension." *Academy of Management Review* 27(2): 185–203.

11. Peter Uvin, Pankaj S. Jain, and L. David Brown. 2000. "Think large and act small: Toward a new paradigm for NGO scaling up." *World Development* 28(8): 1409–1419.

CHAPTER 3

1. All quotations are from senior managers whom we interviewed, unless otherwise specified. Quotations from interviews were lightly edited for clarity and length.

2. Rob Jenkins. 2003. "International development institutions and national economic contexts: Neoliberalism encounters India's indigenous traditions." *Economy and Society* 32(4): 584–610.

3. National Dairy Development Board. "Operation Flood." Retrieved on August 25, 2010, from www.nddb.org/English/Genesis/Pages/Operation-Flood.aspx.

4. Anthya Madiath. 1981. "When tribals awake: The Kerandimals movement. People's participation in development." Gram Vikas.

5. Gram Vikas. 2003. "Institutionalising gender in patriarchal rural communities: Creating spaces through uncontested domains." Gram Vikas.

CHAPTER 4

1. All quotations are from senior managers whom we interviewed, unless otherwise specified. Quotations from interviews were lightly edited for clarity and length. For the case study on the Aravind eye hospital we owe a number of details to the book *Infinite Vision,* by Pavita K. Mehta and Suchitra Shenoy, published in 2011 by Berrett-Koehler Publishers, San Francisco.

2. iMahal Interview Series. "G. Venkataswamy." Retrieved on April 19, 2013, from www.imahal.com/interviews/venkataswamy_06_01/page2.htm.

3. Rangan V. Kasturi. 1993. *Aravind Eye Hospital, Madurai, India: In Service for Sight.* Vol. HBS 9-593-098. Boston: Harvard Business School Publishing.

4. Pavithra K. Mehta and Suchitra Shenoy. 2011. *Infinite Vision: How Aravind Became the World's Greatest Business Case for Compassion.* San Francisco: Berrett-Koehler Publishers.

5. Aravind Eye Care System. "Aurolab, the beginning." Retrieved on June 22, 2015, from www.aravind.org/default/servicescontent/Aurolab.

6. Lions Club International Foundation. "Sight." Retrieved on March 1, 2015, from www.lcif.org/EN/our-work/sight/index.php.

7. Ocular Surgery News India Edition. "Former Aravind administrator guides LAICO, Vision 2020." Retrieved on March 24, 2013, from www.healio.com/ophthalmology/news/print/ocular-surgery-news-india-edition/%7Bfee95b61-e31c-4206-8ef0-23e04fe85dc2%7D/former-aravind-administrator-guides-laico-vision-2020.

8. Aravind Eye Care System. "Aravind activity report 2007–2008, Aravind Managed Eye Care Services." Madurai: Aravind.

CHAPTER 5

1. All quotations are from senior managers whom we interviewed, unless otherwise specified. Quotations from interviews were lightly edited for clarity and length. For the case study on BRAC, we are grateful to Ian Smillie for his wonderful historical biography of BRAC (Ian Smillie. 2009. *Freedom from Want: The Remarkable Success Story of BRAC, the Global Grassroots Organization That's Winning the Fight against Poverty.* Sterling, VA: Kumarian Press).

2. Ian Smillie. 2009. *Freedom from Want: The Remarkable Success Story of BRAC, the Global Grassroots Organization That's Winning the Fight against Poverty.* Sterling, VA: Kumarian Press.

3. Up to 3 million people may have been killed, and about 10 million people may have fled to India. "Bangladesh Genocide Archive." Retrieved on September 5, 2013, from www.genocidebangladesh.org.

4. David Korten, an expert on nonprofit organizations working with the Ford Foundation, after visiting BRAC in 1979; cited in I. Smillie, 2009.

5. BRAC Research and Evaluation Division. 1979. "Who gets what and why: Resource allocation in a Bangladesh village." In *Rural Studies Series.* BRAC Prokashana.

6. BRAC Research and Evaluation Division. 1980. "The Net: Power Structure in Ten Villages." In *Rural Studies Series.* BRAC Prokashana.

7. "In memoriam BRAC's field marshall." *The Daily Star.* October 6, 2010.

CHAPTER 6

1. All quotations are from senior managers whom we interviewed, unless otherwise specified. Quotations from the interviews were lightly edited for clarity and length.

2. Daniel Hoornweg and Perinaz Bhada-Tata. 2012. "What a waste: A global review of solid waste management." Urban development series; knowledge papers no. 15. Washington, DC: World Bank.

3. Iftekhar Enayetullah and A. H. Md. Maqsood Sinha. 1999. "Community based decentralized composting: Experience of waste concern in Dhaka—Case Study #3." New Delhi: Urban Management Program for Asia and the Pacific, All India Institute of Local Self Government.

4. A. H. Md. Maqsood Sinha and Iftekhar Enayetullah. 2002. "Team's entry to the fast 50 social entrepreneurs." New York: Fast Company, New York.

5. Christian Zurbrügg, Silke Drescher, Isabelle Rytz, A. H. Md. Maqsood Sinha, and Iftekhar Enayetullah. 2005. "Decentralised composting in Bangladesh, a win-win situation for all stakeholders." *Resources, Conservation and Recycling* 43: 281–292.

6. Ashoka is an organization that provides start-up financing, professional support services, and connections to a global network of more than 3,000 social entrepreneurs worldwide. For more information, see www.ashoka.org.

7. Waste2Resource. "W2R Fund." Retrieved on July 20, 2015, from http://waste2resource.org/waste2resource/.

8. Lorenzo Santucci, Ingo Puhl, A. H. Md. Maqsood Sinha, Iftekhar Enayetullah, and William Kojo Agyemang-Bonsu. 2015. "Valuing the sustainable development co-benefits of climate change mitigation actions: The case of the waste sector and recommendations for the design of nationally appropriate mitigation actions (NAMAs)." Bangkok: United Nations Economic and Social Commission for Asia and the Pacific.

9. Everett M. Rogers. 1983. *Diffusion of Innovations*, 3rd ed. New York: The Free Press.

CHAPTER 7

1. Albert O. Hirschman. 1967. "The principle of the hiding hand." *The Public Interest* 6: 10–23.

CHAPTER 8

1. Christian Seelos, Johanna Mair, Julie Battilana, and M. Tina Dacin. 2011. "The embeddedness of social entrepreneurship: Understanding variation across geographic communities." In *Research in the Sociology of Organizations*, edited by C. Marquis, M. Lounsbury and R. Greenwood, 333–363. Bingley, UK: Emerald.

2. Abhijit Vinayak Banerjee. 2013. "Microcredit under the microscope: What have we learned in the past two decades, and what do we need to know?" *Annual Review of Economics* 5: 487–519.

3. David Roodman. 2012. *Due Diligence: An Impertinent Inquiry Into Microfinance*. Washington, DC: Center for Global Development.

4. Johanna Mair, Ignasi Martí, and Marc J. Ventresca. 2012. "Building inclusive markets in rural Bangladesh: How intermediaries work institutional voids." *Academy of Management Journal* 55(4): 819–850.

5. Anjali Sarker, Shameran Abed, and Christian Seelos. 2016. "Lessons in scaling and failing: The challenges of scaling up programs aimed at empowering adolescent girls in Bangladesh and Uganda." *Stanford Social Innovation Review* 14(2): 14–15 (Supplement).

sunk cost fallacy, 53
sustainability, 71, 76

Tanzania, 11, 142
technology: bias toward, 204;
telemedicine, 109–10; transfer of, 98
Triodos, 166

Uganda, 11, 142
uncertainty: definition, 23, 24; and
impact-creation logic, 23–25, 31,
32; in innovation, 2, 6, 7, 21, 23–
29, 33–34, 36, 37, 43, 48, 49–50,
51, 53, 114, 123, 124, 154, 174,
179, 181–82, 184, 185, 192, 196,
197, 198–99, 200, 214, 219, 226,
228; vs. predictability, 2; types of
uncertainties, 7, 21, 23–29, 31, 32,
199
UNDP. *See* United Nations Development
Program
UNESCAP. *See* United Nations
Economic and Social Commission
for Asia and the Pacific
UNFCC. *See* United Nations Framework
Convention on Climate Change
unintended consequences, 3, 6, 12,
24, 30, 32, 50, 114, 192, 204; of
innovation failures, 214; in red
zone vs. green zone, 35;
reinforcement of inequality, 27,
65–66, 71, 123
United Nations Children's Emergency
Fund (UNICEF), 161
United Nations Development Program
(UNDP): Sustainable Environmental
Management Program, 158, 160,
163, 168, 173
United Nations Economic and Social
Commission for Asia and the Pacific
(UNESCAP), 160–61, 169
United Nations Framework Convention
on Climate Change (UNFCCC), 164,
170
University of California, Berkeley, 109

Venkataswamy, Govindappa: attitude
regarding external funds, 92; attitude
regarding staff training, 93; attitude
regarding telemedicine, 109; family
members, 93, 94, 98, 102, 112, 116;
as founder of Aravind, 56–57, 89–91,

100, 102, 112, 116, 182; and IOLs,
97–98
Vietnam, 160–61, 169

Waste Concern: vs. Aravind, 10–12,
174, 182, 186–87, 221, 222, 226;
bottlenecks for, 156, 157, 158, 159;
vs. BRAC, 10–12, 159, 168, 182,
186–87, 188, 197, 221, 222, 223,
226; and CDM, 163, 164, 165–68;
composting projects, 153, 154–
61, 163, 164–67, 169, 170, 171;
demonstration plants, 157, 176;
founders, 151–53, 154–56, 158–59,
162–63, 168, 172–73, 176–77, 182,
186, 190, 191, 192, 193, 222; vs.
Grameen Bank, 159, 168; vs. Gram
Vikas, 10–12, 182, 186–87, 188,
222, 226; green zone of, 186–87,
188, 226; identity uncertainty in, 27;
impact-creation logic of, 174, 188;
innovation archetype (innovation for
diffusion), 56, 174–77, 187, 188, 189,
191, 226; innovation pathologies
reduced by, 191, 192, 193; mission,
11, 174; organic agriculture
projects, 170–71; organizational
infrastructure, 221; organizational
innovation at, 160–63; piloting by,
154–55, 157, 172; and plastic waste,
171–72; R&D activities, 154–55,
160, 162, 172, 174, 176, 193, 222;
red zone of, 186; relations with
Asian Development Bank, 162, 166,
167; relations with Bangladeshi
government, 158, 159, 161, 163, 164,
165–66, 167, 169, 171–72, 173–74,
192; relations with funders, 161–62,
165, 166–67, 192; relations with
Gates Foundation, 151, 161, 167–68,
169; relations with people served,
222; relations with People Tree,
170–71; relations with private sector,
156–57; relations with UNDP, 158,
160, 163, 168, 173; relations with
UNESCAP, 160–61, 169; relations
with UNICEF, 161; relations with
WWR, 164, 165, 166; reputation
of, 162–63, 192; scaling through
knowledge transfer by, 56; staff, 11;
training centers, 167, 168, 176, 193;
and W2RF, 169–70